Malcolm Lowry's Poetics of Space

Malcolm Lowry's Poetics of Space

—

Edited by

RICHARD J. LANE AND MIGUEL MOTA

University of Ottawa Press | OTTAWA

u Ottawa

The University of Ottawa Press gratefully acknowledges the support extended to its publishing list by the Government of Canada, the Canada Council for the Arts, and the Ontario Arts Council. This book has been published with the help of a grant from the Federation for the Humanities and Social Sciences, through the Awards to Scholarly Publications Program, using funds provided by the Social Sciences and Humanities Research Council of Canada.

Copy editing: Robbie McCaw
Proofreading: Marionne Cronin
Layout: CS
Cover design: Édiscript enr.
Cover image: Dollarton, North Vancouver, still image from *After Lowry: A Film Essay*

Library and Archives Canada Cataloguing in Publication

Malcolm Lowry's poetics of space / edited by Richard J Lane and Miguel Mota.

(Canadian literature collection)
Includes bibliographical references.
Issued in print and electronic formats.
ISBN 978-0-7766-2340-5 (paperback).--ISBN 978-0-7766-2341-2 (PDF).--
ISBN 978-0-7766-2342-9 (EPUB).--ISBN 978-0-7766-2343-6 (MOBI)

1. Lowry, Malcolm, 1909-1957--Criticism and interpretation.
2. Space in literature. I. Mota, Miguel, editor II. Lane, Richard J., 1966-, editor III. Series: Canadian literature collection

PS8523.O96Z7644 2016   C813'.52   C2016-906249-X
                                        C2016-906250-3

Contents

.

III
CHARTING THE HUMAN LANDSCAPE

.

CODA

.

Introduction

RICHARD J. LANE AND MIGUEL MOTA

G iven that Malcolm Lowry saw himself not only as a writer of words, but also as being written by those words, it is hardly surprising that Lowry criticism has always drawn strong connections between Lowry's writing and his life. Even aside from the two substantial and influential biographies in the conventional sense (by Douglas Day, in 1973, and Gordon Bowker, in 1993), much of the scholarly criticism involving Lowry has had the hint of the biographical about it, even when the principal approach has been formalist or post-structuralist. The most important recent collection of critical essays on Lowry (Frederick Asals and Paul Tiessen's *A Darkness That Murmured: Essays on Malcolm Lowry and the Twentieth Century*, 2000), though clearly encouraging a new, postmodernist reading of Lowry, nevertheless begins with an implicit acknowledgment of the central place of biography in critical approaches to Lowry's work: "His habit of personal mythmaking sometimes obscured with its transformations what (in so far as it could be determined) had actually occurred, but even when Lowry's own fictions were penetrated, dark areas remained, incidents, even periods, wholly or partially mysterious" (11). For its part, Bryan Biggs and Helen Tookey's *Malcolm Lowry: From the Mersey to the World*, published in 2009 to celebrate the centenary of Lowry's birth, offers a suggestively hybrid collection of personal reminiscences, scholarly pieces, fiction, and photographic reproductions of visual works that, while acknowledging the impossibility of fully doing so, nevertheless seeks to "place" Lowry by addressing the geographical, psychological, and creative "voyaging" undertaken by the author throughout his life.

This search for the "mystery" of the life in the work is perhaps inescapable, given the extent to which Lowry turned himself, and has subsequently been turned by others, into a "textual" being. It is perhaps equally unsurprising that such a connection between "textuality" and "identity" wrought such anxiety throughout Lowry's life and work. Sherrill Grace's early assessment of Lowry as "Ortega [y Gasset]'s man in the process of creating (as opposed to finding) his identity through the creation of masks" (*Voyage* 102) resonates in Patrick McCarthy's later insistence that "for Lowry, writing was both his life and a threat to his life: although he seems to have assumed that he could discover or define his identity only through writing, he also feared that the process of composition would leave him without any identity apart from the work" (*Forests* 4). The question becomes, then, not how to extricate Lowry's writing from his life—for that is surely an impossible, perhaps even undesirable, task, the two being so ingrained—but, rather, how to create a critical space within which the relations between writing and life can be both materially located and given imaginative play. One possibility is to see space itself as a category capable of such mobility.

In his essay "Of Other Spaces," Michel Foucault suggests that if the "great obsession" of the nineteenth century was history, then that of the twentieth was space: "The present epoch will perhaps be above all the epoch of space" (Foucault 22). Yet, as Foucault himself insists, space has a history and is implicated in various historical discursive practices and relations:

> The space in which we live, which draws us out of ourselves, in which the erosion of our lives, our time and our history occurs, the space that claws and gnaws at us, is also, in itself, a heterogeneous space. In other words, we do not live in a kind of void, inside of which we could place individuals and things. We do not live inside a void that could be colored with diverse shades of light, we live inside a set of relations that delineates sites which are irreducible to one another and absolutely not superimposable on one another. (23)

How to situate Malcolm Lowry in space, then, given that "space" can mean so much to so many, produced as it is by a seemingly infinite web of relations— especially in an age when the virtual increasingly challenges the material as the place of the imagination?

In her article "The Creative Process: An Introduction to Time and Space in Malcolm Lowry's Fiction," Grace writes intriguingly of Lowry's "fear of space":

> Just as Lowry cannot be fully appreciated without prior knowledge of his voyage theories, those theories cannot be understood without an awareness of Lowry's reverence for time and his fear of space. Over and over again in published works, manuscripts, and notes, Lowry equates time with flow, motion, and a positive Bergsonian sense of duration. Space, isolated from time, he repeatedly views as timelessness or stasis; stasis becomes hell or death, a condition of spatial enclosure, suffocation, and entrapment. . . . His writing, from early stories until his death, expresses a need for time and a terror of space which, when perceived as cut off from temporal flow, threatens to enclose and destroy.

Yet if it is true that Lowry feared space in this sense, it may be equally plausible that space, if formulated differently, offers both Lowry and his readers countless possibilities to explore that infinite web of relations that Foucault posits as defining space; its very heterogeneity contesting the "enclosure, suffocation, and entrapment" suggested above by Grace, and offering up instead the possibility both of moving and of being moved.

The essays in this collection seek to define "space" in just such heterogeneous ways. The authors approach the concept of space in Lowry's work and life from various theoretical and historical perspectives; yet always there is a common, shared sense of space, a sense perhaps best evoked by Gaston Bachelard in *The Poetics of Space*: an understanding of space as an architecture of the imagination. For Lowry's spaces, even when they might be located concretely or geographically, are also always simultaneously imagined, giving voice to what has been termed "the multivalent nature of the novelist's inscape, or landscape of the mind" (Porteous, "Inscape" 123). The latter phrase brings together Gerard Manley Hopkins' aesthetic concept of inscape, which Dennis Sobolev defines as "embodied organized form" (229), and the *paysage intérieur* or disembodied interior landscapes of the French symbolists; in Lowry's unique vision, inner and outer spaces merge to create a new synthesis, where space and mind become one. Douglas Porteous argues that this synthesis can be seen most forcefully in the liminal space of Lowry's Dollarton, British Columbia, where Malcolm and Margerie perched on land and over water as the tide washed under their squatter's shack (that sat on the beach on vulnerable stilts); as Lowry writes in *Hear Us O Lord from Heaven Thy Dwelling Place*, "here in the inlet there was neither sea nor river, but something compounded of both, in eternal movement, and eternal flux and change, as mysterious and multiform in its notion and being, and in the mind as the mind flowed with it, as was that other Eridanus, the constellation in the heavens, the starry river in the sky" (236). Added to this multiform space which merges visionary insight with the material world is the rich symbolism of a paradise lost, the garden created through a "combination of sustaining forest and sea" (Porteous, "Inscape" 126), from which the Lowrys eventually felt tragically banished. Lowry's intensive and extensive use of intertextuality creates an analogous constellation, an architectonic of writing that crosses the boundaries between modernism and postmodernism, leaving the critic to wonder, in relation to Lowry's magnum opus, where exactly this leaves us "in considering the degree to which *Under the Volcano* presages or incorporates elements that we tend now to see as postmodern" (Jewison 142). At the threshold between print and digital cultures, perhaps the question now should be: How does Lowry's spatial dynamic represent a more radical thought than even this previous modernism–postmodernism coupling intimated? Jean Baudrillard argues in The Perfect Crime that such "radical thought is a stranger to all resolving of the world in the direction of an objective reality and its deciphering" (104). As he continues, radical thought "does not decipher. It anagrammatizes, it disperses concepts and ideas and, by its reversible sequencing, takes account both of meaning and of the fundamental illusoriness of meaning. . . . Cipher, do not decipher. Work over the illusion. Create illusion to create an event" (104). In this instance, the event is the publication of Under the Volcano, yet perhaps Baudrillard is too hasty in his demand to "cipher" rather than "decipher," for Lowry's spatial architectonic is grand in vision, opening up new ways of seeing subjectivity, of being, to such an extent that the trope of "decrypting" is more relevant than the cipher/decipher opposition, where decrypting is Henri Lefebvre's "spatial paradigm" of "emergence" and "emancipation" explored in The Production of Space, via the transition from medieval cryptic space to that of a "luminous utopia" (Davis 12–13). Of course, such a transition is essentially about the transformation of imagined, culturally defined spaces, and it is these culturally meaningful spaces, as articulated in the essays below, that cumulatively produce both the fiction of Malcolm Lowry and the fiction that Malcolm Lowry has become.

Focus on spatial dislocation (see Vandamme, Chapter 3) is apparent in many methodological approaches to Lowry, again perhaps none more so than the biographical, which is also closely linked with "claiming" Lowry as a British and/or Canadian author. Dislocation in Lowry's life is figured as "wandering" (Benson and Toye 682), with Lowry also being described as being "a homeless, rootless wanderer" (Porteous, "Deathscape" 34); suffering a "brief imprisonment in Oaxaca" (Mota 683); and being "Evicted From The Paradise Garden" (the title of chapter XXIV of Gordon Bowker's Pursued by Furies: A Life of Malcolm Lowry), that is to say, having to leave the North Shore of Vancouver. City spaces also act to dislocate the human subject, functioning as "both symbols and generators of mental distress," and even a kind of "shorthand" signifying "despair, destruction, and death" (Porteous, "Deathscape" 40). Relief from such a dark world is found in Lowry's self-reflective musings on natural spaces, such as the seascapes and forests of British Columbia, revealing an intensely eco-critical awareness that functions as an escape from the negativity of intense "introversion" (Lowry appears, ever so fleetingly, in a chapter called "The Introverted Novel" in Modernism: A Guide to European Literature, 1890–1930 [Bradbury and MacFarlane]); significantly, this eco-critical awareness correlates with a deep vein of Canadian literary expression concerning the natural world. Laurie Ricou makes the argument that "Canadian literary studies, with their longstanding interest in nature, wilderness, and landscape, might be said to have always been ecocritical" ("Ecocriticism" 324), and

Lowry's "The Forest Path To The Spring" is an exemplary modernist instance of such a mode of writing. In his seminal essay, "The Writing of British Columbia Writing," not only does Ricou open with an epigraph from "The Forest Path," but he suggests that "Lowry's [compositional] method . . . might stand for the processes of British Columbia's writing in general, its prying and filling rich with analogies to intertidal deposition, to exposed aeons of geological layering, to the multiplying growth upon growth of moss upon tree upon nurse log which makes rain forest. Its leafing is interleaving" (109).

The traversing of space in "The Forest Path" is extended and amplified to include seascapes in *October Ferry to Gabriola*, a novel that George Bowering portrays as "the apotheosis of B.C. fiction" (qtd. in Ricou, "Writing" 112). Lowry formulates the complex spatiality in this novel in a 1953 letter to Albert Erskine, his editor at Random House, in which, as Grace notes, "he compares the form of the novel to a triangle" (*Strange Comfort* 47), and that such a "concept of a 'triangle or triad' is crucial to an understanding of the novel's structure as well as to an appreciation of the Cabbalistic ordeal of the protagonist" (48). In mapping narrative through Euclidean geometry, Lowry suggests that the base of the triangle represents the first chapter, but he also registers the word "triad" as relating to chemical theory, to German chemist Johann Döbereiner's notion of "a radical having a valence of three" (47). The range of Lowry's spatial metaphors are obviously extensive—crossing modernist aesthetics, music, and film, as well as philosophy and science—but he formulates these metaphors with precise texts and situations in mind; for example, the triangle/triad represents for him the structure of *October Ferry*, but *Under the Volcano* is differently represented by "the circle" (48). Supplementing Grace's incisive analysis of spatiality in *October Ferry*, then, Lowry's use of Euclidean geometry or space does not simply function as another way of articulating a Platonic "mathematical architecture of being, a transcendental function of ideal numbers" (Badiou 8), but rather is an indication that ontological questions of being had shifted, for Lowry, from unified statements of spatial coherence (the stereotype of the modernist author as a high priest of culture) to the multiplicity of a heterogeneous world. As much as the protagonist "finds" or locates himself in Lowry's fiction through an intense awareness of space, he also at the same time "loses" himself in the poetics of space, be this perceived from aesthetic, ecocritical, or psychoanalytical perspectives.

We imagine space here, then, in various shapes and forms, both internal and external, taking for granted that space has the capacity to figure many different aspects of identity, thereby offering an approach to Lowry that encompasses the broad range of theoretical and "post-theory" methodologies that are of contemporary concern. McCarthy observes that Lowry "could never really let his books go," and this compulsive return to the text neatly encompasses the biographical and the critical: Lowry could not let go "partly because he identified each work so strongly with his own life, and also because he had a compulsive urge to make everything connect to everything else, to fit all of his works within a totalizing design" ("Totality" 182). The modalities of space, then, offer a way of comprehending the intensities of Lowry's textual universe. The essays below address the complex historical and material production of space in Lowry's life and work, and thus involve political, economic, technological, and ideological factors. At the same time, attention is paid to the symbolic experience of space, always necessarily mediated by social exchange. That the production and reproduction of space must of necessity always involve some form of social interaction reminds us that space offers a medium for articulating the many facets of subjectivity, including national origin, geographic mobility, structures of consciousness, ideological formations of belonging and exclusion, and, of course, the human body itself. The essays in this collection, then, approach the representation of space in Lowry's work from numerous perspectives, each assuming its own set of discursive practices: geography, psychogeography, history, culture, media, social exchange. But, crucially, we are reminded also that embodied space incorporates language and discourse; in the case of Lowry's writing, careful attention must be paid to the materiality of representation: the text itself as the space that produces and reproduces the kinds of social exchanges that ultimately define the subject in Lowry's work. Space mediates our connection with the material, but it also maintains a certain fluidity, the promise of a mobility that allows for a continual negotiation of its boundaries and limitations. It is these negotiations with space, in its many forms, that enact both the optimism and anxiety surrounding Lowry's life and work.

Part One of *Malcolm Lowry's Poetics of Space*, "Situating *Under the Volcano*," addresses Lowry's masterpiece from fresh theoretical and historical perspectives. In "Under the Volcano ... the Beach: Malcolm Lowry and the Situationists," Mark Goodall examines Lowry's "inner landscape" through the modernist devices of *dérive*, *détournement*, and psychogeography; in a meandering style that echoes his subject, he argues that "much of Lowry's writing represents an experimental 'drift' through various ambiences," and, indeed, the question of "ambiences" is returned to in one guise or another by many of the contributors to this book. Noting that the situationists called the practice of psychogeography the "Lowry game," Goodall explores how Lowry's "eccentric orbit" led to "new perceptions of space, time and behaviour." In "Lowry, Sebald, and the Coincidental Landscape," Laurence Piercy places Lowry within an aesthetic space of undecidability. Comparing *Under the Volcano* to W. G. Sebald's *The Rings of Saturn*, Piercy not only relates coincidence, repetition, and landscape in Lowry and Sebald, but he argues that both authors share a "venture into the void," where mortality is read via materiality. For example, the ravine in *Under the Volcano* "appears as a commixture of . . . psychological and geographical aspects." Piercy also touches upon Eric Santner and the creaturely, a topic that is further explored later in the collection. The connection between spatial and textual dynamics in Lowry's most famous novel informs Christine Vandamme's "Lowry and Jakobson: Spatial Pyrotechnics and Poetic Writing in *Under the Volcano*," where the concept of "derailing" chronological narrative progression is key to understanding Lowry's poetic writing; a sensitive mapping of the creative process, following Wilderness's dictum, "The whole is an assembly of apparently incongruous parts, slipping past one another," relates another mode of "derailing" in Mathieu Duplay's "Pathologies of Knowledge: David Markson, *Under the Volcano*, and the Experience of Thought." Finally, Charles Hoge, in a comprehensive essay on the phantom dog and liminal spaces, "Phantom Priapusspuss: The Phantom-Dog Tradition in *Under the Volcano*," theorizes that *Under The Volcano* "lives in the same place as the phantom dog," that is to say, "between destinations."

Part Two, "The Spatial Dynamics of Sight and Sound," opens with a fresh perspective on Lowry's well-known connection to film. In "Spectatorial Bodies and the Everyday Spaces of Cinema," Paul Tiessen examines the impact that film and its architectural spaces have upon the body, arguing that "Lowry dramatizes varieties of the spectatorial body, from disembodiment to bodily renewal." Following Tiessen's piece, W. M. Hagen's "Projecting the *Volcano*: The Possibilities of Margerie Bonner Lowry's Film Proposal" offers a detailed analysis and assessment of Margerie Lowry's little-known 1962 film proposal for *Under the Volcano*. Originally intended for the great Spanish director Luis Buñuel, Margerie's proposal is examined here by Hagen as an imagined instance of "what might have been," a suggestion for a film that leads inevitably to other imagined possibilities, other projections. Ailsa Cox, in "Soundscapes in *Lunar Caustic*," argues that Lowry's "images are all placed in dialogue with a range of auditory effects." Drawing deeply upon Mikhail Bakhtin and Julia Kristeva, Cox situates Lowry's use of soundscapes in relation to the disjunction between silent movies and the then-new technologies of sight and sound: "the disjunction between sound and image in *Lunar Caustic* may be related to this awareness of a separation between the visual and auditory channels." The disjunctive splicing between these channels that occurs in the novella "evokes heightened subjective states," which Cox argues are "analogous to the 'asynchrony' of sound film." Turning more exclusively to aural spaces, Catherine Delesalle looks at Lowry's use of jazz rhythms in her "Dwelling In-Between: Rituals and Jazz as Reconcilable

Opposites in 'The Forest Path to the Spring.'" In her reading of Lowry's lengthy short story, Delesalle argues that jazz enables the artist to embrace the "unpredictable emergence" of boundless, unexpected states of being. Finally, in Josiane Paccaud-Huguet's "The Expressionist Gaze in the Psychic Space of *Under the Volcano*," interactions between the visual and the acoustic are brought together in the novel's "forms of looking/gazing," explored intriguingly here with reference to anamorphosis, topography, and "the acousmatic voice."

The essays in Part Three, "Charting the Human Landscape," reflect upon a thread that runs implicitly throughout the collection: how the discourse of the human is given voice in Lowry's work, not only through the representation of geographical and psychological spaces, but also through its concern with the biospatial and biopolitical—through the spaces, in other words, of alternative subjectivities. The first two chapters in this section explore analogous inner spaces: Annick Drösdal-Levillain's "From Liverpool to Eridanus in the Twinkling of an Eye" lyrically connects topography and personal history to map Lowry's "multilayered soulscape," the exilic "paradoxical edgy combination of ex-centeredness and connection to the world" that "perfectly suited Lowry"; and Pierre Schaeffer's "Outgrowing the Alienating Inscape? The Voyage Out in *October Ferry to Gabriola*" charts the shift from "nightmarish inscape" to a more mature "landscape" in Lowry's "road novel," *October Ferry to Gabriola*. While urban spaces are important for virtually all of the contributors, labyrinthine streets and urban crowds form the setting for Pascale Tollance's "The Path to Translation: Ex-isting and Becoming in the Divinely Grotesque Comedy of 'Elephant and Colosseum'." Such a setting provides a key for the "multidirectional nature" of Lowry's narratives. Significantly, Tollance also makes some important critical observations concerning the creaturely, namely that it is constitutive of the human, an idea developed here via Gilles Deleuze. This turn toward varying definitions of the human is picked up by Ryan Rashotte in "Placing Agency in the Cultural Landscapes of *La Mordida*." Rashotte foregrounds Lowry's positioning of his novel's protagonists in what Giorgio Agamben calls the "state of exception," where "the indistinction between law and violence is ... ideologically territorialized." Finally, in the last essay of the collection, Richard J. Lane, in "The Poetics of Exposed, Irreparable Space in Malcolm Lowry's *Lunar Caustic*; or, Reading Lowry through Agamben," develops the state of exception and creaturely aesthetic in the spatial architecture of Lowry's novella. Lane argues that Lowry's spatial dynamic creates a gestalt and complex image, with a heightened graphicness, through which we see the creaturely as situated within the biopolitical. Lane further argues that Lowry's spatial dynamics is deeply ethical, and the ethical impulse remains at the close of his text. The three sections of the book are accompanied by Miguel Mota's "After Lowry"—a documentary film essay that serves as a coda and explores the geographical and imagined space of Dollarton, where in a squatter's shack between sea and forest Malcolm and Margerie Lowry lived, worked, and were happy for many years.

WORKS CITED

Agamben, Giorgio. *Homo Sacer: Sovereign Power and Bare Life*. Translated by Daniel Heller-Roazen, Stanford, CA: Stanford UP, 1998.

Asals, Frederick, and Paul Tiessen, editors. *A Darkness That Murmured: Essays on Malcolm Lowry and the Twentieth Century*. Toronto: U of Toronto P, 2000.

Bachelard, Gaston. *The Poetics of Space*. Translated by Maria Jolas, Boston: Beacon, 1969.

Badiou, Alain. *Being and Event*. Translated by Oliver Feltham, London: Continuum, 2007.

Baudrillard, Jean. *The Perfect Crime*. Translated by Chris Turner, London and New York: Verso, 1996.

Benson, Eugene, and William Toye, general editors. *The Oxford Companion to Canadian Literature*. 2nd ed., Toronto and Oxford: Oxford UP, 1997.

Biggs, Bryan, and Helen Tookey, editors. *Malcolm Lowry: From the Mersey to the World*. Liverpool: Liverpool UP and the Bluecoat, 2009.

Bowker, Gordon. *Pursued by Furies: A Life of Malcolm Lowry*. Toronto: Random House, 1993.

Bradbury, Malcolm, and James McFarlane, editors. *Modernism: A Guide to European Literature, 1890–1930*. London: Penguin, 1991.

Davis, Carmel Bendon. *Mysticism & Space: Space and Spatiality in the Works of Richard Rolle, The Cloud of Unknowing Author, and Julian of Norwich*. Washington, DC: The Catholic U of America P, 2008.

Day, Douglas. *Malcolm Lowry: A Biography*. New York: Oxford UP, 1973.

Foucault, Michel. "Of Other Spaces." *Diacritics* 16, Spring 1986, pp. 22–27.

Grace, Sherrill E. "The Creative Process: An Introduction to Time and Space in Malcolm Lowry's Fiction." *Studies in Canadian Literature/Études en littérature Canadienne*, vol. 2, no. 1, 1977, journals.hil.unb.ca/index.php/SCL/article/view/7852/8909. Accessed 2 July 2013.

———. *Strange Comfort: Essays on the Work of Malcolm Lowry*. Vancouver: Talon, 2009.

———. *The Voyage That Never Ends: Malcolm Lowry's Fiction*. Vancouver: U of British Columbia P, 1982.

Jewison, D.B. "The Uses of Intertextuality in *Under the Volcano*." *Swinging the Maelstrom: New Perspectives on Malcolm Lowry*, edited by Sherril Grace, Montreal and Kingston: McGill-Queen's UP, 1992, pp. 136–145.

Lefebvre, Henri. *The Production of Space.* Translated by Donald Nicholson-Smith, Oxford: Blackwell, 1991.

Lowry, Malcolm. *Hear Us O Lord from Heaven Thy Dwelling Place.* London: Penguin, 1969.

———. *Lunar Caustic.* London: Jonathan Cape, 1977. Originally published in *The Paris Review*, no. 29, 1963.

———. *October Ferry to Gabriola.* Edited by Margerie Lowry, New York and Cleveland: World Publishing, 1970.

———. *Under the Volcano.* 1947. Philadelphia and New York: J. B. Lippincott Company, 1965.

Lowry, Margerie. "*Under the Volcano:* A Film Proposal." *Malcolm Lowry and Conrad Aiken Adapted: Three Radio Dramas and a Film Proposal*, edited by Paul Tiessen, Waterloo, ON: Malcolm Lowry Review, 1992.

McCarthy, Patrick A. "Totality and Fragmentation in Lowry and Joyce." *A Darkness That Murmured: Essays on Malcolm Lowry and the Twentieth Century*, 2000, pp. 173–187.

———. *Forests of Symbols: World, Text and Self in Malcolm Lowry's Fiction.* Athens and London: U of Georgia P, 1994.

Mota, Miguel. "Malcolm Lowry." *Encyclopedia of Literature in Canada*, edited by William H. New, Toronto: U of Toronto P, 2002.

Porteous, J. Douglas. "Deathscape: Malcolm Lowry's Topophobic View of the City." *The Canadian Geographer/Le Géographe canadien*, vol. 31, no. 1, 1987, pp. 34–43.

———. "Inscape: Landscapes of the Mind in the Canadian and Mexican Novels of Malcolm Lowry." *The Canadian Geographer/Le Géographe canadien*, vol. 30, no. 2, 1986, pp. 123–131.

Ricou, Laurie. "Ecocriticism." In *Encyclopedia of Literature in Canada*, edited by William H. New, Toronto: U of Toronto P, 2002.

———. "The Writing of British Columbia Writing." *BC Studies* 100, Winter 1993–94, pp. 106–120.

Sobolev, Dennis. "Inscape Revisited." *English* 51, Autumn 2002, pp. 219–234.

I

Situating Under the Volcano

1

Under the Volcano . . . the Beach: Malcolm Lowry and the Situationists

MARK GOODALL

> I'm back in Paris, and in condition to write, after a series of trips that was longer than I anticipated. But I've at last discovered mescal: it's very good.
>
> —*Correspondence* 391

Not the words of Malcolm Lowry but those of one of Lowry's greatest admirers, French writer and filmmaker Guy Debord. Debord was a key player in the short-lived but highly influential post-war avant-garde groups the Letterist International (LI) and the Situationist International (SI), the latter of which he led.[1] This essay examines the strong relationship between the work and life of Lowry and of Debord, in particular Debord's last and most important film, *In Girum Imus Nocte et Consumimur Igni* (1978). Before proceeding to an analysis of what, arguably, are clear parallels between Lowry's cosmos and Debord's, it may be instructive to refresh the historical and anecdotal links between Lowry's life, writing, and philosophy, and the subsequent actions of Debord and his colleagues in post-war France and Europe. Though the connections between Lowry and Debord range from the biographical (both escaped urbanity by moving to remote areas, to coastal British Columbia and the Auvergne region of France, respectively) to the creative (both wrote what have been called "cinematic" prose), the influence of Lowry on Debord (especially latter Debord) is somewhat overlooked both by Lowry scholars and by historians of the SI. This chapter endeavours to reveal occult (hitherto unknown) but useful connections between Lowry and Debord, and contribute to the vast and daunting realm of material already written about Lowry and his venerated novel, *Under the Volcano*.

THE CONSUL ON THE LEFT BANK

In 1948, the people living in the back streets of the Place Saint-Germain-des-Près could see a strange figure passing: it was Lowry walking day after day with the same slow, regular stride; he was going as in a dream, seeming to look at nothing, nobody. (Francillon 64)

The presence of Malcolm Lowry loomed large in some quarters in post-war Paris. The French translation of Under the Volcano, which Lowry supervised, was a great success with critics and readers and had a strong impact on the Parisian literary and avant-garde traditions. As Lowry's second wife, Margerie Bonner Lowry, observed: "It took the English a while. . . . But in France they just practically cross themselves when they speak of him . . . I've had some of the reviews and they're phenomenal. They just compare him to everybody including Proust, Dante and Shakespeare; the great writers that will live forever" (M. B. Lowry 33). Indeed, some years later, the July/August 1960 issue of the journal Les Lettres Nouvelles was devoted entirely to Lowry. Lowry reciprocated this adoration, and in a letter of March 1, 1950, sent to his French translator, Clarisse Francillon, he praises her translation:

> when the meaning comes through in French as it seems triumphantly to do in your version, the very fact that you have not so much advantage of actual "ambiguity" in the words seems to make the meaning deeper and wider in range and certainly more beautiful in expression. (Lowry, Sursum 2:200)[2]

And in a nod to the cinematic nature of Volcano, Lowry also aligns himself with Jacques Laruelle, the French film director character of the novel: "the whole book could be taken to be M. Laruelle's film—if so, it was my way of paying devout tribute to the French film."[3]

French avant-garde groups, most notably the LI (who often augmented their work with symbols and spoken aspects, "metagraphs") and the SI, were quick to adopt Lowry's novel as both a literary masterwork and as a guide to living. The key figures of the movement, particularly chief theorist Debord, were not only profoundly influenced by the style and themes of Volcano, working these into their own poetic-political statements, texts, and public utterances, but also by Lowry's anarchic personal life and beliefs. Debord saw Lowry as part of a great tradition of English literature (which included Shakespeare, Swift, and Sterne). In a sense, both Lowry and Debord were "men out of their time," drawing on classic and ancient traditions within their own rapidly changing modern milieu (the 1920s for Lowry, the 1960s for Debord). Both were evidently uncomfortable with the changes taking place as a result of advanced capitalism. Debord defined this as the "spectacle," drawing from the texts of the young Karl Marx, who (according to Debord) defined political economy as "the final denial of humanity" (Debord, Comments 39). Both Lowry and Debord hated "fake" experiences such as tourism. Clarissa Lorenz, the wife of Lowry's mentor, Conrad Aiken, once noted that, for Lowry, "conventional tourism was an anathema to him. He preferred his own inner landscape and orbit, sampling the cantinas" (Lorenz 87). The famed situationist techniques of the *dérive* (a mode of experimental behaviour linked to the conditions of urban society), psychogeography (the study of the specific effects of the geographical environment), and *détournement* (rearrangement of pre-existing elements—in short, plagiarism) owe much to the style of Lowry's poetry, fiction, and letter writing.

Much of Lowry's writing represents an experimental drift through various ambiences (such as in the opening section of *Volcano*, where the figures move and shift through the landscape), with Lowry's stream-of-consciousness technique often illustrating the concept of the psychogeographic. Indeed, the practice of psychogeography—a drunken drift through space and time—was dubbed by Debord and his colleagues as the "Lowry game." Admittedly, the French, perhaps bolstered by the violence of their radical milieu, were bolder in their use of experimental techniques. Lowry plagiarized many images and words from esoteric sources. But while the French writers saw plagiarism as a free and radical literary technique (often acknowledging, for example, the influence of Isidore Ducasse: "Plagiarism is necessary . . . it clasps an author's sentence tight, uses his expressions, eliminates a false idea, replaces it with the right idea" [Lautréamont 263]), Lowry, sadly, did not feel so at ease with cultural borrowing, his own form of plagiarism causing him great personal anguish and distress.

Lowry's influence also stretched to the personal and anecdotal. The ultimately tragic figure of letterist Ivan Chtcheglov led a curious Lowryesque existence. Chtcheglov wrote little and was incarcerated in psychiatric hospitals, but composed the brilliant "Formulary for a New Urbanism," which contains, in its allusions to Poe and the mysterious landscape, the difficult beauty of a Lowry work. Ralph Rumney, a painter and former Communist from Halifax (UK), and one of the few English SI members, was nicknamed "the consul" by the French wing, after the protagonist of *Under the Volcano*, who saw Lowry in his imposing figure and aristocratic Englishness. The alcoholic figure moves in and out of reality, perceiving the human condition for "what it is" and recounting the responses to it of a "doomed man." In Paris, Lowry, like Debord, showed a "marked preference for those dim taverns off the beaten track, little frequented unless by a handful of workmen in dungarees" (Francillon 88).

The trap that all humans find themselves within is evident in *Volcano* as it is in the later writings and films of Debord. For both, alcoholism was an antidote, what Lowry called "Gin and orange juice best cure for alcoholism real cause of which is ugliness and complete baffling sterility of existence as sold to you" (Francillon 96), a stingingly prophetic description of Debord's spectacle. The

SI valued heavy drinking as much as theorizing, and it is alcohol that the French writers also took from Lowry and made their own. Debord's increasingly melancholic writings and his description of himself as "someone who had drunk much more than he had written" (Debord, *Panegyric* 29) clearly demonstrates the debt the group owed to Lowry in this regard. As Canadian poet and Vancouver friend Earl Birney said of Lowry, "I doubt if there is another poet, from Li Po to Dylan Thomas, who managed to drink so hard and still write so much and so honestly about drinking" (qtd. in Kilgallin 74).

In search of states outside of the pain of dreary perception and convention, both Lowry and Debord shared an intense, stimulating, and damaging relationship with alcohol. In his memoirs, Debord writes frankly and without shame of his experiences as an alcoholic, quoting the Spanish poet Gracian: "There are those who got drunk only once, but that once lasted them a lifetime" (*Panegyric* 30). Francillon recalls Lowry awoke with a "frenzied impatience," and the "nervous trembling which shook his limbs only stopped once he had drunk the first glass of red wine and water" (87). Debord speaks of what "lies beyond violent drunkenness . . . a terrible and magnificent peace, the true taste of the passage of time." For the protagonist of *Volcano*, the Consul, drunkenness invokes a state of "translucent clairvoyance" (Beckoff 16). Alcohol "frees his language so that it approaches poetry" (17). Debord classified mescal as "incomparable" (*Panegyric* 32). For both Lowry and Debord, drinking was a stirring phenomenon essential to living. For Lowry, "the drunkenness of the Consul is used on one plane to symbolize the universal drunkenness of mankind" (*Selected Letters* 66). Quoting Machiavelli, Debord observed that "if someone judges this way of life shameful, I find it praiseworthy, for we imitate nature, which is changeable" (*Panegyric* 33). But while Debord was defiant about his drinking, Lowry found it shameful. Lowry's "celebrations" of alcohol in his writings are tempered by guilt and remorse. As Hugh, the Consul's half-brother—in fact, a manifestation of the Consul, and Lowry's, alter ego—observes: "Good god, if our civilization were to sober up for a couple of days it'd die of remorse on the third" (121). The disapproval of Lowry's Methodist father, tempered by the need for Lowry to exist on his regular stipends, resulted in further estrangement. This is the eternal struggle between parent and child. Debord knew this, noting: "men resemble their times more than their fathers" (*Comments* 20). Furthermore, both Lowry and Debord hated their fame and sought shelter from it in alcohol. In his poem "After Publication of *Under the Volcano*," Lowry notes, "success is like some horrible disaster" (*Selected Poems* 78). Debord, for his part, quoted Li Po, "For Thirty years, I've hidden my fame in taverns" (*Panegyric* 33).

LI/SI contributors were also drawn to *Volcano* for textual inspiration. Chtcheglov's "Formulary for a New Urbanism" has a complex, Churrigueresque structure: elaborate and ornate, with elements of chiaroscuro, and partly architectural in form, the essay is a lament to a Paris that is now lost (to urban development), decrying the current "boredom" of the city (also a major theme of Debord's film *In Girum*). Chtcheglov considered the *dérive* akin to a form of psychoanalysis and "a good replacement for a mass." Through aimlessly wandering, Chtcheglov finds solace in the strange poetic place names of Parisian locations and shops:

> *Hotel of Strangers*
> *Saint Anne Ambulance*
> *Showerbath of the Patriarchs*
> *Notre Dame Zoo*
> *The swimming pool on the Street of Little Girls*
> (Chtcheglov 1–4)

These peculiar ambiences throw new light on the locations: "Certain shifting angles, certain receding perspectives, allow us to glimpse original conceptions of space, but his vision remains fragmentary" (Chtcheglov 1). What are described are new perceptions of space, time, and behaviour. Using the kinds of techniques and themes expressed throughout Lowry's writings, Chtcheglov draws on the atmospheric writings of the past in order to reinvent the present (Victor Hugo, Dumas, Poe). Debord, in a companion essay, invokes the paintings of Claude Lorrain, which offer a "perpetual invitation to voyage" (Debord, "Introduction" 5–8). Lowry would have felt the same pull gazing out across the oceans.

Patrick Straram, a French-Canadian writer and poet with connections to both the LI and the SI, paid tribute to Lowry in his work *They Write to Us of Vancouver*:

> We still haven't been to Canada! . . . Perhaps in the not too distant future? My behaviour is no longer just enigmatic, it terrorizes, and I cannot be reproached a single gesture, an illicit word. On the contrary, my conduct is exemplary, completely disorienting.

Straram also mimicked Lowry/the Consul's drinking. According to the memoirs of a fellow letterist,

> Straram drank like a fish . . . he was always getting into tight spots . . . and would do really stupid things. Several times he wound up in the cell, even

in the mental hospital. Once he spent a fortnight in there and didn't want to come out. (Mension 54)

But by far the clearest admiration for Lowry is expressed by Debord. In a letter to Straram, sent on the Day of the Dead, 1960, Debord wrote:

> I had the occasion, and the time, to reread [*Under the Volcano*] entirely, toward the beginning of September, on a train between Munich and Gênes. I had found it more fine, and more intelligent, than in 1953 despite loving it a lot then. ("Letter")

This fascination with the book manifested itself in the technique of the *dérive*: "ceaselessly drifting for days on end, none resembling the one before." It seems that for the SI *Volcano* epitomized this form of drift. The novel, for example, begins with precise geographical information, then becomes somewhat fragmentary along Jacques Laruelle's own *dérive* (Lowry, *Volcano* 15–29 passim), taking in sudden changes in direction—if you like, psychogeographically—as well as remembrances of the Taskersons, the Consul's adoptive family, covering a range of English "psychogeographical" locations, and concluding with an "eccentric orbit." Echoing this kind of traverse, in his letter to Straram, Debord wrote:

> One evening, I stopped at Cagnes-sur-Mer where—in the old village, on the hill—I went to see a girl who'd been very important to me for several years. But I neglected to notify her of my passage, and she wasn't there (but what could it say of this sort of return if she had been there?). It is necessary to say that I was perfectly drunk. I passed a very curious evening, going from one bar to another—the place is touristic enough—and at a bend in a very sombre road, I recognized, with a feeling of obviousness, the "barranca," in which I'd almost fallen . . . [goes on to recount various chance meetings] . . . all the chances for communication must be sought after, whatever the cost and whatever the illusions, which aren't frequent or easy. The regret that survives all demonstrations of such "illusions" shows that they aren't condemned to being, to remaining illusions. . . . Thus, the influential game of Lowry, which is subject to favourable conditions (?), suffices to forcefully make appear the significant incidents that otherwise wouldn't even be remarked, certainly not understood as such— and to make appear, at the centre, a sense of this whole day, this *dérive*. ("Letter")

The SI carried out numerous other experiments along these lines. For example, Debord and Raoul Vaneigem spent a day in Sarcelles intoxicated by mescal. "Our crazy walks were a real descent into hell," noted Vaneigem, clearly trying to invoke the spirit of *Volcano* (Vaneigem). For his part, Lowry's famous letter to Jonathan Cape of January 1946, explaining the layers of meaning and symbolism behind his novel, reads like a journey or a walk through the terrain of a great artistic sensibility (*Selected Letters* 57–88). Lowry would continue to influence French culture through the century. Georges Perec, in his essay "Things I Must Really Do Before I Die" (written the year before he did), notes that "Finally, there are things it's impossible to envisage from now on but which would have been possible not so long ago, for example: 36. Get drunk with Malcolm Lowry" (Perec 124).

Debord suffered a "deep unresolved tension between the poetico-artistic part of himself and the intransigent revolutionary" (Forsyth 26–40). He famously scrawled "ne travaillez jamais" on a wall in the Rue de Seine in 1953—a declaration of defiant laziness over any kind of work ethic. This reflects the struggles that Lowry had with his own writing. Day describes Lowry as "a man obsessed by the need to write, while at the same time finding it extremely difficult to write" (Day 5). Lowry, like Debord, produced in his lifetime a published corpus that was pitifully small. The seemingly contradictory nature of both men is evident in Lowry's "preternatural degree of self-awareness, even when face down on the floor of a pub or a cantina" (Day 5). Lowry is described as "a happy man; a suicide" (Day 5), an epitaph that would suit Debord.

Importantly, the SI took from Lowry his superb technique[4] in capturing the human spirit in crisis and the failure of modern man to come to terms with the awfulness of contemporary existence. At the same time, like Lowry and the characters in his works, they seek out and find small fragments of salvation in nature, poetry, love, and alcohol. Lowry's characters commonly enjoy or endure a technique of transient passage through varied ambiences. For the SI, this amounted to a "mode of experimental behaviour linked to the conditions of urban society" ("Definitions"); true, Lowry's characters escape to the wilderness from the city (think of Eridanus in "The Forest Path to the Spring"), but this is not entirely contradictory. Debord later retired to an austere part of the Auvergne, his final parting shot to the spectacle he had always despised.

The above is but a brief outline of some of the ways in which Lowry influenced a microcosm of the French post-war avant-garde. In order to further explore the importance of Lowry to this group, we turn now to Debord's 1978 film *In Girum Imus Nocte et Consumimur Igni* to observe further particular symbolic elements at work.

CIRCULAR TIME: IN GIRUM IMUS NOCTE ET CONSUMIMUR IGNI

"The Road of Excess leads to the palace of wisdom"
(William Blake, The Marriage of Heaven and Hell)

In addition to its effects on the writings of the LI/SI, Lowry's influence also stretched to other media. Debord's melancholic film In Girum Imus Nocte et Consumimur Igni (1978) is about the triumphs and tragedies of life. The title of Debord's film is taken from a medieval Latin palindrome, the kind of word play that Lowry liked. This famous macaronic verse, called the devil's verse, is a riddle in the form of a palindrome—literally, a puzzle inside a puzzle. It translates as "we wander in the night, and are consumed by fire," or "we enter the circle after dark and are consumed by fire," and is said to describe the movement of moths. Others believe that it is about the mayfly, that short-lived insect known to circle fire only to be consumed by flame. The beginning of the palindrome can also be translated as "go wandering" instead of the literal "go in a circle"; strolling or wandering around, clearly relating to the dérive favoured by the LI/SI.

Here again the Lowry-esque techniques come to the fore. The film makes liberal use of détournement and the dérive, repositioning existing elements into new forms. Debord was influenced by films such as Hiroshima Mon Amour (1959), where documentary and fiction are combined, where maps and ephemera are used to aid a dreamlike form of reality that captures the "anguish of decay."[5] The symbols of fire and circularity are powerful (rewatch/reread; Lowry always said that his work needed to be read many times before the full meaning could come through). We recall the words of Lowry's masterpiece: "Time was circumfluent again too, mescal-drugged" (Volcano 364).

Lowry's novel opens up with a cinematic, cosmic view of the world, gradually focussing in on characters and their trials. It is structured around a form "considered to be like that of a wheel, with 12 spokes, the motion of which is something like that, conceivably, of time itself" (Lowry, Selected Letters 67). For Debord and his colleagues in the early stages of the history of the SI, cinema was just another revolutionary tool, what Réne Viénet called "the newest and without doubt the most useful means of expression of our epoch" (Viénet 213–16). Film was to be used to expose the mediated state of the contemporary world. Détournement was the key practical method of making cinema. It seems, however, following Lowry, that in his later works, especially In Girum, Debord transcended film as a revolutionary tool to create a poetic, critical biography of the modern world. Although the film does incorporate various critiques of modern society (the very first scene is of an audience enjoying a "pseudo experience"), and deals with the alienation of the individual in capitalist systems, this is connected to the personal experience of an "important subject," Debord himself. Interestingly, a number of Debord's films existed as books before they were seen as films, further cementing the relationship between film, fiction, and literature.[6] The film contains many citations from other films and literary texts, and like Lowry's approach, draws on layers of Dantesque quadrival meanings.[7]

Debord intended In Girum to be a document of a world decaying as a result of the "widespread historical amnesia which defined the society of the spectacle" (Hussey 317). This marks the later works of Debord, which oscillated—like Hugh and the Consul in Under the Volcano—between political theory and poetic lament. Part of the film is a coruscating attack on advanced capitalism, on the spectacle. The rest is a lament for the lost youth of postwar rebellion. Debord was acutely aware of the tradition of ancient France and sought, like twelfth-century troubadours, an art that reconciled the aristocratic and the democratic.[8] The film combines footage of film re-enactments of moments in European history with contemporary elements and poetic narration spoken by Debord himself, laced with quotations from Bossuet, Clausewitz, and Dante, read aloud, as Lowry liked to do in dictating his stories and poems to Margerie.

The overall theme of Debord's film reflects Lowry's obsessions. In one of Lowry's last published stories, "Strange Comfort Afforded by the Profession," Wilderness, the "hero," "despondently recognizes that the grand heroic life-style of Keats and Shelley is gone from the world. Modern writers are like bank clerks" (Binns 19). Lowry's lament at the crassness of the modern world is symptomatic of his later works and is also the theme of Debord's film. Both Lowry and Debord deliberately confuse the objective and subjective worlds of the writer and reader. Debord moves in In Girum from an objective critique of the modern capitalist world to subjective reflections on his own life and times, as does Lowry in Under the Volcano. Both texts support an impressionistic and yet modern form that is both "inward and outward looking" (Binns 41). It is not that Lowry and Debord share direct themes or politics, but that the spirit of Lowry is embedded in the very poetry of the film.

The film's opening pulls no punches in lambasting modern man in the guise of the movie-going public. Debord notes:

How harshly the mode of production has treated them! With all their 'upward mobility' they have lost the little they had and gained what no one wanted. They share poverties and histories and humiliations from all the past systems of exploitation without sharing in the revolts against those systems. . . . They are nothing but numbers on charts drawn up by idiots. (*Cinematic Works* 135–36)

Such words echo the kind of despair found in Lowry's writing. In the novella *Lunar Caustic*, Lowry's protagonist, Bill Plantagenet, perceives a

> mischievous world over which merely more subtle lunatics exerted almost supreme hegemony, where neurotic behaviour was the rule, and there was nothing but hypocrisy to answer the flames of evil, which might be the flames of judgement, which were already scorching nearer and nearer. (*Lunar Caustic* 317)

Elsewhere, Debord notes the connections between the destruction of the natural world—Lowry's *paradise*—and the destruction of mankind: "A society that is ever more sick, but ever more powerful, has recreated the world—everywhere and in concrete form—as the environment and backdrop of its sickness: it has created a *sick planet*" (*Sick Planet* 81). This clearly echoes the way in which the tragedy of Lowry's characters is mirrored by the catastrophes of the external world.

The defiance of the true artist is evident throughout Debord's film. The opening lines, "I will make no concession to the public in this film" (*Cinematic Works* 133), state this unambiguously. Debord wishes to supersede film language: "I do not wish to preserve any of the language of this outdated art, except perhaps the reverse shot of the only world it has observed and a tracking shot across the fleeting ideas of an era" (146). There is no desire to make a work that is user friendly. Debord's paraphrasing of Swift, "It is no small satisfaction to present a work that is beyond all criticism" (147), echoes Lowry's own defence of his working methods.

To support the overall themes of the film, Debord utilizes a number of powerful symbolic elements, many of which can also be found in Lowry's work. These are worth exploring in detail.

WATER

"The entire film," notes Debord, "is based on the theme of water. Hence the quotations from poets evoking the evanescence of everything, who all used water as a metaphor for the flowing of time" (*Cinematic Works* 223). The sequences of the film not *détourned* were shot in Venice by a small crew. Most of the shots are tracking shots of buildings and the flowing of water along the canals. Of course, Lowry's obsessions with the sea are well known. Lowry was fascinated by Scandinavia and the Norwegian writer Nordahl Grieg, and the Consul himself longs for a water-wreathed northern paradise in *Under the Volcano*. Indeed, large sections of that novel (especially chapter 5) are filled with images and descriptions of lakes, waterfalls, and rain much needed in the Mexican locale of the novel. The Consul's relationship with water is tragic: "The regenerative water, the mysterious river Eridanus that can put out the flames and cool the body is never reached" (Beckoff 24). Yet in Debord's film, "the water of time remains, and ultimately overwhelms and extinguishes the fire" (*Cinematic Works* 224), rendering it therefore more symbolically hopeful.

At one point in the film, during a section on past time and the "restless and exitless present" (165), Debord quotes Ecclesiastes: "All the rivers run into the sea; yet the sea is not full; unto the place from whence the rivers come, thither they return again" (166). Though the reference in *In Girum* is to the river Seine in Paris, locality of so many situationist adventures, the image conjures up also the circularity of time as evoked by the Ferris wheel in *Under the Volcano*. The film ends with allusions to the sea: "this civilization is on fire; the whole thing is capsizing and sinking. What splendid torpedoing!" (191) Humanity is dying—an appalling collapse which Debord participated in and which Lowry, imagining he would, depicted in his writings.

FIRE

In Girum is a film about water, but it is also about fire and, according to Debord, of "*momentary brilliance*—revolution . . . youth, love, negation in the night, the Devil, battles and unfulfilled missions where spellbound 'passing travellers' meet their doom; and *desire within this night of the world*" (223). Fire, for Lowry, was "the element that follows you around" (*October Ferry* 123). As Clarissa Francillon observed, speaking of Malcolm and Margerie, "Ineradicably, fire was to be inscribed along the whole course of their existence" (Lowry, *Psalms and Songs* 93). Lowry's fascination with the occult, through his acquaintance with Charles Stansfeld Jones (aka Fred Achad, and the "magical child" of Aleister Crowley), led him to believe that his "playing about" with the occult had put him in bad repute with certain demonic forces and that it was his destiny to be pursued by the element of fire. Famously, many of Lowry's works, including his manuscript for the novel *In Ballast to the White Sea*, were destroyed by fire.[9] In *Under the Volcano*, the Consul's letters are burned by Laruelle, and in her dying dream, Yvonne (the Consul's estranged wife) witnesses his manuscript go up in flames. According to Percy Cummins, a neighbour of the Lowrys at Dollarton who witnessed the burning of their shack, "His mind must have been a fiery furnace for all he thought about was fire" (Kilgallin 38). Lowry's doomed man (the Consul), like much of Lowry's actual work, is destined to be destroyed by flames. Lowry knew Eliot's *Four Quartets* well, and his words about "Time past and time future" (Eliot, *Collected Poems* 192; "We only live, only suspire / Consumed either by fire or fire" [191]) ring out in the title and theme of Debord's film: "It has become ungovernable, this wasteland where new sufferings are disguised with the name of former pleasures and where people are so afraid. They turn in the night, consumed by fire" (*Cinematic Works* 191).

TIME

> [*Under the Volcano*] should be seen as essentially trochal, I repeat, the form of it as a wheel so that when you get to the end . . . you should want to turn back to the beginning again. (Lowry, *Selected Letters* 88)

Perhaps the most important aspect of Debord's film in relation to Lowry is its cyclical structure. The authors of both *Under the Volcano* and *In Girum* invite the "reader" to go back to the beginning and start again.

In his famous letter to Jonathan Cape, who had conditionally agreed to publish *Under the Volcano*, Lowry began a defence of his technique by claiming that the slow start to the novel would be redeemed for the reader by "the reports which had already reached his ears of rewarding vistas further on" (*Selected Letters* 58). At the same time, Lowry was keen to stress the importance of the circularity of the novel; that in regard to the ending, "the beginning . . . answers it, echoes back to it over the bridge of the intervening chapters" (59). At screenings of Debord's deliberately interminable first anti-film, *Hurlements en Faveur de Sade* (1952)—a film made up of black-and-white screens with only random voices as a stimulus—each screening was prefaced by the promise of "something dirty." This "playing with time" was central both to Debord's films and to Lowry's art. A. C. Nyland notes that "in his later work Lowry showed great skill in presenting the passage of time" (Nyland 143). Action exists merely to "arrest the flow of thought and to make the reader conscious of the passing of time" (143). Lowry's books formed part of what Beckoff describes as a "cosmic never-ending voyage" (Beckoff 7). The theme of circularity is stated in the palindrome form of the title of Debord's film, which is capable of "perfectly uniting the form and content of perdition" (Debord, *Cinematic Works* 166), a state of eternal punishment and damnation into which a sinful and impenitent person passes after death. George Woodcock notes that "the present cannot escape the past, that the impotence of man's present merges with the guilt of his past, is symbolically best expressed in a cinematic style where the circularity of the form, imitating the circular motion of the reel, can manipulate the overlapping and merging of time" (Woodcock 140). In a piece for LIGHT, the journal of the literary spiritualist organization the Discovery Group, during a discussion on Lowry between Rosamond Lehmann and Kathleen Raine, it was noted that "All he has to do now, is to acknowledge that he undertook more than he can manage spiritually, and he will have to come back and do the whole thing over again."

It seems Lowry was fated to repeat incidents from his life and work.

MUSIC

Another key aspect of Debord's film is its musical soundtrack. Only three pieces of music are used: two pieces by the baroque composer Francois Couperin and a jazz instrumental by Art Blakey and the Messengers. The music by Couperin (from his Concerts Royaux [Royal Concerts]), has a courtly, majestic quality to it, evoking a past age of aristocratic elegance and eloquence, invoking perhaps the classical texts that were an important symbol against the crassness of contemporary lived experience. But it is the use of Blakey that speaks most loudly to Lowry's life and work; for it is jazz, of course, that represents the kind of ambience that Lowry immersed himself in, loving and trying to imitate and evoke its tenor in his difficult, stirring, and often beautiful words. The Blakey piece in Debord's film is used to stimulate memories of a specific milieu: the Left Bank culture of Paris (a place which Lowry enjoyed too). Specifically, Saint-Germain-des-Prés was for Debord a symbol of liberation and decadence, where African American musicians such as Blakey were welcomed and frequently performed. Debord's use in this instance of the Messengers' live recording of Benny Golson's "Whisper Not" contributes significantly to the melancholia of the film.[10] Like Lowry before him, Debord knew the value and importance of jazz in painting a picture of modern life that is both poetic and destructive. The film, as we know, follows the dérive, the letterist concept of the drift, wandering, which in this case might be understood as a kind of improvisational jazz performance. Lowry's work is full of the dérive.

CONCLUSION

Debord's own contempt for the cinema, expressed strongly in his film, echoes Lowry's own disenchantment with the American film industry, disgusted as he was with "the poor quality of writing which was expected of him" (Lowry, Psalms and Songs 92). This desire, perhaps even nostalgia, for an ideal and idealized space permeates the work of both men. While Debord's film begins ferociously, it edges slowly toward a lamentation for a lost world, moving toward an exposition on passion and a regret over how ingrained routines render true emotion obsolete. Lowry examines a similar loss in his work: the phrase "one cannot live without love" resonates throughout *Under the Volcano*. In *Girum Imus Nocte et Consumimur Igni* examines the "cafés of lost youth" and reflects on the friends of Debord who have died, disappeared, or gone mad: "Suicide carried off many. 'Drink and the devil have done for the rest' as a song says" (*Cinematic Works* 164). The suicide of Lowry's friend Paul Fitte stood as a symbol for Lowry of this tragic youth ("the brilliant youth of Saint-Germain-des-Près . . . were drowned in the flowing waters of their century" [Debord, *Cinematic Works* 224]). *Volcano* and *In Girum* depict humanity as looking into the abyss, "or simply down the drain" (Lowry, *Selected Letters* 68).

In the film, the figure of Debord functions, as in Lowry's own use of his own "self" in his writing, neither as "facile autobiography [n]or narcissist indulgence" (Levin 103) and is, in fact, reminiscent of an earlier Debord project, *Eloge de ce que nous avons aimé* (*Homage to the Things We Loved*), a film that celebrates his friends (e.g., Chtcheglov) and, more generally, life (food and drink). Debord expresses his love for games (his kriegspiel), just as Lowry was fond of numbers; this is their occult sensibility at play. Debord plays with the language of cinema just as Lowry plays with the language of words. Both writers contribute to a study of the "battering the human spirit takes" (Lowry, *Selected Letters* 63). Incorporated into *In Girum* are blank screens, found footage and photographs, quotations, sections from Debord's other earlier films. This echoes Lowry's use of quotations throughout his work, but especially perhaps in *Volcano*. But the difficulties of reading/watching Debord's film and Lowry's stories are transcended by the experience of the reader actually engaging with the text. Levin points out that Debord's films formed a "third avant-garde" that "synthesizes a formal modernism . . . and semiotic and ideological reflexivity" (108), a combination of ancient texts with new ideas and personal poetics. Lowry achieved something very similar in his own work.[11]

The final shot of Debord's film shows the narrow canal of the city opening out to a vast expanse of empty water. This is ambiguous, but has hope.[12] Lowry, for his part, expressed his own ambivalent feelings in his masterpiece: "Though tragedy was in the process of becoming unreal and meaningless it seemed one was still permitted to remember the days when an individual life held some value and was not a mere misprint in a communiqué" (*Volcano* 11). The final words of the film we hear are:

Preparing an era for a voyage through the cold waters of history has in no way dampened these passions of which I have presented such fine and sad examples.

(Debord, *Cinematic Works* 193)

This is followed by the title:

TO BE GONE THROUGH AGAIN FROM THE BEGINNING.

Debord quoted Marx: "You can hardly claim that I think too highly of the present time. If I nevertheless do not despair of it, it is because its own desperate situation fills me with hope" (*Cinematic Works* 192). If "Lowry's work expressed the poles of human possibility—whether to be actively part of society, fighting to change it, or whether to be outside it altogether as an addict, visionary and drop-out" (Binns 21), then a glimpse at the life and works of Debord will confirm that he followed the latter.

The epitaph on Keats' tombstone in the Protestant cemetery in Rome reads:

Here lies one whose name was writ in water

Such would stand, evident in the majesty of these experimental works, as a fine tribute to the works of Malcolm Lowry and Guy Debord.

NOTES

1. The English-language versions of the group names are used here.
2. *Sursum Corda!: The Collected Letters of Malcolm Lowry* (Jonathan Cape: London), vol. 2, 200.
3. Ibid., 201.
4. Gerald Noxon notes (in Kilgallin 112) that "it was necessary that (Malcolm's) writing should have a perfectly wrought surface meaning, in the sense of the term established by Flaubert" and "a sound dramaturgy of classical origin." Debord reflected this style in his prose.
5. Kilgallin notes that this too was the way to approach Lowry's novel: armed with a form of "alternative consciousness" (130–31).
6. The published script is included in *Guy Debord: Complete Cinematic Works, Scripts, Stills, Documents*—see Works Cited.
7. These meanings are, according to Kilgallin, (i) literal, (ii) allegorical, (iii) tropological, and (iv) anagogical (Kilgallin 151).
8. In this, he followed not only the chansons of modern troubadour Georges Brassens but also the English author Ford Madox Ford, who also sought refuge in southern France from the ugliness of contemporary life and art.

9. Though *In Ballast to the White Sea* was long thought to have been destroyed by fire, in fact a surviving manuscript existed, in the hands of Lowry's first wife, Jan Gabrial, and an edition has recently been published by the University of Ottawa Press—see Works Cited.

10. The recording can be found on *Art Blakey Et Les Jazz-Messengers Au Club St. Germain*, Vol. 1 (RCA LP 430.043, France, 1959). The Messengers' line-up includes Lee Morgan (trumpet), Benny Golson (tenor saxophone), Bobby Timmons (piano), Jymie Merritt (bass), and Art Blakey (drums).

11. Interestingly, Debord's final published text was a slim volume called *Des Contracts*, simply a reproduction of three contracts between Debord and his main financier, the film producer Gérard Lebovici. It seems that Debord's life and works were defined as much by these "correspondences" as Lowry's were by his letters. These envoi documents become an important part of the expression of creativity for each writer.

12. It is also reminiscent of the final scene of Alexander Sokurov's film *Russian Ark* (2002). Also of note is George Robertson's 1961 two-part film on Lowry, made for the CBC TV Vancouver series *Explorations*, where Lowry's words are expressed as paths where one loses one's way and as movements through space.

WORKS CITED

Beckoff, Samuel. *Malcolm Lowry's Under the Volcano: A Critical Commentary*. New York: Monarch P, 1975.

Binns, Ronald. *Malcolm Lowry*. London: Methuen, 1984.

Chtcheglov, Ivan. "Formulary for a New Urbanism." 1953. *The Situationist International Anthology*. Edited and translated by Ken Knabb, Berkeley, CA: The Bureau of Public Secrets, 1989.

Day, Douglas. "Preface." In Malcolm Lowry, *Dark as the Grave Wherein My Friend Is Laid*. Harmondsworth: Penguin, 1972.

Debord, Guy. *Comments on the Society of the Spectacle*. London: Verso, 1990.

——. *Correspondence*. Cambridge: Semiotext(e), 2009.

——. *Guy Debord: Complete Cinematic Works, Scripts, Stills, Documents*. 1978. Edinburgh: AK P, 2003.

——. "Introduction to a Critique of Urban Geography." 1955. *The Situationist International Anthology*. Edited and translated by Ken Knabb, Berkeley, CA: The Bureau of Public Secrets, 1989.

——. "Letter to Patrick Straram." 2001. *Not Bored*. www.notbored.org/debord-31 October1960.html, 2005.

——. *Panegyric*. London: Verso, 2004.

——. *A Sick Planet*. Oxford: Seagull Books, 2008.

"Definitions". *Situationist International Anthology*. www.bopsecrets.org/SI/1.definitions. htm.

Eliot, T. S. *Collected Poems*. London: Faber, 1974.

Forsyth, Lucy. "The Supersession of the SI." *The Hacienda Must Be Built: On the Legacy of Situationist Revolt*. Edited by Andrew Hussey and Gavin Bowd, Huddersfield, UK: AURA, 1996.

Francillon, Clarisse. "My Friend Malcolm." *Malcolm Lowry: Psalms and Songs*. Edited by Margerie Bonner Lowry, New York: Plume Books, 1975.

Hussey, Andrew. *The Game of War*. London: Jonathan Cape, 2001.

Kilgallin, Tony. *Lowry*. Erin, ON: P Porcepic, 1973.

Lautréamont, Comte de. *Maldoror and Poems*. Translated by Paul Knight, Harmondsworth, UK: Penguin, 1978.

Lehmann, Rosamond, Kathleen Raine, et al. "Discovery Group: Virginia Woolf and Malcolm Lowry", *Light: a Journal of Psychic and Spiritualist Knowledge and Research* 97, No. 4, 1977.

Levin, Thomas Y. "Dismantling the Spectacle: the Cinema of Guy Debord." *On the Passage of a Few People Through a Rather Brief Moment in Time: The Situationist International 1957–1972*. Edited by Elizabeth Sussman, Cambridge, MA: MIT P, 1989.

Lorenz, Clarissa. "Call it Misadventure." *Malcolm Lowry: Psalms and Songs*. Edited by Margerie Bonner Lowry, New York: Plume Books, 1975.

Lowry, Malcolm. *In Ballast to the White Sea: A Scholarly Edition*. Edited by and with an introduction by Patrick A. McCarthy, annotations by Chris Ackerley, Ottawa: U of Ottawa P, 2014.

——. *Lunar Caustic*. Harmondsworth, UK: Penguin, 1979.

——. *Malcolm Lowry: Psalms and Songs*. Edited by Margerie Bonner Lowry, New York: Plume Books, 1975.

——. *October Ferry to Gabriola*. Harmondsworth, UK: Penguin, 1979.

——. *Selected Letters of Malcolm Lowry*. [1965] Edited by Harvey Breit and Margerie Bonner Lowry, Philadelphia: Lippincott, 1985.

——. *Selected Poems of Malcolm Lowry*. San Francisco: City Lights Books, 1962.

——. *Sursum Corda!: The Collected Letters of Malcolm Lowry*. 2 vols. Edited by Sherrill Grace, Toronto: U of Toronto P, 1995, 1996.

——. *Under the Volcano*. Harmondsworth, UK: Penguin, 1963.

Lowry, Margerie Bonner. "Interview." *Malcolm Lowry Newsletter* 5, Fall 1979.

Mension, Jean-Michel. *The Tribe*. London: Verso, 2002.

Nyland, A. C. "Malcolm Lowry: the Writer." *Malcolm Lowry: Psalms and Songs*. Edited by Margerie Bonner Lowry, New York: Plume Books, 1975.

Perec, Georges. *Species of Place and Other Pieces*. Harmondsworth, UK: Penguin, 1999.

Straram, Patrick. "They Write to Us of Vancouver." *Potlach* No. 2, June 1954. www.cddc.vt.edu/sionline/presitu/potlatch2.html#vancouver

Vaneigem, Raoul. "Raoul Vaneigem, Refusals and Passions." *Not Bored.* www.notbored.org/vaneigem-interview.html, 2003, 2014.

Viénet, René. "The Situationists and the New Forms of Action Against Politics and Art." 1967. *The Situationist International Anthology.* Edited and translated by Ken Knabb, Berkeley: The Bureau of Public Secrets, 1989.

Woodcock, George. *Malcolm Lowry: The Man and his Work.* Vancouver: U of BC Press, 1971.

2

Lowry, Sebald, and the Coincidental Landscape

LAURENCE PIERCY

In its use of baroque style, Malcolm Lowry's *Under the Volcano* traces the complex and shifting dynamics between the individual, the landscape, and history. Using the exemplary work and critical afterlife of W. G. Sebald, this chapter maps the spatial intricacies of Lowry's text through comparison. I focus on Sebald's *The Rings of Saturn*, a text well recognized for drawing links—historical, textual, psychic, ephemeral—between disparate human and natural events. This centripetal vision becomes the vehicle for investigating the oblique nature of cause and influence that frames our relations with the past, with the environment, and with ourselves. Although these texts are entirely different in scope and style, they approach these complex relations in similar ways. Coincidence and pattern play a distinct role in both texts, and become a model through which the respective narrators reflect on the limits of knowledge. These questions underlie a distinct interaction with the landscape that traces the shifting grasp and loss of control of the individual in space. Loss of control in this guise is poised against human antagonism, both in the political turbulence of Lowry's Mexico and in Sebald's encompassing vision of historical victimhood. These contiguities are supported by shared references to the English physician, polymath, and author Thomas Browne. The allusions to Browne are thematically important, though the diverging rhetorical uses of his arguments by Sebald and Lowry also point to some fruitful differences between these complex texts.

In both *The Rings of Saturn* and *Under the Volcano*, behind the experience of nature lies the possibility of transcendental design. Sebald's use of Browne's quincunx, a geometrical pattern, "composed by using the corners of a regular quadrilateral and the point at which its diagonals intersect," poses a structure that is found by Browne to occur throughout the natural world, and "might be multiplied without end" to "demonstrate *ad infinitum* the elegant geometrical designs of Nature" (Sebald 20–21). The quincunx, proliferating through animate and inanimate things, also implicates human materiality in its scope as it is "also observable in some part of the skin of man" (Browne, "Garden" 166). Though we see these patterns in "the order of things," Sebald is clear that "we cannot grasp their innermost essence" (Sebald 19). The existence of an order manifest in infinite geometrical patterning seems too complex to attribute to accidental or even coincidental causality. In light of this, Browne concludes that its existence indicates the intervention of design, which in turn indicates the divine. This means that any repetition within "transient Nature" is "a reflection of eternity" because it gestures toward the actions of the divine, and, in this, gestures to the possibility of knowledge beyond the physical sphere (Sebald 19). In his secular reading of Browne, Sebald removes God from these patterns, and cosmic geometry appears as the evidence of how little we know of natural life. In this reading, the proliferating quincunx is less an image of eternity than evidence of our eternal ignorance.

Under the Volcano is also framed within the mysterious workings of the cosmos. Michael Wutz reads the infernal machine, the mechanistic images of the wheel that occur throughout the novel, as "multiple concentricities" which lock "microcosmic" happenings into "cosmic" revolutions and create a clear causal relation between the individual and the universe (102). This point in Wutz's reading is not dissimilar from Frank Livingstone Huntley's discussion of the circle motif in Browne, where Ezekiel's "wheels within wheels" define the relationship of man to God:

> [In] the metaphor God is the large circle about us, and man is the smaller circle within and related to that larger movement by natural law. Man carries within him the illimitable spaces of the universe, and hence is not a forgotten speck unfixed in the void. (Huntley 358)

Yet doubt also intrudes into the interlocking cosmic structure of Under the Volcano. Lowry's wheels and circles proliferate to the point where the causal relations between them are scarcely observable. As Wutz suggests, "their oscillating radii . . . delineate the maelstrom of causalities that are only partly accessible to human observation" (102). The clockwork becomes too complex to evidence any direct link between heaven and earth. Between the cosmos and the individual, Sebald and Lowry both repeatedly place coincidence as a possible, though ultimately flawed, signifier of secret knowledge. Lowry's use of a cabbalistic number system is not dissimilar from the structural play of coincidence within The Rings of Saturn.[1]

As Bianca Theisen notes, these patterns represent the "codes and numbers that for pre-rationalist thought could offer direct access to a hidden reality" (564). In a secular view, these coincidences, as with the quincunx, are separated from the knowledge that they promise to reveal. The removal of divine design from these systems further confuses the epistemic problem. Without design, it becomes unclear that coincidence can offer any knowledge, or whether it is simply the interpretive fantasy of the individual imposed on pattern in nature. If coincidence still signifies the hope of knowledge, it is also tempered with the recognition of our limits of comprehension.

Coincidence, then, is a way of negotiating the narrator's ability to understand the environment in which he exists, and the fluctuating sense of immediacy that permeates this. Anne Fuchs develops this to delineate three ways in which the Sebaldian narrator interacts with the landscape: firstly, the landscape is seen as a repository of human experience, "a record of the history of human arrogance" (Fuchs 130); secondly, a "more phenomenological dimension" describes the stark "autonomy of nature"; and finally, an intermediary point marks the "natural history of destruction" (132). This latter reading recognizes human violence and technological incursion as "a kind of historical experiment that anticipates the point at which the course of human history is subsumed back into the history of nature," and describes a point at which the autonomy of nature becomes oppositional, and a feedback loop of destruction occurs in specific reaction to human incursions on the landscape (137). As this final point makes clear, human history and the history of nature are not separate, but mutually shaping.

An episode in *The Rings of Saturn*, in which the narrator meets a likeminded figure, Michael Hamburger, is especially rich in the interconnections between individual and landscape. A description and dream recollection of the narrator's walk across Dunwich Heath occurs immediately before his appearance at Hamburger's house. On this journey, the narrator's confused path through the "bewildering terrain" of the heath repeatedly results in a sense of lost dizziness (Sebald 173). It is unclear whether these paths originate from the landscape or from human construction, whether the signposts are deliberately misleading or whether the idiosyncrasy of the landscape prevents the signposts from signifying accurately. What is certain is that the atmosphere increases the sense of confusion that arises from the "endlessly winding paths" (173):

> The low, leaden sky; the sickly violet hue of the heath clouding the eye; the silence, which rushed in the ears like the sound of the sea in a shell; the flies buzzing about me—all this became oppressive and unnerving. (172)

The paths across the heath repeatedly force the narrator to "retrace long stretches of that bewildering terrain," creating repetitions which actively disorientate him (172). From the heath, Sebald moves to a companionate image, though one that signifies human design, "the yew maze at Somerleyton," which, in the narrator's dream, "represented a cross-section of my brain" (173). The maze can represent the brain, but not describe it completely. The landscape is even further removed from the involutions of the maze, which creates "a pattern simple in comparison" with the paths over the heath (173). Through these comparisons, Sebald sketches the limits of comprehension, moving from the fathomable complexity of the yew maze to the unknown involutions of the mind and the natural world.

Through recalling the Somerleyton yew maze, the narrator directs us back to the Somerleyton episode earlier in the book, which is itself rich with the complexities of knowledge. Somerleyton Hall, far from offering an accessible history, now "imperceptibly nearing the brink of dissolution and silent oblivion," signifies "many ages" and geographical locations:

> [One] is not quite sure whether one is in a country house in Suffolk or some kind of no-man's-land, on the shores of the Arctic Ocean or in the heart of the dark continent. (36)

The ruinous building becomes the catalyst for various associative links that trace, at one point, the cataclysm of the Second World War ("German cities going up in flames, the firestorms setting the heavens alight" [38]) and, at another point, the mysterious collision of two American fighter planes close to the estate (40). These historical events arise from the experience of the building, an occurrence that Anne Fuchs describes as a "historical . . . reading" of the landscape (Fuchs 130). This network of traces is incomplete; signs do not offer historical understanding in themselves but provide connections which work, as they do in Claude Lévi-Strauss's "social bricolage," to give a sense of an idea (Lévi-Strauss 20). Sebald's technique divests bricolage of its aspiration of meaningful connectivity, and deflates the illusion of coherence, which offers "some sort of sense when there isn't, as we all know."[2] The coincidental patterns that recur through human history appear, like the quincunxial patterns in nature, to trace the limits of our understanding.

Following this, Sebald probes coincidental occurrences as manifestations of the mind's complexity. Tracking his life against Hamburger's, the narrator notes their respective friendship with another figure, Stanley Kerry. He observes that "at the time we met him, in 1944 and in 1966 respectively, we were both twenty-two," an "incomprehensible" coincidence (Sebald 187). This is framed within a series of "elective affinities" through which "one perceives oneself in another human being," affinities which connect humans over time, but are personal and deeply ambiguous: "Does one follow in Hölderlin's footsteps, simply because one's birthday happened to fall two days after his?" (182). While the dream scene on Dunwich Heath draws the symbols of human and nature into a single shifting vision, coincidence becomes the means of separation between nature and the individual consciousness. The narrator presents this in an image of clear delineation:

> Perhaps there is in this as yet unexplained phenomenon of apparent duplication some kind of anticipation of the end, a venture into the void, a sort of disengagement, which, like a gramophone repeatedly playing the same sequence of notes, has less to do with damage to the machine itself than with an irreparable defect in its programme. (187–88)

The repeated event, like the repeating notes from a broken record, is the imposition of coincidence on the universe, rather than the traces of secret knowledge. This recognition provides the basis for a secular readirg of repetition that situates the individual within a matrix of historical and personal similarities through which they attempt, to no avail, "to fathom the imponderables that govern our course through life" (182). Coincidence appears as an attempt to understand mortality, "the end" (188). Emerging from human materiality, coincidence becomes a way of interacting with the unknowns of the body and the natural world.

The "venture into the void" resonates throughout Sebald's text. In its figurative sense, the void marks the endpoint of knowledge, the "abyss of ignorance" (19). Describing both the limits of our knowledge of the natural world and of our own materiality, the abyss stands at the point of urgent but unknown interaction between the earth and the body. At this point, where the individual and the natural world are brought together, they are also unfathomably different. In Sebald's section on Browne, we find another image of ignorance: "the invisibility and intangibility of that which moves us" (18). The double meaning of this phrase both traces the patterns of the individual within history, the "imponderables that govern our course through life," and implies that we are also physically moved, displaced by nature (182). Here, these experiences are brought together to the point where they symbolize each other. Elsewhere, Sebald breaks this symbolic loop by emphasizing the phenomenal alterity of nature, though he does this through the same imagery of the void: "As darkness fell," Dunwich was "clawed away" into the sea, a destructive "abyss . . . a whirlpool of whitish brown waters" (158). These different figures of the void reveal the shifting ground between signification and actuality, and the complex way in which this underwrites our knowledge.

We see a similar shift between the natural and symbolic in *Under the Volcano*, where the abyss also appears in a similar geopsychic role. The ravine, or *barranca*, which runs through Quauhnahuac, imposes repetition on the Consul's daily travels around the town: "One was . . . always stumbling upon the damn thing" (Lowry, *Volcano* 134). Here, the topography of the town is both a physical determinant and a psychologized, symbolic pattern that structures the Consul's walks. Because of this, it is hard to trace the distinctions between mind and nature that underwrite the uncanny "unintended recurrence" of the ravine at every turn (Freud 237). This is further complicated when the Consul recognizes how he psychologizes the ravine, and the figurative "pitfalls" of the coming day are literalized by his close encounter with the *barranca* (Lowry, *Volcano* 134). The "frightful" aspect of the "cleft" then appears as a commixture of these psychological and geographical aspects (134), a sense that reveals itself in a confused (and hilarious) hyperbolic display: "Thou mighty gulf, insatiate cormorant, deride me not, though I may seem petulant to fall into thy chops" (134).

The blurred boundary between the symbolic and real finds close expression in the shared reference to Thomas Browne's *Religio Medici, Hydriotaphia,* and *The Garden of Cyrus* in both *Under the Volcano* and *The Rings of Saturn*. As Theisen notes, Sebald uses Browne to set up "the contrast between life and death, stability and volatility as a nexus" (Theisen 564), into which contradictions he reads a negative episteme that shows earthly life as tending toward the darkness of ignorance.

> [Nothing] endures, in Thomas Browne's view. On every new thing there lies already the shadow of annihilation. For the history of every individual, of every social order, indeed of the whole world, does not describe an ever-widening, more and more wonderful arc, but rather follows a course which, once the meridian is reached, leads without fail down into the dark. (Sebald 24)

Each individual is implicated in the rise and fall of "every social order" and the "whole world," and common ignorance governs these cycles. Building on the idea developed earlier, that materiality is inextricable from ignorance, Eric Santner also recognizes a link between materiality and the patterns of human history:

> Sebald's "baroque" sense of the object world is that for him materiality does not merely signify the "natural" corruptibility of all things earthly; rather, this corruptibility is an index of their participation in the violent rhythms of human history. (Santner 114)

Into the abyss of ignorance, then, Santner develops recognition of intersubjective engagement; our common mortality should preclude solipsism.

In direct contrast to Sebald's use of Browne, the Consul's reference to "Hydriotaphia" recasts mutability not as a call for engagement, but as an abdication of interpersonal responsibility. His argument emerges from an "illusion [of speech]," a "whirling cerebral chaos" in which he develops associations "like Sir Thomas Browne, of Archimedes, Moses, Achilles, Methuselah, Charles V, and Pontius Pilate" (Lowry, *Volcano* 309). In a parody of baroque prose, in which associative leaps create a sense of levitation, the Consul's thoughts abruptly ground in a confused, inelegant sophistry, arguing for an abdication of political and interpersonal responsibility. The Consul recalls an earlier event, in which he and Hugh witness an Indian dying in the road. Dwelling on this, the Consul asks, "why should we have done anything to save his life? Hadn't he a right to die, if he wanted to? . . . Why should anybody interfere with anybody?" (311) The Consul perhaps talks, like Sebald's Thomas Browne, of human mutability to put forward a historical viewpoint. In this instance, it is easy to imagine the historical argument being developed to rid himself of responsibility for the Indian. The excerpts that correspond to the associations that he draws from "Hydriotaphia" certainly seem to support this:

> How many pulses made up the life of Methuselah were work for Archimedes: common counters sum up the life of Moses his man. Our days become considerable, like petty sums, by minute accumulations; where numerous fractions make up but small round numbers, and our days of a span long make not one little finger. (Browne, "Hydriotaphia" 126)

> But in this latter scene of time we cannot expect such mummies unto our memories, when ambition may feat the prophecy of Elias, and Charles V can never hope to live within two Methuselahs of Hector. (128)

> To be nameless in worthy deeds exceeds an infamous history: the Canaanitish woman lives more happily without a name than Herodias with one. And who had not rather have been the good thief than Pilate? (129)

Expanding his policy of non-involvement from the case of the Indian to a wider view of nation building and social dissolution, the Consul develops Browne's emphasis on human transience to become the image for the decline of society: "Read history. . . . What is the use of interfering with its worthless stupid course? Like a *barranca*, a ravine, choked up with refuse" (Lowry, *Volcano* 311). The simile of a *barranca*, an image which appears everywhere in *Under the Volcano*, here provides a veiled link to Browne's burial urns, the burned remains that, when unearthed near Browne's home in Norfolk, precipitated the writing of *Religio Medici, Hydriotaphia,* and *The Garden of Cyrus.* The simile partly suggests the Consul's throwaway use of Browne as a justifying allusion. More importantly, it pairs the avoidance of human understanding with the symbolization of the landscape, and in doing so occludes a sense of underlying reality. In this general turn away from the world, Sue Vice recognizes the Consul's symbolizing tendencies as digressions that remove "the discourse from what is happening" and point "straight back to the bottles and misery" (Vice 104).

The symbolizing tendency is also at work in Laurelle and Hugh. Laruelle's description first images the volcanoes, "terrifying in the sunset," and desolation, "fields were full of stones: there was a row of dead trees," which arouse a "sense of being, after all these years . . . still a stranger" (Lowry, *Volcano* 15). Yet the strangeness of the image turns into familiarity where, "if you looked a little bit farther . . . you would find every sort of landscape at once, the Cotswolds, Windermere, New Hampshire, the meadows of the Eure-et-Loire," "Cheshire" or "even the Sahara" (15–16). The changeable beauty of the landscape, "fatal or cleansing as it happened to be" (16), is marked by Sharae Deckard as a "deployment of rhetorical tropes and myths of Mexico as a depraved Eden" (Deckard 52). Indeed, the cooption of the Mexican landscape as a blank canvas for Laruelle's global snapshots certainly develops an image of rhetorical imposition. Interestingly, it seems to be "look[ing] a little farther" beyond the immediate landscape that allows this as, later in the novel, Hugh enacts a similar conceit (Lowry, *Volcano* 15). Reading the "wild strength" of the land, Hugh hears "a presence born of that strength whose cry his whole being recognized as familiar, caught and threw back into the wind" (128). Hugh *as* echo reflects the grandeur of the landscape, which bolsters his political and personal idealism, and arouses in him "the passionate, yet so nearly always hypocritical, affirmation of one's soul" (128). Once affirmed, his "soul" transcends the immediate landscape. Self-affirmation comes with a look beyond the immediate, outside the enclosure of the valley:

> It was as though he were gazing now beyond this expanse of plains and beyond the volcanoes out to the wide rolling blue ocean itself, feeling it in his heart still, the boundless impatience, the immeasurable longing. (128)

Yet the hostile otherworldliness of the immediate landscape that Laruelle first recognizes is echoed in another of Hugh's descriptions. At this point, Hugh describes the landscape outside the bus as lunar, "like driving *over* the moon"

(240; emphasis in original). This is not a throwaway simile, but is brought back to the actual volcanic debris, "pines, fircones, stones, black earth," that testify to "Popocatepetl's presence and antiquity" (241). From this, Lowry moves to a strained understanding of the volcano:

> Why were there volcanic eruptions? People pretended not to know. . . . [Because] the watery rocks near the surface were unable to restrain the growing complex of pressures, and the whole mass exploded; the lava flooded out, the gases escaped, and there was your eruption.—But not your explanation. No, the whole thing was a complete mystery still. (241–42)

The volcano seems to evade understanding, even if this is grudgingly admitted. This description moves on to the ambiguous human reactions to the "complete mystery" of the volcano. "In movies of eruptions," despite mass panic, "people are always seen standing in the midst of the encroaching flood, delighted by it," "smoking cigarettes" while buildings crumble (242). The eruption and the unfathomable human reaction are not oppositional, but mysteriously interacting. The limit of Hugh's volcanic knowledge appears at the same point at which human behaviour evades him, and both of these things are made more obscure in their inexplicable meeting.

Hugh moves on, away from the volcano and into another landscape, where there stands "a ruined church, full of pumpkins, bearded with grass. Burned, perhaps, in the revolution" (242). Out of the shadow of the volcano, the atmosphere on Hugh's bus changes to "a sense of gaiety" (242). The burned church continues the fire trope of the volcano, but in contrast, peculiarly seems to offer up an instantly fathomable causality. The complex history of revolution and political turmoil that the church alludes to is left untested. However, this elision becomes evident almost immediately when the bus narrowly misses the bleeding Indian lying in the road, jolting Hugh from another nostalgic vision "of England," imposed on the "winding" Mexican road (243). The brutality of the Indian's injury appears to have a similar effect as the mysterious workings of the volcano. Faced with the Indian, "Hugh and the Consul stood helplessly" (245). Hugh's inaction comes from not "knowing what should be done" in Mexico, and when he does attempt to examine the Indian, he is stopped by "the law" (245). As Deckard suggests, "they can neither speak for the Indian nor fathom his suffering" (Deckard 56). The tortured inaction of Hugh and the Consul is set amongst the practiced inaction of the other onlookers, whose "ingenuity" is manifest in their ability to erect obstacles to "doing anything about the Indian" (Lowry, *Volcano* 248). They eventually descend into political arguments that make "no sense" (248). Hugh's dumb confrontation with the volcano pervades his interaction with Mexico at large.

Brian Rourke gestures toward the limits of comprehension in Under the Volcano in his description of the all-encompassing ambitions of the book, in which causality and difference are submerged under the textual play of the novel:

> Subjectivity, historical discourse, and memory appear as products of a textual machine that is itself part and product of a monistic, inorganic, and non-subjective network that connects society, bodies, even an entire cosmos. (Rourke 21)

A similar description comes from Sherrill Grace, who describes a "condition of containment" in the novel, which is both "suggested by the Consul's destructive withdrawal inside his own circumference and by the images of containment . . . dominating the narrative" (Grace 154). Both critics describe the sense of claustrophobia and dominating focalization that control the novel. Yet, as I have suggested, even within this machinery Lowry is gesturing to the natural and historical sublime that escapes the comprehension of his characters.

As with Sebald, coincidence is also developed by Lowry as a way of mediating the relation between his characters and the landscape. This is especially complex in the final two chapters of the novel, which describe the near-simultaneous death of Yvonne and the Consul. Before these complexities are developed, Lowry consolidates the link between Mexican history and its landscape that arises through their mutual incomprehensibility. Again, a phenomenological reading of nature is gestured to, this time from an episode in which the landscape is approached with glib surety. Yvonne reflects on how "merrily Mexico laughed away its tragic history" (Lowry, Volcano 256), and from this, turns to a particularly favourable view of Popocatepetl:

> [The] traitorous mirror of the bright enamel compact. It reminded her that only five minutes ago she had been crying and imaged too, nearer, looking over her shoulder, Popocatepetl.
> The volcanoes! How sentimental one could become about them! (257)

Yvonne's sentimentality is mediated through the mirror; the image of the volcano is doubled and indirect, "even more beautiful for being reflected" (258). When the mirror cannot compact the landscape, Yvonne responds with further sentimentality: she simply could not "get poor Ixta in, who, quite eclipsed, fell away sharply into invisibility" (258). Yvonne's viewpoint is developed with a particularly optimistic turn, revealing that she had never "given up, or ceased to hope, or to try, gropingly, to find a meaning, a pattern, an answer—" (270). Yvonne's persistent hope is that pattern should still yield knowledge. This position is eroded in the final chapter of the novel, where Lowry's textual play constructs coincidence as an oppositional force to the characters. This is developed with an increasingly hostile image of the landscape. As the denouement nears, the "pitch-massed cloud banks" that appeared in Yvonne's mirror become increasingly malignant storm clouds. The clouds are stacked up against the volcano, increasing its bulk and making it mobile: "Before him the volcanoes, precipitous, seemed to have drawn nearer ... the whole precipitous bulk of Popocatepetl seemed to be coming towards them, travelling with the clouds, leaning forward over the valley" (316).

This enclosure becomes the scene for coincidence, in which extra-narrative comment is balanced against contrivance in the plot. The series of events that leads Yvonne and the Consul to die almost simultaneous deaths is also a confused chain of causes, in which human influence is combined with the natural conditions for chance. In the storm, the "mental door," which is first an attitude of trust in chance, "the entrance and the reception of the unprecedented, the fearful acceptance of the thunderbolt that never falls on oneself," becomes the perspective through which Yvonne is made aware "that something [is] menacingly wrong" (335). The obscure sense of safety seems corrupted by the Chief of Rostrums' gunshot, which combines with the setting in an oppressive echo:

Lightning flashed like an inchworm going down the sky and the Consul, reeling, saw above him for a moment the shape of Popocatepetl, plumed with emerald snow and drenched with brilliance. The Chief fired twice more, the shots spaced, deliberate. Thunderclaps crashed on the mountains and then at hand. (373)

The landscape shifts from the sublime to an accomplice in the inexplicable movements of the political machine. In this, there is movement between what Fuchs recognizes as the "phenomenological" relationship and the "natural history of destruction," in which human folly is reflected and magnified by the movements of nature (Fuchs 132).

This relationship becomes more complex when, following the simultaneous gunshots and thunderclaps, the horse is released and rears, and, "tossing its head ... plunged neighing into the forest" (Lowry, Volcano 374). The Chief's actions and the enclosed landscape are indistinguishable causes at this point, but as the horse moves into the forest, the topography becomes a determining force that steers the course of events. The claustrophobic wooded setting of Yvonne's death implies a natural limitation that directs the horse, which is "terrified by the storm," to Yvonne, and she falls into its path when "pitched forward" off a "dark slippery log" (335). Here, the conceits of the narrative are carefully balanced against the plausibility of the space of the wood playing such a decisive role. In a letter to Jonathan Cape, his nominal publisher at the time, Lowry defends this balance by arguing that, in "these parts," such chance is magnified, "where the paths in forests are narrow" (Lowry, *Selected Letters* 83).

This measured conceit is also entwined with the obscure questions of pattern and transcendentalism, most clearly signified by the horse with "the number seven branded on the rump."[3] If, as I have previously argued, the cosmic pattern of the book can be seen not in conjunction with divine design, but as a reflection of the patterns both human and natural that evade our understanding, then the occurrence of the horse with the number seven branded on its side reflects back on the coincidental deaths as a locus of ignorance. The interrelation of human and natural causes performs a rhetorical move that blurs the boundary between the oppositional elements, offering oblique enquiry, not only into the separate forces at work but, in a Brownian move, to the point of death, where these elements become hopelessly entangled.

Both Lowry and Sebald use coincidence as a way of exploring individual control within the natural and social environments. Pattern moves from being a way of seeing the world, a way of finding out about the world, to become a point of disconnection between the individual and his environment. For Lowry, coincidence is detached from the understanding of the characters to become obliquely connected with the events that escape their control and crowd in upon them. Coincidence becomes a way for Lowry to intermingle the spatial and social constraints of the Mexican scene. In the episode of the dying Indian, this is wrought specifically to trace the extent to which the Consul is willingly or forcibly ethically disenfranchised. Sebald interrogates the relationship between the individual and the suffering of others more explicitly, but also deeply implicates this in the complex relationships between humans and their environment. In addition, Sebald uses coincidence as a trope of comprehension, but, unlike Lowry, he presents it as a hopeful gesture of imposition upon the natural world. This effort is ultimately unsuitable, but failure itself gives way to the vital comprehension of our own limitations, an attitude that Sebald associates with a turn away from control and toward intersubjectivity.

NOTES

1. See Epstein, *The Private Labyrinth of Malcolm Lowry: Under the Volcano and the Cabbala.*
2. Quoted in Sheppard, 425.
3. Lowry calls the number seven "the fateful, the magic, the lucky good-bad number" in the letter to Cape (*Selected Letters* 77). The number, of cabbalistic significance, occurs throughout the book.

WORKS CITED

Browne, Sir Thomas. "Hydriotaphia." *Religio Medici, Hydriotaphia, and The Garden of Cyrus.* Edited by R. H. A. Robbins, Oxford: Clarendon P, 1997, pp. 91–134.

——. "The Garden of Cyrus." *Religio Medici, Hydriotaphia, and The Garden of Cyrus.* Edited by R. H. A. Robbins, Oxford: Clarendon P, 1997, pp. 135–190.

Deckard, Sharae. *Paradise Discourse: Exploiting Eden.* London: Routledge, 2010.

Epstein, Perle S. *The Private Labyrinth of Malcolm Lowry: Under the Volcano and the Cabbala.* New York: Holt, Rinehart and Winston, 1969.

Freud, Sigmund. "The Uncanny." *The Standard Edition of the Complete Psychological Works of Sigmund Freud.* Edited by James Strachey in collaboration with Anna Freud, vol. 17, London: Vintage, 2001, pp. 217–252.

Fuchs, Anne. "'Ein Hauptkapitel der Geschichte der Unterwerfung': Representation of Nature in W.G. Sebald's *Die Ringe des Saturn.*" *W.G. Sebald and the Writing of History.* Edited by J. J. Long and Anne Fuchs, Würzburg: Königshausen & Neumann, 2007, pp. 121–138.

Grace, Sherrill E. "The Luminous Wheel." *Malcolm Lowry: Under the Volcano.* Edited by Gordon Bowker, Basingstoke, UK: Macmillan, 1987, pp. 152–171.

Huntley, Frank Livingstone. "Sir Thomas Browne and the Metaphor of the Circle." *Journal of the History of Ideas,* vol. 14, no. 3, 1953, pp. 353–364.

Lévi-Strauss, Claude. *The Savage Mind.* Translated by Weidenfeld and Nicolson, London: Weidenfeld and Nicolson, 1966.

Lowry, Malcolm. *Selected Letters of Malcolm Lowry.* Harmondsworth, UK: Penguin, 1985.

——. *Under the Volcano.* London: Penguin, 2000.

Rourke, Brian. "Malcolm Lowry's Memory Machine: An Eclectic Systemë." *Journal of Modern Literature,* vol. 29, no. 3, 2006, pp. 19–38.

Santner, Eric L. *On Creaturely Life: Rilke, Benjamin, Sebald.* London: U of Chicago P, 2006.

Sebald, W. G. *The Rings of Saturn.* Translated by Michael Hulse, London: Vintage, 2002.

Sheppard, Richard. "Dexter – sinister: Some Observations on Decrypting the Mors Code in the Work of W.G. Sebald." *Journal of European Studies,* vol. 35, no. 4, 2005, pp. 419–463.

Theisen, Bianca. "A Natural History of Destruction: W.G. Sebald's *The Rings of Saturn.*" *MLN* vol. 121, no. 3, 2006, pp. 563–581.

Vice, Sue. "Fear of Perfection, Love of Death and the Bottle." *Malcolm Lowry Eighty Years On*. Edited by Sue Vice, New York: St. Martin's P, 1989, pp. 92–107.

Wutz, Michael. *Enduring Words: Literary Narrative in a Changing Media Ecology*. Tuscaloosa: U of Alabama P, 2009.

3

Lowry and Jakobson: Spatial Pyrotechnics and Poetic Writing in Under the Volcano

CHRISTINE VANDAMME

When reading *Under the Volcano*, one cannot but be struck by the extraordinary reflexivity of the novel, as well as its dense and multiple metaphorical networks. These give birth not only to an extremely rich and singular textual space but to a multitude of concomitant and possibly divergent interpretive and identificatory lines, as if the text could replicate itself endlessly, but with a slight variation each time, depending on the hermeneutic route the reader decides to follow. Such spatial dynamic makes Lowry's prose here very similar to poetry, and it is precisely this question of both *spatial* and *poetic* writing in *Under the Volcano* that this chapter will consider.

The linearity of sentences in Lowry's novel is consistently and systematically disrupted by a form of derailment or sudden disconnection, which then gives way to a poetic revolution in all senses of the word: Lowry's writing starts spinning words, syntagms, sentences, and motifs instead of linking them up or threading them into a predictable series of sentences, a predefined succession of actions, a logical plot. The chronological line is always used as a reassuring decoy—the essence of the book is elsewhere.

Such spatial and poetic writing becomes increasingly prevalent as the novel progresses, with chapter 10 undeniably illustrating it best: sentences and paragraphs keep derailing along with narrative progression, as if words, syntagms and voices had suddenly started exploding, as if the reader were irresistibly sucked into the bursting core of the volcano-like novel.

Such disruption of the syntagm is a sure sign of poetic writing, according to Roman Jakobson, and it is also coupled with a never-ending process of repeated selection. The two mechanisms go hand-in-hand and fuel each other, as will be shown in applying Jakobson's theory of language onto Lowry's text—an approach that provides illuminating insight into both the narrative structure of the novel and the type of reading it requires and encourages. This will ultimately have to be analyzed in relation to the type of identificatory, political, and ethical positioning such experimentation on narrative form and reader response suggests.

SPATIAL AND POETIC WRITING

Joseph Frank was the first critic to explicitly refer to modernist writing as "spatial," and his definition applies usefully to *Under the Volcano*, with its emphasis on the existence of a network of "images and symbols which must be referred to each other spatially throughout the time-act of reading" (Frank 439). In fact, *Under the Volcano* may be defined as spatial not only in this modernist sense of openness and emphasis on the reader's freedom and responsibility in the interpretive process, but also in its postmodernist use of the spatiality of language and text to make new meanings and ethical positionings emerge.

One can start by considering the opposition Jakobson establishes between prose and poetry in his famous article on two types of aphasia, "Two Aspects of Language and Two Types of Aphasic Disturbances." According to Jakobson, poetry mostly works with metaphorical processes, while prose tends to privilege metonymy. He also states that poetry favours selection and substitution, where prose would turn more willingly to combination and contexture:

> The development of a discourse may take place along two different semantic lines: one topic may lead to another either through their similarity or through their contiguity. The metaphoric way would be the most appropriate term for the first case and the metonymic way for the second, since they find their most condensed expression in metaphor and metonymy respectively. ("Two Aspects" 254)

But Jakobson also explicitly points out that the *poetic function* is not only to be found in poetry, since it may also characterise any work of prose as long as what constitutes the sequence, whether syntactic or narrative, is of a metaphoric nature rather than a metonymic one, as long as "equivalence is promoted to the constitutive device of the sequence":

> The selection is produced on the basis of equivalence, similarity and dissimilarity, synonymy and antonymy, while the combination, the build-up of the sequence, is based on contiguity. The poetic function projects the principle of equivalence from the axis of selection into the axis of combination. Equivalence is promoted to the constitutive device of the sequence. ("Linguistics" 27)

And it is precisely this kind of poetic writing, foregrounding metaphorical processes, that chapter 10 of *Under the Volcano* so evidently displays. The dominant point of view in the chapter is that of the Consul and, more importantly still, the Consul under the influence of alcohol, the fire of mescal that will bring about multiple successive explosions. It is no coincidence that the chapter begins with the word "mescal": "'Mescal,' the Consul said, almost absent-mindedly. What had he said? Never mind. Nothing less than mescal would do" (Lowry, *Volcano* 281). From this moment on, the diegetic line, the succession of paragraphs, the sequence of sentences, and the order of words in the sentence will be disrupted by the sudden and unexpected irruption of elements from the paradigmatic axis: memories, voices, metaphors, which ignite the Consul's mind through complex associations of ideas. In other words, as per Jakobson, the axis of *selection* perturbs the axis of *combination*.

Such diegetic and syntactic derailment is a direct result of the Consul's alcohol, as exemplified by the second paragraph of chapter 10:

> Nevertheless, the Consul thought, it was not merely that he shouldn't have, not merely that, no, it was more as if he had *lost* or *missed* something, or rather, *not precisely lost, not necessarily missed.*—It was as if, more, he were *waiting* for something, *and then again, not waiting.*—It was as if, almost, he *stood* (instead of upon the threshold of the Salón Ofélia, gazing at the calm pool where Yvonne and Hugh were about to swim) once more upon that black open station platform. (281; italics added)

The sentence is repeatedly interrupted, as if the axis of selection couldn't come to rest in the absence of the appropriate word. First, the Consul cannot find any suitable verb to place after "he shouldn't have," and, therefore, instead of looking for a word that would be satisfactory, he thinks of verbs that reflect his state of mind but which require another syntax, another combination, which is no longer built on the group of words "I shouldn't have" but on "it was as if." So we pass from a syntagm built on contiguity, "I-do-something," to a syntagm which actually reflects the activity of selection itself: "it was like this or like that," which is simply a question of *equivalence*, not a question of *contiguity*.

The rest of the paragraph is also built on this uninterrupted substitution of synonyms or similar terms, such as the following verbs: "lose" ("lost"), "miss" ("missed"), "wait" ("waiting"), "stand" ("stood"). Mescal seems to overactivate the selection process for the Consul to such a degree that he finally loses contact with any specific context, with the "hic and nunc" situation in Salón Ofélia. The reader has been imperceptibly transplanted from the Salón Ofélia to a mysterious, anonymous station platform, from a dialogue between the Consul and Cervantes, the owner of the cantina, to a remembered scene, real or imaginary, involving a certain Lee Maitland, whom the Consul is supposed to have "lost," "missed," or "waited" for as he "stood" on the platform.

The derailment of the sentence then comes to a standstill, but the image of the train supposed to bring Lee Maitland into the station also starts derailing in a more literal sense, with great visual and even filmic vividness, before finally, so to speak, provoking an ultimate derailment of the syntax:

> First the distant wail, then, the frightful spouting and spindling of black smoke, a sourceless towering pillar, motionless, then a round hull, as if not on the lines, as if going the other way, or as if stopping, as if not stopping, or as if slipping away over the fields, as if stopping; oh God, not stopping; downhill: clipperty-one clipperty-one: clipperty-two clipperty-two: clipperty-three clipperty-three: clipperty-four clippperty-four . . . (282)

Lowry knew exactly what he was doing when he chose the train motif; it cannot but evoke the linearity of the sentence based on contiguity: subject–verb–complement. The excerpt seems at first to correspond to the classic narrative structure identified by the Russian formalists as a chronological series of actions and events: "first" a wail, then a spouting, then a hull. Such a logico-temporal line is quickly disrupted, though, when the wagon words and the wagon actions start going off the rails of the sentence, and then spin round in the directionless world of endless "possibility,"[1] in Dickinson's sense of the word: the sentence and its "as if" mode start saying both one thing and its opposite, as if the train stopped or didn't stop (stopping/not stopping). In a sense, the train represents the faculties of articulation and combination of the sentence as it goes off the rails ("as if not on the lines") because the selection process is unable to reach a balance and eventually stop.

The *wagon words* of the *train sentence* are replaced by syntagms that are numeric variations of "clipperty," an imaginary word built on the morpheme "clip." "Clipper" suggests that the logico-temporal structure of the sentence has been cut down or "clipped," so to speak, only to be replaced by an artificial sequence. The repetition of "clipperty" gives it the appearance and the effect of an onomatopoeia, as if the only solution after the failure of selection was a series of purely mechanic morphemes: "clipperty-one clipperty-one: clipperty-two clipperty-two: clipperty-three clipperty-three." The sentence thus retrieves a form of articulation, but of a contrived nature, as sheer perception of time passing, progressing, inexorably.

Such disruption of the axis of combination does not only manifest itself at the level of the sentence or syntax; it is also to be seen on the more general level of diegesis. Mescal seems indeed to disconnect the Consul from the place and time of the narrated scene. This might account for the unexpected repeated reference to the "Suspension Bridge," as if to indicate to the reader that the Consul is indeed suspended outside diegetic time and place. He is, at the time, physically in the Salón Ofélia, a few metres only from Yvonne, who has just come back to him after leaving him several months before. Yet the Consul is alone. While Yvonne and Hugh prepare to go swimming, he remains inside, in the cantina's toilet, from where he can hear snippets of the conversation between Yvonne and Hugh without taking part. But he is already plunged into the memory or hallucination of the train, which he waits for indefinitely and to no avail. And this memory, which is supposed to take place in Oakville, reveals its true nature, a form of dream or hallucination borne out of alcohol, whose details evoke a process of Freudian condensation. Oakville is Oaxaca, the town that the Consul associates with divorce and suffering (48–49); it is also "the Farolito" in Parián where, at four o'clock in the morning, the Consul writes a desperate letter to Yvonne that she will never receive, just as in this pseudo memory he waits, at four in the morning, for a mysterious Lee Maitland, who will never come:

> That was Oakville.—But Oaxaca or Oakville, what difference? Or between a tavern that opened at four o'clock in the afternoon, and one that opened (save on holidays) at four o'clock in the morning? (284)

Oakville and Oaxaca echo each other typographically with the same initial vowels "o" and then "a," and a similar consonant evoking a cross, visually speaking, in "k" and "x." As a result, Oakville crystallizes the sense of loss and of futile waiting for a train—and, above all, for a return to the rails of life. The only train the Consul is now waiting for, despite Yvonne's return, is that of death, as Lowry actually points out in his famous letter to Jonathan Cape: "The opening train theme is related to Freudian death dreams and also to 'A corpse will be transported by express'" (Lowry, Sursum 1:521).

In the examples above, the poetic principle breaks up the linearity of sentences and diegesis so as to produce spatial effects of both initial fragmentation and explosion, and then new spatial configurations of meanings and symbolic networks. In other words, alcohol seems to have stimulated the associative faculties of the Consul so much that syntax starts derailing and spinning, as does the diegesis itself, which is then articulated on other connexions, which are metaphorical and associative rather than contiguous. It is precisely this highly metaphorical and poetic texture of the chapter that needs to be scrutinized, as the disruption of the syntactic and diegetic combination gives way to an extraordinary explosion of possibilities on the axis of selection.

In the following sentence, for instance, there is no denying mescal contributes to disjoin the habitual articulations of both the sentence and the diegesis, while at the same time reinvesting them with a fireworks of concomitant metaphoric lines which, instead of contradicting or destroying each other, make up a coherent and striking network of spun metaphors:

> The Consul, cooler, leaned on the bar, staring into his second glass of the colorless ether-smelling liquid. To drink or not to drink.—But without mescal, he imagined, he had forgotten eternity, forgotten their world's voyage, that the earth was a ship, lashed by the Horn's tail, doomed never to make her Valparaiso. Or that it was like a golf ball, launched at Hercules' Butterfly, wildly hooked by a giant out of an asylum window in hell. Or that it was a bus, making its erratic journey to Tomalín and nothing. Or that it was like—whatever it would be shortly, after the next mescal. (*Volcano* 287)

The path of life motif here takes on various successive forms: a "world's voyage" on a ship "lashed by the Horn's tail" and "doomed never to make her Valparaiso," in other words, lashed by Hell's tail and destined never to reach the valley of Paradise ("Valparaiso"), and, finally, the flight of a golf ball. Such a superimposition of various forms of the path of life underlines the profuse vitality of the associative and metaphoric resources of language, but more significantly still, they concur to outline a similar vision of the journey of a man's soul, which, like a frail and noble vessel, bravely faces the sea, Cape Horn, and the successive holes of the golf course in its quest for eternity, paradise, or any form of the absolute. All these metaphors illustrate the same struggle man has to fight "for the survival of [his] consciousness" (217). They exemplify the hardships of a consciousness fighting against itself, against its own familiars. Such a series of spatial metaphors based on the journey motif is highly representative of the modernist paradigm that undeniably informs the late modernist *Under the Volcano*: the whole narrative structure is based on the existential and political quest of the Consul, Geoffrey Firmin, in the wake of previous modernist wanderings: Mrs. Dalloway's strolls in London, Leopold Bloom's peregrinations in Dublin, or the reader's own erratic progression in Eliot's *The Waste Land*. Frank's "spatial form" and Jakobson's "poetic function" are indistinguishable in such examples because they impose a similar type of involvement on the part of the reader: "[the] chapters are knit together, not by the progress of any action . . . but by the continual reference and cross-reference of images and symbols which must be referred to each other spatially throughout the time-act of reading" (Frank 439). In other words, the textual space has to be crossed again and again by the reader so as to knit the chapters together in the progressive build-up of the text's interpretive web. But there is another typically modernist feature at work here, a conception of meaning and identity as transitory states, transitory "explosions in the mind," which is why the reader cannot do without the spatial progression in the text without the progressive weaving of the interpretive web and its subsequent tearing apart before weaving yet another in its place:

> The main defect of *Under the Volcano*, from which the others spring, comes from something irremediable. It is that the author's equipment, such as it is, is subjective rather than objective, a better equipment, in short, for a certain kind of poet than a novelist. . . . The conception of the whole was essentially poetical. . . . But poems often have to be read several times before their full meaning will reveal itself, explode in the mind, and it is precisely this poetical conception of the *whole* that I suggest has been, if understandably, missed. (Lowry, *Sursum* 1:500)

In this excerpt from the famous letter to Cape, Lowry insists on the necessity to read his novel as one would a long poem in prose: it should ideally be read in one go to bear in mind, as much as possible, this impression of a complete object, a whole whose metaphoric echoes between various events, themes, or even words or syntagms could not but *explode* in the reader's mind. But even though the links between the various successive metaphors of the path of life are quite obvious in the passage quoted above, it is often much more difficult to identify such echoes between syntagms, sentences, or even paragraphs in the rest of the novel, where they tend to remain, as it were, "suspended." Nevertheless, the explosion motif sheds a very interesting light on the type of articulation of the chapter and on the mode of reading it requires. Indeed, the links between events, themes, and even words in the same sentence or in succeeding paragraphs are omnipresent, but only implicitly, and it is only in the reader's mind that they will ultimately reveal themselves.

The chapter reads as if its internal logic was that of the Consul's stream of consciousness; but given the alcohol, everything becomes confused, and voices, real or imaginary, present or past, passages from tourist folders or books the Consul is reading, are juxtaposed without any clear transition or hierarchy. Such a narrative choice compels the reader both to accept fragmentation and to look for some miraculous spark that will suddenly illuminate the obscure connections between such fragments so that, in the end, they may "explode" in his or her mind.

Lowry was aware of such a creative and interpretive process at work in the chapter when he claimed it contained "strange evocations and explosions" (*Sursum* 1:522). The chapter is made up of a patchwork of excerpts from exchanges between different people in separate places and times, passages from tourist brochures, words heard on the radio, and so on. But behind such an impression of a field of ruins after some explosion, there reside very potent links between events, words exchanged, heard, or read. And we might qualify the very meaning of those fragments as "explosive" as far as such links are only ignited retrospectively as some form of time bomb.

In the whole chapter, the axis of combination and contexture is consistently broken up: sentences stop abruptly, various voices are telescoped, whether they are real or inner voices, present or past, alive or dead. Whereas previous chapters give the reader the impression, or at least the illusion, of a relatively stable and unified point of view, with one predominant voice, that of the represented conscience,[2] in chapter 10, the axis of contexture is all the more frequently interrupted as voices proliferate. Here, the Consul's conscience seems to disintegrate under the influence of alcohol and tends to turn into a figurative "echo chamber."[3] The proliferation of voices transforms the chapter into a cacophony of voices, where no origin or source for the voice can be identified. Voices speak with no identified locutor. And this is when a "poetic" reading has to be used: the reader is summoned to remember where he saw this or that sentence or word and to assign each of those to a character in particular.

In chapter 10, the dialogue between Hugh and Yvonne appears on the same plane as the voices the Consul hears from his "stone retreat" (*Volcano* 294), a noble euphemism designating in fact the toilet of the Salón Ofélia. The Consul has just left Yvonne and Hugh, but he can still hear their conversation. No typographical device is at hand for the reader to guess whether the quoted words are those of Hugh and Yvonne, other voices heard in the bar, imaginary voices, or voices from the past. In the following passage, it is difficult to identify with any certainty who the locutors are, even though some passages obviously refer to the present dialogue between Hugh and Yvonne and others to a past conversation between the Consul and Yvonne:

"you say first, Spaniard exploits Indian, then, when he had children, he exploited the halfbreed, then the pure-blooded Mexican Spaniard, the criollo, then the mestizo exploits everybody, foreigners, Indians, and all. Then the Germans and Americans exploited him: now the final chapter, the exploitation of everybody by everybody else—"

Historic Places- SAN BUENAVENTURA ATEMPAM
In this town was built and tried in a dike the ships used for the conquerors
in the attack to Tenochtitlán the great capital of the Moctezuma's Empire.

"Mar Cantábrico."
"All right, I heard you, the Conquest took place in an organised community
in which naturally there was exploitation already."
[. . .]
"I'm watching you . . . You can't escape me."
"—this is not just escaping. I mean, let's start again, really and cleanly."
"I think I know the place."
"I can see you."
"—where are the letters, Geoffrey Firmin, the letters she wrote till her
heart broke—"
"But in Newcastle, Deleware, now that's another thing again!"
"—the letters you not only have never answered you didn't you did you
didn't you did then where is your reply—"
"but oh my God, this city—the noise ! the chaos ! If I could only get out !
If I only knew where you could get to !"
[. . .]
"It will be like a rebirth."
"I'm thinking of becoming a Mexican subject, or going to live among the
Indians, like William Blackstone." (299–301)

The first sentence of this passage is placed just after an excerpt from a tourist
folder, and the two suppressed passages between square brackets also belong to
a tourist brochure. The whole dialogue between Hugh and Yvonne is thus interspersed with excerpts from newspapers or magazines that the Consul is reading in the toilet while listening absentmindedly to Hugh and Yvonne. In a sense,
those are dead voices. There is no doubt certain sentences do not belong to Hugh
and Yvonne's dialogue and appear suddenly and unexpectedly, thus disrupting
the continuity of the dialogue. For instance, the first sentence of the passage
quoted above refers to a Spanish ship, the *Mar Cantábrico*, which served to provide
Republicans with weapons from the United States during the Spanish Civil War;
but in January 1938, following its capture by Nationalist forces, the Spanish crew
was executed and the weapons were used against the Republicans. To that extent,
such an isolated syntagm sheds ironic light on Hugh's committed speech, but
one must note no locutor can be attributed to it since its link with the previous
sentence, as well as the next, is extremely elliptic. It is as if the words came from

nowhere, and yet such a reference to *Mar Cantábrico* is subtly related to the ships mentioned in the preceding tourist folder. Those ships were built on Mexican soil to attack Montezuma; in both cases, a place which seemed to correspond to resistance to invasion, the Mexican soil on the one hand and the Republican ship on the other, turn out to serve oppression.

What such an example leads us to conclude is that the derailing of the dialogue is not fortuitous. The irruption first of the excerpt from a tourist folder and the appearance of such an apparently heterogeneous syntagm as *Mar Cantábrico* weaves, in fact, subtle metaphoric connections between Hugh's speech and the realization that appearances can be misleading; in all three cases, a paradox emerges, opposing rather simple appearances to a much more complex truth, just as Hugh's political commitment is often presented as a narcissistic indulgence in heroic poses that can be as disastrous, in the end, as the *Mar Cantábrico* enterprise.

The reader is made to understand he is following the Consul's stream of thoughts, or at least his incoherent succession of thoughts and readings, which keep leaping from one "incongruous part"[4] to the next through metaphorical shortcuts. The very "stammering" of some excerpts from the tourist folders is further proof that such an interpretation is right: this is an undeniable indication that the Consul is reading them, stumbling on certain sentences or words due to his drunken state (297–98). And when the dialogue is taken up after being interrupted once more, it is no longer the conversation between Hugh and Yvonne that is prolonged but another dialogue with the irruption of new voices— including that of "the idiot . . . in the dirty grey suit" (283). The sentences "I'm watching you. . . . You can't escape me" and "I can see you" have already been pronounced by the latter a few pages earlier at the very beginning of the chapter (283). Similarly, the sentences referring to the Consul's letters are those of the Consul's *familiars*, his inner voices in other words, the ones he hears when he drinks too much. The exact same words are used in chapter 3 when one of his familiars whispers in his ear: "—'Have you forgotten the letters Geoffrey Firmin the letters she wrote till her heart broke . . . the letters you not only have never answered you didn't you did you didn't you did then where is your reply but have never really read' . . . the voice might have been either of his familiars" (91). As to the last part of the passage, it repeats Yvonne's dream of a rebirth, a new start with the Consul in a little house by the sea:

"This isn't just escaping, I mean, let's start again really, Geoffrey, really and cleanly somewhere. It could be like a rebirth."
"Yes. Yes it could."

"I *think* I *know*, I've got it all clear in my mind at last. Oh Geoffrey, at last
I think I have."
"Yes, I think I know too." (277–78; italics added)

The very last sentence of the passage about living with the Indians, in answer to
Yvonne's "it will be like a rebirth," suggests the Consul's desire to leave "civili-
sation" behind and adopt Indian culture instead. The references to William
Blackstone, who had gone to settle with the Indians, are numerous (51, 126, 135).

The whole excerpt thus makes it very clear that such a juxtaposition of voices
telescopes times and places which are incompatible in the diegesis and yet very
close as far as specific images and metaphors go: living in British Columbia or
with the Indians is equivalent in each case to the idealization of an elsewhere that
escapes traditional routes. Once again, spatial form and poetic function revolve
on the same network of images centering on the quest motif, which implies, on
the one hand, omnipresent fragmentation and dislocation, and, on the other, the
contrary longing for an idealized place of possible fulfilment, however ironically
such a topos may be presented. The ironic tone is suggested by the refusal on the
part of the Consul to really settle on one place and identity in particular. When
he finally seems to make up his mind, the choice of place, of identity, of political allegiance, remains open: either Mexican (as opposed to foreign exploiters,
English included?) *or* Indian (as opposed to the long series of exploiter-invaders
as listed by Hugh?). Just a few lines earlier, the Consul refers to American colo-
nization and William Penn's settlement in Newcastle, Delaware, as if he were
drawing an implicit comparison with his and Yvonne's desire to start a new life,
yet refraining from any judgment, simply stating in a provocative tone: "But in
Newcastle, Deleware, now that's another thing again!" (300). And his refusal to
take any sides or situate himself spatially or politically is even more obvious in
the following passage:

"I'm thinking of becoming a Mexican subject, or going to live among the
Indians, like William Blackstone."
"Napoleon's leg twitched." (301)

The reader is first startled and obliged to stop for a moment to try and make
sense of such a statement. It seems reasonable to interpret the Consul's words
here as another typical tongue-in-cheek provocation on his part, as if he were
aware of his sudden urge, an itch to intervene in other people's lives which he
indirectly compares to the conquering spirit of Napoleon. The odd juxtaposition
of the two sentences thus suggests he could be thinking to himself, "I, Geoffrey

Firmin, intend to go and live with the Indians and rescue and save them, against their own will, if need be," just as Napoleon imagined he was rescuing other European peoples in his series of military conquests. The image of Napoleon's twitching leg also turns Geoffrey's supposedly noble and altruistic mission into the whim of an impatient child, or of some invalid who would find some gratification and consolation in such grandiose schemes, and thus sheds an ironic light on the Consul's own posturing.

But even more importantly, what the novel ceaselessly suggests is that questions relating to space or place, whether private or public, individual or political, "neutral" or committed, are essentially linguistic and imaginary. The excerpt studied above is emblematic of a displacement from the idea of presence, origin, and "transcendental" place to the concept of voice as a substitute for such a place. Just as in the rest of the novel, there is a multiplication of voices, which is symptomatic of a dissociation between the source of the voice and the voice itself, but it is here pushed to the extreme. As a result, the "living voice" or "phenomenological voice," which implies both presence and identity, and which is central in Western metaphysics and culture, is here put at a distance.[5] Voice is no longer a sign of presence or truth but rather threatens the very concept of presence and identity; neither the Consul nor the other characters master their voice, they are possessed by it. In other words, voices occupy a place that the Consul is no longer able or willing to occupy, and to that extent he is representative of the blank place left once the humanist subject and conscience have disappeared.

Such a loss of identity is often conveyed in the novel through a strong depersonalization of the protagonists, as is testified by a very unusual use of pronouns, passing imperceptibly from the specific mode to the generic mode as if they were interchangeable, as if the individual had become a mere channel through which voices could flow, his own but also that of others. Similarly, choices of life seem to come from external and impersonal sources just as much, if not more, than from personal ones, as the following passage clearly demonstrates:

(Why did I stop playing the guitar? Certainly not because, belatedly, *one* had come to see the point of Phillipson's picture, the cruel truth it contained . . . *They* are losing the Battle of the Ebro—And yet, *one* might well have seen *one's* continuing to play but another form of publicity stunt, a means of keeping *oneself* in the limelight, as if those weekly articles for the *News of the World* were not limelight enough! Or *myself* with the thing destined to be some kind of incurable "love-object," or eternal troubadour, jongleur, interested only in married women—why?—incapable finally of love altogether . . . *Bloody little man. Who,* anyhow, no longer wrote songs.

While the guitar as an end in itself at last seemed simply futile; no longer even fun—certainly a childish thing to be put away—) (179; italics added)

The hesitation between deictic pronouns such as "I," "myself," and anaphoric pronouns such as "one," "oneself," or "they" is an undeniable sign of a fluctuating identity that only works on the mode of a specular relationship to objects (the "guitar," for instance), to imaginary identifications (the romantic young man, both sailor and musician, the committed journalist fighting for the Republicans, but also the immature cowboy, the flirt). Hugh is unable to find his own voice, his own "space" or place—he keeps borrowing other people's voices, his guitar's melodious voice or the newspapers' jarring voices. He seems to be born from the interweaving of various discourses or symbolic spaces in Lacan's sense of the term, what originates and constitutes the characters' imaginary identifications.

Yvonne experiences the same sort of enactment of a scenario that has been previously written for her: she relives the tragic destiny of a film heroine, Yvonne Griffaton,[6] as if the latter had already "scribbled down"[7] Yvonne's line of life. It is quite significant to note all her life revolves around the signifier "star," a signifier which is very charged symbolically in Hollywood, where she started her career: she will study astrophysics before becoming a film star and finally die under a shower of stars in the night sky. Her fate seems to have been written for her as that of a shooting star. Those voices of the symbolic (the cinematographic voice, the cultural voice, the political voice), all those codes, as it were, turn the novel into a stereophonic or, more precisely, stereographic novel, as Barthes would have it in *The Rustle of Language*: "We can say metaphorically that the literary text is a stereography: neither melodic nor harmonic, it is resolutely contrapuntal: it mingles voices in a volume, not in a line, not even a double one" (93). Lowry's writing is not linear but voluminous, and such volume requires a musical composition above all. He says as much in his letter to Cape:

> It can be regarded as a kind of symphony, or in another way as a kind of opera or even a horse opera (western). It is hot music, a poem, a song, a tragedy, a comedy, a farce, and so forth. It is superficial, profound, entertaining and boring, according to taste. It is a prophecy, a political warning, a cryptogram, a preposterous movie, and a writing on the wall. (*Sursum* 1:506)

Lowry could have chosen to follow one privileged line corresponding to the diegetic line, the flow of the stream of consciousness, or a generic line (novelistic, poetic, musical, operatic), but he deliberately had them coexist in a peculiar volume of voices whose simultaneity sparks infinite poetic explosions in the reader's mind that are creative and liberating, contrary to the final conflagration in the very last scene.

The novel thus shows that man is always tempted to let himself be guided by inner voices which he does not necessarily control, or by public voices which are conveyed by culture or politics, but it does not correspond to any glorification of nihilism or fatalism; it is, on the contrary, a way of alerting readers against imaginary identifications that are, more often than not, misleading and alienating, as is the case for Hugh and Yvonne. Just as, for Jakobson, poetry is what protects us from the rust that tends to freeze our formulations of love and hate, and life in general,[8] for Lowry, poetic writing and spatial form make the usual poverty of the combination axis explode. Such explosions and evocations thus reintroduce the richness, the creative vitality, and the inventiveness of the selection axis, protecting all of us thereby from, among other things, the rust of political complacency and blindness when faced with the monological temptations of either fascism or nihilism.

NOTES

1. I use "possibility" in Dickinson's sense of the word in her poem "I dwell in Possibility":

     I dwell in Possibility—
     A fairer House than Prose—
     More numerous of Windows—
     Superior—for Doors—(Miller 233)

2. See Sherrill Grace's thorough analysis of the equation between each chapter and a point of view, in particular, as one of the consequences of a growing "spatialization" and reflexivity of the narrative structure, from one version to the next (Grace 39–40).

3. Patrick O'Donnell uses the term "echo chamber" in a very illuminating article on the use of voice in *Under the Volcano* (O'Donnell 124).

4. I borrow this famous expression from Lowry's highly reflexive and metadiegetic short story "Through the Panama," in which the narrator, Sigbjørn Wilderness, quotes Lawrence about Joyce's *Ulysses*: "The whole is a strange assembly of apparently incongruous parts, slipping past one another" (34, 97).

5. Derrida has often pointed out the Western tendency to give greater authenticity and validity to the voice rather than to the letter as a means to enhance the illusion of complete adequation between a locutor's words and his presence and identity. This is what he calls the "living voice" ("vive voix") or "phenomenological voice" in *Speech and Phenomena*, his seminal book on the privilege accorded to voice in its "transcendental flesh"—"the voice phenomenologically taken, speech in its transcendental flesh" (16).

6. Yvonne remembers the film *Le destin de Yvonne Griffaton*, a film she had fully identified herself with (*Volcano* 266). Such identification process was all the more potent as
the girl's existential questionings in the film were eerily close to hers: was the past
going to "repeat itself in the future," was she predestined to live one "tragedy" after
another? (267)

7. The film is French and the heroine's last name, *Griffaton*, evokes *griffon* and therefore
griffonner, which means "scribbling down."

8. Jakobson says, "It is poetry which protects us against automatization, against the rust
which threatens our formulation of love and hate, of revolt and reconciliation, of faith
and negation." I have translated the last part of Jakobson's article on poetry "Qu'est-
ce-que la poésie?" (Jakobson, "Qu'est-ce que" 47), which is to be found in the French
translation of the article, but not in the abridged English translation found in *Selected
Writings*.

WORKS CITED

Barthes, Roland. *The Rustle of Language.* Translated by Richard Howard, Berkeley:
U of California P, 1989.

Derrida, Jacques. *Speech and Phenomena and Other Essays on Husserl's Theory of Signs.*
Translated by David B. Allison, Evanston, IL: Northwestern UP, 1973.

Frank, Joseph. "Spatial Form in Modern Literature." *Sewanee Review*, vol. 53, no. 2,
Spring 1945, pp. 221–240; vol. 53, no. 3, Summer 1945, pp. 433–456; vol. 53,
no. 4, Autumn 1945, pp. 643–653.

Grace, Sherrill E. *The Voyage that Never Ends: Malcolm Lowry's Fiction.* Vancouver:
U of British Columbia P, 1982.

Jakobson, Roman. "Linguistics and Poetics." *Selected Writings*, vol. 3, *Poetry of Grammar
and Grammar of Poetry*, The Hague: Mouton, 1981, pp. 18–51.

——. "Qu'est-ce que la poésie?" *Huit questions de poétique*, Paris: Seuil, 1977, pp. 31–49.

——. "Two Aspects of Language and Two Types of Aphasic Disturbances." *Selected
Writings*, vol. 2, *Word and Language*, The Hague: Mouton, 1971, pp. 239–259.

——. "What is poetry?" *Selected Writings*, vol. 3, *Poetry of Grammar and Grammar of Poetry*,
The Hague: Mouton, 1981.

Lowry, Malcolm. *Sursum Corda!: The Collected Letters of Malcolm Lowry.* Edited by Sherrill
E. Grace, vol. 1, 1926–1946, Toronto: U of Toronto P, pp. 1995–1997.

——. "Through the Panama." *Hear Us O Lord from Heaven thy Dwelling Place.* London:
Jonathan Cape, 1961, pp. 29–98.

——. *Under the Volcano.* 1947. London: Picador, 1993.

Miller, Cristanne, ed. *Emily Dickinson's Poems as She Preserved Them.* Cambridge, MA:
Harvard U P, 2016.

O'Donnell, Patrick. *Echo Chambers: Figuring Voice in Modern Narrative.* Iowa City:
U of Iowa P, 1992.

4

Pathologies of Knowledge:
David Markson, Under the Volcano,
and the Experience of Thought

MATHIEU DUPLAY

L owry scholars are familiar with David Markson's 1978 pioneering book *Malcolm Lowry's Volcano: Myth, Symbol, Meaning.* However, while they acknowledge its historical importance, few are aware of the crucial role it played in the other career of its author, a highly regarded novelist known for experimentation. Based on Markson's ground-breaking MA thesis, which he completed in 1952, the book manuscript was "finished in its present form . . . in 1972," he says in the afterword (215), or shortly after the publication of *Going Down* (1970), Markson's first "serious" novel and one in which he deliberately set out to emulate Lowry's achievement (Markson, personal communication). Thus, the book's eventual 1978 publication can be said to have marked the close of a twenty-five-year period during which the aspiring novelist sought to come to terms with the shadow of his great predecessor, and, in particular, with the way in which *Under the Volcano* manages to bring a vast wealth of heterogeneous and largely abstract material, what Markson calls "intellectual odds and ends" (personal communication), into an "organic structure," a textual space compatible with the demands of traditional narrative (*Malcolm* 6).

The reason this development took so long may be that the task, as he saw it, was eminently problematic. Critical distance, it seems, was the key issue. According to Markson, the chief difficulty consisted in striking the right balance between two contradictory forces: on the one hand, the near-overwhelming pull of Lowry's novel, in which the author seeks to order the totality of past, present, and future experience of subjectivity into a single, all-embracing pattern, so that later writers would appear to have no other option than to produce imitations of *Under the Volcano*; and, on the other, the centrifugal tendencies apparent in a novel that, by drawing on extremely diverse sources, not only appears to defy closure but suggests that the point of writing lies in its disjointedness and consequent unpredictability. This put Markson in the uneasy position of having to distance himself from a text that appears to encompass everything because, by heavily relying on discontinuity, it suggests that no space is out of bounds, least of all the totally unexpected.

In his critical study of *Under the Volcano*, Markson states that the book captures, in more or less allusive form, "the essence of man's creative tradition—which is man" (*Malcolm* 6); according to Markson, nothing lies outside the scope of the novel, whose analogic nature and ability to reveal otherwise hidden connections easily give the impression that the reader's own reactions merely extend and enrich the overall pattern: "Any man's myth increases me, for I am 'Mankinde'" (*Malcolm* 5). However, if whatever is said or written in response to *Under the Volcano* is in a sense absorbed into the text itself—if, in other words, Lowry's novel leaves its readers no space for personal expression, having pre-emptively laid claim to all the available terrain—then they can never become novelists in their own right, unless they either minimize its importance to them or attempt to usurp the place of its author, a bold yet self-defeating gesture. As Markson revealed in 2008, "I guess at the beginning I would have liked to write *Under the Volcano* . . . or my version of it; I was aiming at it in a small way, my feeble way, when I did *Going Down*" (personal communication). If to write is to try and return to a point of origin (however problematic), as Markson's novels repeatedly suggest, conscious imitation is certainly not an appropriate strategy, and it is a far cry from his self-deprecating use of the phrase "at the beginning" to the grand opening sentence of *Wittgenstein's Mistress* (1988), possibly the most ambitious of his later works: "In the beginning, sometimes I left messages in the street" (*Wittgenstein* 7), the narrator recounts, as she prepares to describe a post-apocalyptic universe where there is no one left to imitate, since she claims to be its sole surviving inhabitant. This hard-earned freedom may owe much to the experience of writing *Malcolm Lowry's Volcano*; for if it is true that "not many writers are going to feel close to [Lowry]," as Markson also states (personal communication), that is to say if, as a rule, one must choose between becoming a writer and undue proximity to *Under the Volcano*, then an excursion into criticism may have been necessary for Markson in order to establish the sense of distance, the space between, without which his later novels would never have come into being.

While *Malcolm Lowry's Volcano*, despite its reverential tone, marks an ambiguous moment of leave-taking, distance is not synonymous with indifference; Markson certainly suggested as much when he pointed out in the course of the same interview: "After I had done *Wittgenstein's Mistress* I really was just experimenting, and I owe my willingness to take that chance to my reading of *Under the Volcano* and *The Recognitions*, in spite of the fact that my books are not at all like Lowry's and Gaddis's." In other words, the novels Markson completed between

1978 and his death in 2010 no longer reflect a desire to "write" *Under the Volcano*; their ambition is rather to do justice to Markson's *reading* of Lowry, to carry on the task begun in *Malcolm Lowry's Volcano*, if by other means than those of academic criticism, and in a rather different spirit, since the point is less to emphasize the impressive economy of means with which Lowry imposes order and a form of closure on heterogeneous cultural data than to rediscover the sense of unpredictability and adventure which, from the start, characterized his endeavour. Kate, the narrator of *Wittgenstein's Mistress*, tirelessly comments on earlier sections of her own autobiographical manuscript, frequently pointing out omissions and errors. As a result, a rhetoric of epanorthosis—or the deliberate rewording of earlier statements—comes to predominate in this novel, with often disconcerting results since this constant process of supplementation allows the narrative to wander freely in all directions while ostensibly contenting itself with the unambitious task of clarifying what has already been said. In this chapter, I would like to argue that a similar relationship exists between Markson's last five novels—*Wittgenstein's Mistress* (1988), *Reader's Block* (1996), *This Is Not A Novel* (2001), *Vanishing Point* (2004) and *The Last Novel* (2007)—and Lowry's *Under the Volcano*: while they all, to some extent, gloss the earlier text, they are faithful not so much to its encyclopaedic quest for order as to the element of unpredictability which, in Lowry's novel, counteracts the totalizing impulse and foregrounds discontinuity and dissociation at the expense of the overall pattern, thus opening up a space for creative intervention. Not only do Markson's later works demonstrate how literary innovation may be possible after, and in response to, *Under the Volcano*, they also make an implicit point about Lowry's book by suggesting that the surprising analogies on which it so constantly relies are predicated on the essential disjointedness of all thought. In other words, Markson's later novels imply that the true value of the "cohesive surface sequence" lauded in *Malcolm Lowry's Volcano* (6) lies in the manner in which it simultaneously raises and dispels skeptical questions about our ability to know, about the desire for a comprehensive ordering of knowledge that, on one level, *Under the Volcano* seeks to gratify, and its source in our fascination for what Markson, quoting Joyce, calls the myth of the "complete man" (5) unconstrained by the usual limitations of the human condition.

❧

While unpredictability and intermittence are key thematic concerns of Markson's writings—"In the beginning, sometimes"—they most obviously characterize the unusual narrative form adopted in his later fiction. These deliberately "nonlinear," "discontinuous," and "collage-like" novels (Markson, *Reader's Block* 14) consist of an accumulation of micro-narratives, frequently based on fact and culled from a wide range of more or less arcane sources. Typically, Markson's later novels are divided into brief paragraphs separated by blanks; occasional allusions are made to one or two characters about whom virtually nothing is known—for instance, in *Reader's Block* a writer interestingly nick-named "Reader" and "Protagonist," the central figure in the novel he is attempt-ing to compose. The one exception is *Wittgenstein's Mistress*, a more traditional first-person narrative, where a degree of continuity is preserved and traces of plot and characterization can be detected. All this largely conforms to Sigbjørn Wilderness's familiar dictum, "The whole is an assembly of apparently incon-gruous parts, slipping past one another—" (Lowry, "Panama" 97), and encour-ages readers to follow the cumulative process whereby meaning arises out of the "gradual accretion of allusive detail," much as Markson does in his study of *Under the Volcano* (*Malcolm* 8). The difference is one of emphasis, for while a sense of the whole is much in evidence in these novels, which betray an increasing preoc-cupation with finality, death, and creative closure—"There is always more time than you anticipate. / Said Malcolm Lowry. For whom there wasn't" (Markson, *Last Novel* 187)—the reader is struck by the deliberate open-endedness of texts in which incongruity and slippage are viewed positively as means of making room for the emergence of the unpredictable. "Well before the end, . . . Lowry's mul-tiple clusters of meaning will have become virtually *dehiscent*; there, the effort is to keep them from spilling off the page," Markson warns in the introduction to *Malcolm Lowry's Volcano* (8). In his own later novels, dehiscence is apparent from the very first line, enhanced by a strategy which, by stripping the main narra-tive, such as it is, of all save a strictly metafictional function, allows the rest of the text to wander with complete freedom since no subject matter can possibly appear irrelevant where the act of writing itself, rather than the material on which it relies, is the one constant preoccupation.

On the face of it, this change of perspective would seem to alter the very essence of the reading experience by drawing attention away from the emotional issues that Lowry's fiction so squarely confronts. According to Markson, *Under the Volcano* owes its greatness to the fact that, despite its complexity and intellec-tual sophistication, it remains "a novel first of all, with its own profoundly literal impact" (*Malcolm* 6). By contrast, his own works appear to foreground epistemo-logical questions related to the nature of knowledge. In *Wittgenstein's Mistress*, the narrator's hopeless love affair seems to be not so much with a long-dead thinker as with philosophy itself, and, more specifically, with a mode of questioning that responds to the perplexities caused by the use of language in the pursuit of truth.

That novel hinges on the question of skepticism: the narrator's admission that she was once mad, and her categorical but problematic claim that she has in the meantime recovered her sanity, cast doubt on the mind's relation to the rest of the world, and her extreme sensitivity to the vagaries of verbal expression challenges the possibility of truthful discourse as it reveals that the inherent ambiguity of words stands in the way of all attempts at interpretation: "Time out of mind. Which is a phrase I suspect I may have never properly understood. / Time out of mind meaning mad, or time out of mind meaning simply forgotten?" (*Wittgenstein* 7). The subject of enunciation—which, as in Markson's later novels, also presents herself as the agent of writing—thus appears to have been banished to a dimension of exteriority from which nothing can rescue her; as she no longer enjoys any kind of intimate connection with anything, let alone with the words she uses, she is literally as well as figuratively "out of her mind" and refers to herself in the same tone of cool detachment as when she talks about the faraway countries she has visited as a tourist. This gives rise to a pervasive sense of unreality, as the reading/writing subject wanders in a textual world devoid of echoes, where no account is taken of its presence, except perhaps negatively, in the blanks and ellipses that pervade the narrative. Nothing, one is tempted to conclude, could be further removed from *Under the Volcano*, described by Markson as "a tragedy in which [Lowry's] subjectivity serves to create a *drama* of the consciousness rather than a mere representation of its workings" (*Malcolm* 7).

This, however, would involve a simplification, for the quotation from Kierkegaard that prefaces *Wittgenstein's Mistress* implies that this novel and its successors describe not the elimination of subjective thinking but, rather, its triumph: "What an extraordinary change takes place . . . when for the first time the fact that everything depends upon how a thing is thought first enters the consciousness, when, in consequence, thought in its absoluteness replaces an apparent reality" (*Wittgenstein* 5). The apparent contradiction can be resolved by pointing out that Markson's later novels indeed raise the question of skepticism, but in order to answer it in a Wittgensteinian or possibly a Heideggerian mode, to mention another one of Kate's favourite philosophers. According to Stanley Cavell,

> An admission of some question as to the mystery of the existence, or the being, of the world is a serious bond between the teaching of Wittgenstein and that of Heidegger. The bond is one, in particular, that implies a shared view of what I have called the truth of skepticism, . . . namely, that the human creature's basis in the world as a whole, its relation to the world as such, is not that of knowing, anyway not what we think of as knowing. (Cavell 241)

In other words, the problem of skepticism is not a matter of speculative concern that requires an answer in the nature of a solution, but the epistemological "cover" of existential anxiety, "the attempt to convert the human condition, the condition of humanity, into an intellectual difficulty, a riddle," or, to put it bluntly, "the conversion of metaphysical finitude into intellectual lack" (Cavell 493). Markson's fiction sees through the skeptical fallacy and summons the discourse of epistemology in order to comment not on what is known, but on "how a thing is thought." In the novels, intellect is neither reduced to its cognitive function nor confined to a dimension of transcendental ideality; it is an experience whose full significance can be grasped only in anthropological terms as one of the ways in which the person, in a given context, explores the immediate possibilities of the human condition—if not indeed as an affection of the subject, which, like fatigue or disease, arises from the action of forces originating outside the consciousness. All this clearly echoes *Under the Volcano*, where knowledge per se matters less than the *magic* of cognition, its performative impact on the persons seeking it, and the murderous rage it arouses in those who, failing to acquire the learning they covet, are forcibly reminded of their own finitude, of what they most ardently wanted to evade. "Hitler, [the Consul] pursued, . . . merely wished to annihilate the Jews in order to obtain just such arcana as could be found behind them in his bookshelves" (Lowry, *Volcano* 186). This explains why tragedy plays such an important role in Markson's fiction as well as Lowry's, either directly, in the narrative of the Consul's final hours, or indirectly, when Kate, the narrator of *Wittgenstein's Mistress*, recalls that "Irene Papas was an effective Helen in the film of *The Trojan Women*" (93) or refers to Maria Callas singing *Medea* (104); for, as Cavell also points out, "Tragedy is the place we are not allowed to escape the consequences, or price, of [skepticism's attempt to evade the truth about the human condition]: that the failure to acknowledge a best case of the other is a denial of that other, presaging the death of the other . . . and the death of our capacity to acknowledge as such, the turning of our hearts to stone, or their bursting" (Cavell 493).

True, the problem of skepticism and its role in the Consul's demise are already referred to in *Malcolm Lowry's Volcano*, where Markson discusses Lowry's interest in George Berkeley, and especially in his response to the skeptical objection that nothing conclusively proves our ideas of external objects to originate outside our minds (*Malcolm* 186–88). However, the argument Markson offers in his commentary on the final chapter of *Under the Volcano* is significantly weakened by his contention that Berkeley's philosophy is treated by the Consul as a source of entertaining conundrums about the number of drinks he has consumed (186), or else taken as "a point of departure for speculations about the *potential* of perception: if consciousness is all, where might consciousness go?" (187) If Cavell's intuition is correct, this reformulation of the debate in strictly epistemological terms actually bolsters the skeptical thesis that Berkeley was attempting to rebut and makes the allusion appear superfluous, save perhaps as an indirect clue to the nature of the self-imposed blindness that leads the Consul to his doom. A stronger interpretation would point to the ontological implications of the famous adage *esse est percipi* (to be is to be perceived), especially in the light of a novel such as *Wittgenstein's Mistress*, whose narrator does not exist for others since she claims to be the only surviving human being, and who is sure of her own existence only in so far as she is the object of her own unreliable perception: "There is only one mirror in this house, incidentally. / What the mirror reflects is . . . an image of myself, of course. / Though in fact what it has also reflected now and again is an image of my mother. / What will happen is that I will glance into the mirror and for an instant I will see my mother looking back at me" (*Wittgenstein* 67). If *to be* is the same as *to be perceived*, and perception includes self-awareness, the condition of human existence lies in a form of twofold passivity: I am what is perceived, the object of perception, in which, as such, no activity is to be detected; and if I then wonder *what* I am, the answer has to be that I am that which does the perceiving, the recipient of impressions arising from some external source. In other words, *to be* is *to be affected*, and the source of all knowledge—of myself and the rest of the world—is identical to what one could call the *pathos* of existence, that is to say, in the etymological sense of the term, to that which causes me to suffer whatever befalls me in life.

Markson's later novels take this argument one step further and suggest that knowledge as pathos is always suspiciously close to becoming pathological: even in its highest manifestations, consciousness is prone to various disorders, as is indicated by Kate's madness or, in *Reader's Block*, by the narrator's obsessive concern with the anti-Semitism of numerous major thinkers, writers, and artists. While this could be taken to mean that thought should never be trusted implicitly, and that, being inextricably linked to somatic processes liable to decline, disease, and death, it does not enjoy any of the special privileges usually ascribed to "mental" phenomena, it also implies that rationality and rational expression are worthwhile only to the extent that they are rooted in a form of life and acknowledge the risks to which they are therefore exposed. This is not skepticism, but a sober appraisal of the human mind's inescapable limitations, and to recognize that literature, philosophy, and art do not redeem human nature from its inherent foibles does not detract from their value, but rather reveals in what it actually consists.

"To recall consciousness to its necessary modesty is to take it for what it is: a symptom, and nothing but a symptom, of a deeper transformation, a symptom of the activity of forces wholly other than spiritual" (Deleuze 36). The closest parallel to Deleuze here is not Berkeley but Nietzsche, whose concern is not skepticism so much as nihilism, and who sees rejection of idealism as the price to pay for a re-evaluation of thought in terms that do not depreciate it by contrasting it with life as actually lived by feeling, breathing people. Interestingly, this comparison suggests a better reason than the one Markson explicitly adduces for the fact that, to Lowry's Consul, philosophy is little more than a "point of departure" (*Malcolm* 187); for as Nietzsche provocatively claims in the 1887 Preface to *The Gay Science*, "The unconscious disguise of physiological needs under the cloaks of the objective, ideal, purely spiritual goes to frightening lengths—and often I have asked myself whether, taking a large view, philosophy has not been merely an interpretation of the body and a *misunderstanding of the body*" (23–24). If this intuition is correct, then it may be preferable to leave theoretical thinking aside and turn to other modes of interaction with the world, as Markson did when he gave up criticism to embark on the most productive phase of his career as a creative writer. In any case, narrative is far better suited than argument to a symptomatology of consciousness, if only because the interplay of conflicting forces to which thought owes its existence gives rise to inherently unstable situations, whose unfolding constitutes the "drama" Markson perceives in *Under the Volcano* (*Malcolm* 7). All the better, indeed, if this narrative is poetic; that is to say, if it not only encourages the reader to approach thought and language as objects of sensory perception, but suggests that rationality and meaning arise from just such an experience and are worthwhile only to the extent that they do not deny their empirical origin.

Under the Volcano occupies just such a narrative space: a novel not so much about knowledge as about the embodied experience of knowledge and discourse, the re-evaluation, on properly experiential grounds, of a mode of learning whose air of abstraction and intellectuality is thus exposed as a dangerous illusion—or, figuratively speaking, about a consciousness tormented by an idea as Prometheus was by the eagle, or as cabbalists can be hounded by demons which, as Jewish mystics well know, primarily reside in language: "Erekia, the one who tears asunder; and they who shriek with a long drawn cry, Illirikim; Apelki, the misleaders or turners aside; and those who attack their prey by tremulous motion, Dresop. . . . The flesh in-clothed and the evil questioners. Perhaps you would not call them precisely rational. But all these at one time or another have visited my bed" (Lowry, *Volcano* 185–86). Therein, it could be argued, lies the pathos of the Consul's tragedy, whose ability to let words affect him in the flesh renders him acutely sensitive to the deceptions of fine talking and the dangers of *ignoratio elenchi*—"the fallacy of supposing a point proved or disproved by argument which proves or disproves something not at issue" (309)—to which no philosopher is forever immune. However, his apparently cynical posture also enables him to uncover rationality's roots in experience of the body, and thus to suggest a way in which the disorders that affect consciousness could one day be healed, perhaps by a saving drink: "Tequila, no, that is healthful . . . and delightful. Just like beer. Good for you" (216). To one who wishes to solve the problems of humankind, this may sound like an inauspicious beginning; yet as the retrospective light cast on *Under the Volcano* by Markson's deliberately unassuming narratives suggests, a "necessary modesty" may be the key to this most imposing of all novels: for when it is read, despite its tragic tone, as a salutary farewell to all delusions of grandeur, "it seems to be written in the language of the wind that brings a thaw: it contains high spirits, unrest, contradiction, and April weather, so that one is constantly reminded of winter's nearness as well as of the triumph over winter that is coming" (Nietzsche 3).

WORKS CITED

Cavell, Stanley. *The Claim of Reason: Wittgenstein, Skepticism, Morality, and Tragedy.* Oxford: Oxford UP, 1979.

Deleuze, Gilles. *Nietzsche and Philosophy.* Translated by Hugh Tomlinson, London: Continuum, 2006.

Lowry, Malcolm. "Through the Panama." *Hear Us O Lord From Heaven Thy Dwelling Place.* 1961. Vancouver: Douglas & McIntyre, 1987.

——. *Under the Volcano.* 1947. London: Picador, 1993.

Markson, David. *The Last Novel.* Berkeley, CA: Shoemaker & Hoard, 2007.

——. *Malcolm Lowry's Volcano: Myth, Symbol, Meaning.* New York: Times Books, 1978.

——. Personal communication. September 4, 2008.

——. *Reader's Block.* Normal, IL: Dalkey Archive P, 1996.

——. *Wittgenstein's Mistress.* Normal, IL: Dalkey Archive P, 1988.

Nietzsche, Friedrich. *The Gay Science.* 1882. Edited by Bernard Williams, translated by Josefine Nauckhoff, Cambridge: Cambridge UP, 2001.

5

Phantom Priapusspuss: The Phantom-Dog Tradition in Under the Volcano

CHARLES HOGE

The phantom dog is a ubiquitous, borderless, folkloric presence. Comprised of hundreds of variants assembled across centuries of human history, the phantom dog resists easy definitions and taxonomical assignments, but one feature is fairly consistent: it is almost always encountered "on the road," usually along a footpath, by nocturnal wayfarers. It is an entity of the liminal space, between destinations, neither aligned with the home of the self nor the away of the other, but always in the territory that connects the two. This status of existence "between the registers" matches nicely with Malcolm Lowry's *Under the Volcano*—which similarly resists easy classification and, of course, shares a liminal environment with phantom dogs—as the text chronicles a journey along a series of roads, among other things, and many of the most important textual events transpire in the spaces provided by the road. One may say that the text lives in the same place as the phantom dog. As a liminal entity, the phantom dog presents itself as a domesticated animal with no attachment to domestication; the phantom dog *belongs* to nobody, and is never interpreted as a wolf or other wild canine, so tension is created in that it defies our expectations by lacking any connection to human ownership. Lowry's text offers perhaps a similar questioning of ownership, as the sliding nature of the narration complicates any consideration of identity in regard to the speaker; access to the characters' thoughts sometimes spills from the mind of one character into that of another, and overall attempts to situate a consistent voice speaking across the landscape of the text are problematic. This chapter explores the specific intersections between *Under the Volcano* and the phantom-dog tradition, and hopes to emerge with an understanding of how the text may participate in that tradition, specifically, how protagonist Geoffrey Firmin's fate might be interwoven, illuminated, and even accelerated within the liminal textual spaces occupied by phantom-dog figures.

The phantom dog is a multivalent folkloric entity whose variants across Britain, Ireland, and Scotland have been recorded and analyzed by folklorists for more than a century. Various angles of interest have motivated the cataloguing and interpretation of phantom-dog narratives, from the late-Victorian desire to collect the sort of vanishing oral traditions that scientific and industrial developments were devouring to the twenty-first-century impulse of cryptozoologists to locate a solid record of a previously undocumented "hidden animal." Barbara Allen Woods' 1959 study *The Devil in Dog Form: A Partial Type Index of Devil Legends* and Melissa Westwind's 2013 *Monster Dogs: The History of the Beast of Dartmoor* provide the most comprehensive studies of the phantom-dog figure. Though both of these seminal studies acknowledge the fragmentary nature of extant records of phantom-dog narratives, and neither offers a specific point of origin for the shadowy figure, they both thoroughly explore a tangled network of source material and find within it a consistently unnatural creature of the liminal plane. In doing so, they track the phantom dog lurking as far back as Cerberus in Greek mythology, developing to appear in packs in accompaniment with the Wild Hunt throughout medieval sources, shifting in the post-medieval era to the form of the avenging "hell hound" and finally solidifying into the solitary semi-corporeal haunter of lonely paths that it becomes by the nineteenth century. It is in this form that we encounter a modified iteration of the phantom dog within the story world of *Under the Volcano*.

As a liminal creature, the phantom dog is frequently regarded as a supernatural harbinger of ill tidings, though the specific tragedy being forecast is never known until it occurs. It provides pre-emptive confirmation that something bad lies ahead but does not allow enough information for the percipient to anticipate or avoid it. Phantom dogs' association, either as messengers or occasionally as protectors, with "the dead and dying" (Trubshaw i) seems to make their persistent attachment to Geoffrey and the text itself painfully meaningful. The notion, too, that the gaze of or attention from the dog "may mean that the dog's appearance in front of a particular witness is intentional and has some personal significance for the witness" (Bord and Bord 95) hints that such creatures in *Under the Volcano* may carry personalized (but unknown) meanings with them as they follow the characters, specifically Geoffrey Firmin, the Consul, throughout the text.

Though Lowry's text may be seen as something of a phantom dog in itself, a relationship with the literal entity of the phantom dog is reflected more tangibly in several instances by the pariah dogs that seem to dog the footsteps of Geoffrey and, occasionally, other spaces within the text. The very first mention of pariah dogs appears to assign them a supernatural association, which quietly points the reader in the direction of the phantom-dog tradition. In referring to the haunting night-time sounds of his current environment, Geoffrey's conscience notes that "the howling pariah dogs, the cocks that herald dawn all night, the drumming, the moaning that will be found later white plumage huddled on telegraph wires in back gardens or fowl roosting in apple trees, the eternal sorrow that never sleeps of great Mexico" (Lowry 37). This passage equates the dogs with images of preternatural affiliation. The cocks that crow all night represent a disordered world. They deceive people into believing that the "safe" space of daytime has dislodged the "dangerous" night when, in fact, it has not; thus, folks are called out into the world, expecting daytime when it is actually still nighttime, which is the time occupied by the largely nocturnal phantom dogs. Similarly, the idea of these ghostly bird noises dovetailing into a description of a somnambulistic sorrow that haunts the country creates an image of unity between the natural world and the psychic landscape, and phantom dogs, frequently associated with sadness of this type, are almost always closely connected to, even imprisoned by, their immediate physical environment. It is important, too, that this sorrow is never able to rest within the confines of "great Mexico," and this notion of unfulfilled satisfaction intertwines with the folklore of the supernatural phantom dog, which typically is stuck in the area between life and death, forever a creature of both spaces and neither space simultaneously, so that it can reach across with knowledge from the land of the dead to deliver its hazy messages to the land of the living.

The pariah dogs appear almost always with descriptors that mark their desperate conditions; they are "hideous," "starving," and appear to be "skinned." But they have no traceable owners. It seems likely that Lowry is playing with the double meaning of pariah, not only to supply the name of the dogs' subspecies but also their social status within the communities they haunt. This second meaning certainly appears to align them with the phantom-dog tradition. An early glimpse of the pariah dog may be used to illustrate this possible relationship. "A hideous pariah dog [is described as having] followed" Geoffrey and Yvonne through the gates to the home they used to share (Lowry 67). This dog's appearance is greeted by Geoffrey's unclear and trailed-off declaration of "strange . . . " (67). "Strange" is a catchword with a long history of association with the phantom-dog phenomenon; perhaps the best-known phantom-dog-related historical document, Abraham Fleming's 1577 pamphlet describing the demonic dog that attacked parishioners at a church service in Bungay, introduces the monster as a "Straunge and Terrible Wunder," for example. If we can assume that Geoffrey is referring to the dog with this "strange" remark, the hint of its supernatural nature might be planted, especially in conjunction with the narrator's claim that it is "hideous." Typically, the phantom dog foretells disaster for the witness, but here it might serve the purpose of reminding Geoffrey that disaster has already befallen his relationship with Yvonne. It is the converse of the forerunner in Lowry's world here; it is the after runner.

The phantom dog is frequently associated with "places of death," including the sites of murders and executions. The horrifying legend of the Black Dog of Newgate, in which a monstrous dog appeared on the prison grounds after a young prisoner accused of witchcraft was murdered and cannibalized by inmates in 1596, may be the most prominent of these. It is perhaps not too much of a leap to see the house Geoffrey and Yvonne shared as a "place of death," with their relationship seemingly dead and their memories and dreams cannibalized, as the symbolic victim the pariah dog's presence illuminates. The looming presence of the Spanish Civil War and its battlefields are frequently evoked in Lowry's text, and these sites of mass human tragedy have certainly generated narratives of phantom dogs as well. Specifically, the Allied trenches of the First World War were said to be plagued by a horrible, giant dog, the devilish "Hound of Mons," which stalked the no man's land to kill isolated soldiers and savage their bodies (Paijmans 40–41). This phantom dog's bloodthirsty behaviour deviates from the tradition, but it seems a subspecies at least of the phantom dog in that its territory is spectacularly liminal, as it inhabits the literal wasteland boundary that separates the two fighting sides. Though the alleged phantom dog in Lowry's text is hardly such a murderous creature, it may occupy the same emotional environment: a location in which human anguish has been prominent, and one in which the notion of war powerfully overhangs.

It should be mentioned here that the phantom dog is frequently referenced with the chromatic descriptor "black," though a review of purported sightings reveals that the color black is not a necessary characteristic, as a wild diversity of coloration and shapes is evident within the phantom-dog tradition. In fact, occasional folkloric references exist to "black" phantom dogs that are, according to their actual descriptions, not black at all, yet the name still accompanies the creatures. (Westwind's examination of nineteen phantom-dog narratives, from across the English countryside and spanning the twelfth to the nineteenth centuries, revealed that only ten referred to the dogs specifically as black [195]). Some sightings in fact disfigure or remove the shape of the dog altogether, and describe a headless dog, an invisible animal, or even a giant calf as the "phantom dog." The lack of consistency that accompanies the phantom-dog tradition thrives within Lowry's text, as a typical phantom dog, if such a thing even exists, is certainly not what we encounter here. In fact, these dogs, while laden with foreboding meaning, frequently disfigured morphology and placement in liminal places, are not black, and, in one very important incident, the phantom does not even manifest itself in canine form.

In fact, Lowry might invert the "dogness" of the phantom tradition altogether in his presentation of Geoffrey's encounter with his neighbour Quincey's cat, which seems to appropriate, despite its apparent morphology, the necessary attributes of the traditional phantom dog. Significantly, the early nineteenth century added to the lore of the phantom-dog shape-shifting abilities, in which the form of large cats was specifically considered a possible disguise (Waldron and Reeve 70); Quincey's cat, read within this tradition, could be a manifestation of a phantom dog. Interestingly, within the realm of cryptozoology in Britain, phantom cats have almost entirely replaced phantom dogs; this thriving phenomenon, termed "ABC" (alien big cats), has generated countless recent sightings, photographs, and discussion. Though it's admittedly a specious leap, it's a tempting one: one almost feels that Lowry's possible "phantom cat" prefigures this development, this "phantom shift" from canid to felid. Jennifer Westwood, in "Friend or Foe? Norfolk Traditions of Shuck," offers that

> Today the Norfolk Black Puma, reported from 1993 onwards, is often mentioned in the same bated breath as Shuck [a popular term for the "hellhound" phantom-dog variant]. I am sometimes asked if I think that they are one and the same, and the answer is yes, in a way I do. For all the cages we try to put him in, Shuck remains protean, unpredictable, wild, a survivor. (Westwood 76)

Moreover, "the connection between these 'big cats' and black [phantom] dogs is that it has been suggested that the cats are a modern manifestation having the same origin as the black [phantom] dogs" (Bord and Bord 110). To apply the phantom-dog identity to a cat, then, is not necessarily out of order, and reflects a folkloric shift of which, of course, Lowry could not have been aware, post-dating the writing of his novel by several decades.

But Quincey's cat, after all, is phantom-doglike, as it does enter the narrative within a liminal space, namely, the land that serves as a boundary between Geoffrey's property and Quincey's. Though it is identified as Quincey's cat quite clearly in the dialogue, its behaviour does not seem to validate such a claim of ownership (indeed, one might argue that all cats by nature refute claims of ownership, just as do phantom dogs). Importantly, the cat's "owner," Quincey, does not speak to it, but Geoffrey does, unleashing a torrent of references that flirt with the idea of phantomness and align it as a candidate for the phantom-dog position. Importantly, a prominent feature of the phantom-animal phenomenon involves the danger invoked by anyone who speaks to the creature; death seems to come quickly to those who acknowledge the phantom by speaking directly to it. Thus, Geoffrey's very interaction with the cat has perhaps activated supernatural forces working toward his destruction.

He playfully renames the cat Priapusspuss and Oedipusspusspuss (Lowry 141), and this Greek-based conflation of a god of fertility with a literary figure marked as a corruption of fertility (particularly regarding the consequences of marrying one's mother) creates a cyclical notion of generation and degeneration. Mathematically, this particular arrangement invariably favours degeneration, as Oedipusspusspuss is one "puss" heavier than Priapusspuss. It is possible that Geoffrey's renaming of Quincey's cat creates a signal pointing toward his own demise, a signal he is not capable of recognizing, even though it is he who has drunkenly put it forth. And he drives the last nail into the coffin of assigning this cat as a harbinger when he calls it Xicotancatl, ascribing it the name of another ill-fated historic personage, this time a sixteenth-century Aztec luminary, either a father or son but in both cases doomed by proximal contact with Hernán Cortés and his bloodthirsty conquistador forces. The cat's identity, then, is tilted strongly toward the tragic, and such a trajectory seems to match that of Geoffrey's, unbeknownst to him. In case any ambivalence remains as to the meaning of the cat, Geoffrey punctures it by playing again at renaming the cat Catastrophe (142), spurred by a "knocking" sound he hears in the door of his own mind, perhaps as a subtle, unrecognized nudge in the direction of awakening. In any case, he again foreshadows his own destiny through this ascribed identity for the cat. It is significant that Geoffrey reads such meaning from his encounter with the cat, because this interpretive work is exactly what people within the folkloric tradition who come across phantom dogs are compelled to do.

But this role of "doom-foreteller" is not the only one the phantom dog, or cat, occupies in folklore, and this diversity of functions is represented in Lowry's text as well. While typically read as harbingers of doom or pyschopomps (creatures which escort the dying to the afterlife), some phantom-dog figures act in ways that bring to the phenomena a protective element. These guardian phantom dogs appear to travellers in potential danger in order that their presence might deter potential malefactors. Westwood cites several cases in which the phantom dog, for example, stands in the path of a vehicle which otherwise would have killed the percipient (Westwood 59), acts "as guardian and guide to women rush-gatherers out late at night," or simply escorts lonely wayfarers through dangerous areas (68). When Hugh and Yvonne detach from Geoffrey to take a scenic horseback trip around the countryside, they are accompanied by "an affectionate scrubbed woolly white dog belonging to the farm" (Lowry 109). This dog is unlike the typical phantom variety in that it lacks the black coloration, and is described as friendly and as "belonging" to the farm; however, it does seem to fulfill the protective role that the phenomenon occasionally embodies. During the journey Hugh feels that he should keep the foals walking along with them safe, but "actually the dog was guarding all of them. Evidently trained to detect snakes, he would run ahead then double back to make sure all were safe before loping off once more" (110).

Later, as the group crosses a river, the dog swims ahead of the rest, and though the speaker attaches to him the condition of feeling "fatuously important" (111) as he does so, we see that he does make safe the trail before the travellers. River crossing is read folklorically by many cultures as a journey to the afterlife, and the symbolic value of the accompaniment of a phantom dog along this trip emphasizes the connection further. But what afterlife has been reached? Perhaps the transition is simply the attainment of Hugh's awareness of the reality regarding his status with Yvonne. And, in a larger sense than the notion of defense from snakes, what protection has been granted by the dog? The latter question is perhaps easier to answer: after the crossing, Hugh internally confronts his own temptation, and floods his battle with images of serpents, highlighted by the observation that a dead garter snake was indeed trodden upon during the journey. Maybe the "protection" the dog offers, through its presence, provides Hugh enough of a figurative and amusing distraction to derail his temptation concerning Yvonne. Even after Yvonne and Hugh stop for drinks, the dog resumes his duty as soon as they leave. "The dog ran ahead of the foals though he never failed to dodge back periodically to see all was well. He was sniffing busily for snakes among the metals" along their path (121). This dog continues to protect but is perhaps slightly less diligent; although still searching for snakes, standing in for temptation, he now allows himself to get ahead of the travellers, as though he has more confidence that, after crossing the river, they are safer now than they were at the beginning of the journey, when Hugh's temptation was more virile within him.

Perhaps the last image of this dog is the strongest support for its phantom nature. "Behind them walked the only living thing that shared their pilgrimage, the dog" (131; emphasis in original). This observation melts into a vision, seemingly Yvonne's, which fuses into something belonging in Geoffrey's head, as he emerges as the central character as the chapter solidifies. The apparent ability to occupy, or walk through, multiple human minds, and to create a transition that unites them on a level deeper than consciousness, certainly seems to place the dog, as "the only living thing" along at this point other than the human characters, on the supernatural plane. Finally, it should be noted that the phantom dogs which slink around Geoffrey's periphery never offer a protective radiance. Tragically absent for Geoffrey is a "helper" phantom dog like the Guatemalan *cadejo*, for example, a supernatural canid haunter of burial spaces (de Guerrero 28) that was known to protect drunks from harm ("Cadejo").[1] In fact, as will be discussed later, a phantom dog seems to pin Geoffrey down into the environment that will frame his death, and reappears physically only as a carcass thrown into a ditch after his own corpse. In short, there is no protection, supernatural or otherwise, given for Geoffrey.

After Señora Gregorio leaves Geoffrey's presence at the cantina, he watches as several men enter, as well as a three-legged "starving pariah dog with the appearance of having lately been skinned [which] squeezed itself in after the last man; it looked up at the Consul with beady, gentle eyes. Then, thrusting down its poor wretched dignity on its chest, from which raw withered breasts drooped, it began to bow and scrape before him" (Lowry 238–39). This dog seems to fit within the template for the phantom-dog tradition; three-legged phantom dogs, for example, are found within the Scandinavian folklore of the Wild Hunt (Woods 57). However, elements of this encounter powerfully contradict many of the defining characteristics of the traditional phantom dog. Firstly, the dog's presence in the cantina, and not out on the road, is unusual; only very rarely do phantom dogs leave their liminal haunts and enter human spaces. Furthermore, the notion that the dog appears to be starving is significant, perhaps indicating Lowry's attempt to add to and possibly subvert the folkloric tradition from which the figure might be borrowed, as it brings a layer of corporeal depth to the dog that is absent from most phantom-dog encounters. Also, the sympathy-inducing frailty of a living animal is a quality missing from the supernatural aura that accompanies most traditional phantom dogs. The "gentle" eyes of the dog create a compassionate gaze which stands in dramatic contrast to the traditional phantom dog, whose saucer-sized eyes almost universally glow a sinister red. Lowry has taken one of the strongest components of the phantom-dog tradition that allows percipients to know that they are not in the presence of a "normal dog," the frightening, otherworldly eyes, and turned it completely on its head: this dog's eyes are also unlike those of a "normal dog," but the compassion they radiate places their owner at the *opposite end* of the spectrum from the phantom phenotype. The fact, further, that this dog proceeds to "bow and scrape" before Geoffrey is unusual in its anthropomorphic nature, but it also cuts against the grain of the phantom-dog tradition, as phantoms very rarely supplicate themselves to their human percipients. If anything, phantom dogs tend to be the aggressors across the folkloric history of their encounters with humanity.

This supplication seems to inspire Geoffrey to speak to the dog, which perhaps foreshadows a window into his approaching death. First he commands the dog to leave; "dispense usted, por Dios" (Lowry 239), Geoffrey commands in a whisper, as though addressing a demon during an exorcism, possibly underscoring his belief in the dog's attachment to the supernatural. Immediately following this, though, "wanting to say something kind, [he] added, stooping, a phrase read or heard in youth or childhood: 'For God sees how timid and beautiful you really are, and the thoughts of hope that go with you like little white birds—" (239). However, this magnanimity vaporizes, as he "stood up and suddenly declaimed to the dog: 'Yet this day, pichicho, shalt thou be with me in—' But the dog hopped away in terror on three legs and slunk under the door" (239). This declaration, and the dog's reaction, should not be overlooked. Geoffrey flirts with images, borrowed from long ago in his own history, of love, just as he seems to envision a life with Yvonne and away from the grave he feels he is digging himself here. These thoughts vanish with frightening speed, and the declaration hints, though cut off by the dog's terrified retreat, that the two figures are destined to unite in death, as of course the last line of the novel confirms to us is the case. The dog perhaps reveals its supernatural prescience of this through its withdrawal; it does not wish to join the doomed Geoffrey, as he has seemed to invite it to do. Yet the destiny of the text itself cannot be sidestepped, as a dog (perhaps not this specific dog, but a dog nonetheless) will join Geoffrey's body in the ditch into which it will be deposited. Passing under the door is a significant detail, as well. We recall that the phantom dog is prone to appearing "along the road," in transitional spaces, so its passing through the transitional space of a door might prefigure Geoffrey's impending passage from life to death. This three-legged phantom dog is maybe a very subtle forerunner, then. And again, the folkloric tradition suggests that Geoffrey's very act of speaking to the phantom dog carries with it some degree of peril.

Geoffrey's association with phantom dogs runs deeper than their proximity to him and his loved ones. Hugh confronts him in regard to what seems to be his sabotaging a possible reunion with Yvonne by reminding him of all the damage he has caused her, and cajoles him with the fact that he would be lucky to get her back in his life "after all your howling" (227). Geoffrey's mode of communication is reduced to that of a dog, and, more importantly than its value as an insult is the connection it suggests between Geoffrey and the dogs that appear to follow him. That the vocalized manifestation of his wildness, this "howling," is the very thing Hugh thinks is likely to chase Yvonne away, is of course meaningful, as Geoffrey's phantom-doglike nature is marked by another human character as an instrument of sabotage against the attempted rehabilitation of his life with Yvonne.

If the connection between Geoffrey and the phantom dog tradition is one that Lowry intends us to notice, then the next step in investigating their presentation would involve the extrapolation of any messages, literal or figurative, their appearances might announce. Charla White offers a seemingly directly applicable connection, in that, typically, "the black [phantom] dog does not exhibit aggressive behaviour; rather it just follows and projects a feeling of fear and despair," and that witnesses frequently become "despondent and notice a severe decline in vitality making their ability to observe their surroundings or the black dog nearly impossible" (White). Evidence of this emotionally charged sensory incapacitation is clearly present throughout Geoffrey's character. Every above-mentioned symptom matches with Geoffrey, insofar as we have been exposed to his emotional condition in the text; he is already wracked by fear, despair, and a fuzzy grasp on his physical surroundings, and does not seem to require the emotionally contagious presence of a phantom dog to inspire such dark and dismal feelings. The phantom dog, here, does not so much create these feelings of depression, as they were clearly present before the encounter, but it certainly throws a spotlight onto them.

The violently spectacular thunderstorm that tears and sears the landscape throughout chapters 11 and 12 evokes the atmosphere preceding the most intense and well-known encounter with a phantom dog. On Sunday, August 4, 1577, a wild morning thunderstorm raged as church services started in the English villages of Bungay and Blythburgh. Suddenly, according to contemporary pamphleteer Abraham Fleming, a huge black dog exploded through the door and into the church, stalking down the aisle and killing two men either by mauling them viciously or simply by brushing against them, depending on which version of the story is considered, before vanishing. (The coat of arms for the village of Bungay depicts the phantom dog standing atop a bolt of lightning. Though not created until 1953 [Westwood 72], this graphic association of the dog with the powerful storm that announced its presence helped to centralize the storm so literally in the narrative that the two become virtually inextricable.) This murderous visitation was essentially repeated moments later in the church at Blythburgh. It may be too much to claim that Lowry directly references this incident, but the circumstantial evidence is weirdly compelling. After all, Geoffrey has just recently visited a Quauhnhuac church dedicated to "the Virgin for those who have nobody with" and characterized by the notion that "only the bereaved and lonely went here" (Lowry 300). Geoffrey prays to be allowed to suffer, asks that he be permitted to "sink lower still," and eventually calls out for forces to "destroy the world!" (300) Such tragic and violent imagery is not far, perhaps, from describing the scenes at Bungay and Blythburgh. In fact, the Calvinist rhetoric in Fleming's 1577 pamphlet seethes with admonishments that its sinful English readers are balanced on the precipice of a world facing destruction akin to that suffered by Sodom and Babylon. Moreover, it may not be too much of a stretch to assert that the Farolito cantina is a sacred space for Geoffrey and, as chapter 12 begins, he is, very much like the churchgoers at Bungay and Blythburgh, under violent assault by the supernatural.

"The Consul now observed that on his extreme right some unusual animals resembling geese, but large as camels, and skinless men, without heads, upon stilts, whose animated entrails jerked along the ground, were issuing out of the forest path the way he had come" (356). After shutting his eyes against this, then, glancing a second time, he sees these visions replaced by commonplace sights. But the mood is set, and the parading of these monsters from a Hieronymus Bosch painting into the sacred heart of the text, even if they are ultimately illusory, seems to grant the supernatural some territory here. Moments later, Geoffrey envisions the inevitable trajectory of his night as one in which he will be wracked by terrifying images, sounds, and battles with demons, including an idea of troubled sleep, "interrupted by voices which were really dogs barking, or by his own name continually repeated by imaginary parties arriving, the vicious shouting, the strumming, the slamming, the pounding, the battling with insolent archfiends, the avalanche breaking down the door" (356). Each of these notions contains echoes of the Fleming account. The barking of dogs is literal enough; phantom dogs are occasionally said to possess humanlike voices, though this element is apparently absent in the 1577 encounters. The calling out of specific names by supernatural entities is also reported, though again not at Bungay and Blythburgh, but the notion that the phantom dog's appearance delivers a dire message of sorts for specific people is undeniably present throughout the phenomenon. The violent, noisy imagery, culminating in a fight with "archfiends," seems to offer an active description of the 1577 attacks. Finally, the breaking down of the door might be seen as a direct parallel to the method by which the phantom dog gained entry to the church at Bungay. (In one variant, huge claw marks remained on the Bungay church door, perpetual souvenirs of the encounter.) Again, it is too far to assert that Lowry directly evokes the incidents Fleming documented, but the coincidences of the imagery, even if nothing else, are too suggestive to disregard.

To this point in the text, dogs are present, but the act of ascribing a phantom nature to them is not unassailable: they are not overtly supernatural in either appearance or behaviour, and their association with the folkloric tradition is suggested, more than demanded, by a careful consideration of their recurrence and liminal placement within the landscape of the text. They could certainly be actual, physical dogs, no strangers to the landscape of 1940s Mexico. However, as the narrative begins to speed itself toward Geoffrey's death, his relationship with the clearly identified phantom-dog figure becomes impossible to ignore. Geoffrey sits at the cantina in Parian, viciously haunted by his past and future, and feeling that he has yet to hit the bottom of his descent, lying instead on a metaphoric ledge, horribly injured but not dead, stationed halfway down a cliff face. This moment of vulnerability allows the phantom black dog to take a clear supernatural place in the scene. "And it was as if a black dog had settled on his back, pressing him to his seat" (377). Though somewhat neutered by the "as if" simile, the image of the dog here is undeniable. The ever-present dog has solidified its nature as a phantom in that it has finally become black, and it has also become invisible, adopting another characteristic of the phantom-dog phenomenon. It is no longer a pariah, detached from the fate of the one whom it is destined to follow. Quite literally, it is now attached to Geoffrey. More important than these morphological similarities to the folkloric archetype, though, is that the dog has now become an active forerunner figure; deeper than being a simple harbinger of the imminent death of the person to whom it appears, this phantom black dog actually physically traps the percipient within the environment that will frame his death. Geoffrey cannot leave the site of his impending demise because the dog, the very figure that has followed him throughout the text, refuses to allow it, and becomes the spectral canine stand-in for "the monkey on his back." *Stay here in the cantina,* the message seems to be, *even though it is going to kill you, Geoffrey Firmin.* American blues pioneer Robert Johnson sang of the phantom dog: "the days keeps on worryin' me; there's a hellhound on my trail" (Westwood 77). Beset by worries, Geoffrey realizes his troubles may finally be over because the "hellhound" has found him, in the bar, of course. He signals his tacit acknowledgement of this, bowing down his head, buried in this terrible moment, that "there is nowhere to fly to" at this point (Lowry 377).

The phantom dog returns to the text, this time in the most corporeal form imaginable, in the novel's last line: "Somebody threw a dead dog after him down the ravine" (391). On a literal level, a connection may be made between many ancient cultures' symbolic attachment of dogs with death and the after-life. According to Alby Stone's "Infernal Watchdogs, Soul Hunters and Corpse Eaters," dog remains have been found at the bottoms of Roman-era wells and pits in Britain in manners that strongly suggest their association with the underworld (Stone 39); Iron Age sites in Britain have uncovered dog skeletons that appear to have been placed amid burials to serve as ritual guardians for the deceased. The dead dog that accompanies Geoffrey's corpse into the ravine might be meant as a similar sacrifice, especially given the relationship between Geoffrey and the pariah dogs that the text presents. (Of course, this issue could be examined more thoroughly if we knew anything at all about the "somebody" who threw the dog into the ravine.) We should not leave the consideration of this subject without again mentioning Cerberus, the mythical three-headed dog that guarded the entrance to the Greek underworld. None of the pariah dogs in Lowry's text are assigned any triple-headed markers to align them easily with this tradition, of course, but the three-legged dog Geoffrey encounters earlier in the cantina at least establishes, via its missing appendage, the significance of the number three. (Interestingly, the number three here results from a loss rather than an addition. Unlike Cerberus, whose three heads represent a morphological excess compared to a "normal" corporeal dog, this dog's three-leggedness represents an absence, in terms of a "normal" corporeal dog's quadrupedal structure. This phantom dog, in other words, is marked by the subtractive rather than the additive, dismemberment instead of enhancement.)

Significantly, though, the covering of Geoffrey's makeshift grave with the carcass of a dog sets forth a scenario in which one need not squint that hard to see the suggested post-mortem conflation of the protagonist with the phantom dog. Precedent exists for this in the folklore that surrounded fifteenth-century alchemist Cornelius Agrippa, whose own "familiar," a supernatural black dog named Monsieur, vanished mysteriously into a river upon its master's death (Sax 318). In this context it is tempting to read Geoffrey as the alchemist of the world of the text, and thus, as in Agrippa's case, his "familiar" must expire when he does. But if the phantom-dog figure has been intended as an indecipherable supernatural messenger, warning Geoffrey of his impending death, it is perhaps as punctuation on the "final message" that its body is delivered into Geoffrey's grave. With the death of the one to whom the message is intended, the phantom dog no longer has a role in the world of the text and can, with symbolic significance of association, be discarded into the same pit that contains the carcass of the protagonist. The dog is no longer a forerunner, but now truly an after runner, in that it follows him into the ravine of death instead of leading him there itself. The bodily nature of the dog's corpse removes it from the realm of the phantom and plugs it, irredeemably, into the "real world." So here, in the dying gleam of the narrative, Geoffrey and the phantom black dog, as dead bodies, become one. What is to be gathered from this implied connection? Perhaps Geoffrey's hyperactive self-analysis and fractured meta-awareness of his own impending death throughout this last day of his life have made him, truly, the phantom dog of his own fate. Geoffrey Firmin, the Consul, at the end, may be his own forerunner, mapping his own trajectory between the registers and toward the grave, across a landscape pockmarked with phantom dog and cat figures aimed at containing him, as a border collie contains its flock, within the narrative path that leads inevitably to the end of his life.

ACKNOWLEDGEMENTS

I would like to thank my patient and meticulous peer readers, Bill Hoge and Rob Gilmor, for their wonderful insight and support, and acknowledge my gratitude to Sheryl and Kirk Salloum, who, via a truly serendipitous encounter in Oxford, introduced me to the world of Malcolm Lowry.

NOTE

1. "Cadejo," *Monstropedia*, http://monstropedia.org/index.php?title=Cadejo. Accessed 25 Sept. 2015.

WORKS CITED

Bord, Janet, and Colin Bord. *Alien Animals*. Harrisburg, PA: Stackpole Books, 1982.

de Guerrero, E. A. P. "Games and Superstitions of Nicaragua." *Journal of American Folklore*, vol. 4, no. 12, Jan.–Mar. 1891, pp. 35–38.

Lowry, Malcolm. *Under the Volcano*. New York: Harper Perennial Modern Classics, 2007.

Paijmans, Theo. "The Hound of Mons." *Fortean Times* 243, Jan. 2009, pp. 40–41.

Sax, Boria. "The Magic of Animals: English Witch Trials in the Perspective of Folklore." *Anthrozoos: A Multidisciplinary Journal of the Interactions of People & Animals*, vol. 22, no. 4, Dec. 2009, pp. 317–332.

Stone, Alby. "Infernal Watchdogs, Soul Hunters and Corpse Eaters." *Explore Phantom Black Dogs*, edited by Bob Trubshaw, Loughborough, UK: Heart of Albion P, 2005, pp. 36–56.

Trubshaw, Bob, editor. *Explore Phantom Black Dogs*. Loughborough, UK: Heart of Albion P, 2005.

Waldron, David, and Christopher Reeve. *Shock! The Black Dog of Bungay; A Case Study in Local Folklore*. Hidden Publishing, 2010.

Westwind, Melissa. *Monster Dogs: The History of the Beast of Dartmoor*. Melissa Westwind, 2013.

Westwood, Jennifer. "Friend or Foe: Norfolk Traditions of Shuck." *Explore Phantom Black Dogs*, edited by Bob Trubshaw, Loughborough, UK: Heart of Albion P, 2005, pp. 57–76.

White, Charla. "The Black Dog." *The Shadowlands*. 2012. theshadowlands.net/blackdog.html. Accessed 26 Sept. 2015.

Woods, Barbara Allen. *The Devil in Dog Form: A Partial Type-Index of Devil Legends*. Berkeley: U of California P, 1959.

II

The Spatial Dynamics of Sight and Sound

6

Spectatorial Bodies and the Everyday Spaces of Cinema

PAUL TIESSEN

From the late 1920s, by which time the practice of regular moviegoing had long been widely established, right through to the 1950s, Malcolm Lowry expressed interest in the peculiarities of moviegoers and of the everyday protocols of moviegoing. He might have picked up his categories of exploration from older modernists who, in the late 1920s, paid considerable attention to relationships between the cinema and the bodies, or body parts, of its spectators. For them, the subjectivity of a moviegoer, as a twentieth-century Everyman, could be understood by the functioning of spectatorial bodies in the spaces in and around movie theatres.

For example, in her scrutiny of the physical body in relation to the screen, Virginia Woolf noted in 1926 the disjunction between what the moviegoer's helpless eye proposed to the body and what the body palpably felt: "We see life as it is when we have no part in it. . . . The horse [on the screen] will not knock us down. . . . The wave [on the screen] will not wet our feet" (Woolf 308). More hyperbolically, Wyndham Lewis, in The Childermass, observed that an untutored eye without recourse to touch was unable to find its spatial bearing in processing movie-like images swarming the eye: "What are these objects that have got in? signal the muscles of the helpless eye: it distends in alarm: it is nothing but a shocked astonished apparatus" (Lewis 15). But some modernists challenged the worriers about the fate of the body. In her lusty 1927 attack on the "vast horde of the fair-to-middling intellectuals" who wrung their hands over screen images' alleged threats to the body, H.D. mocked the view that cinema was "a Juggernaught crushing out mind and perception in one vast orgy of the senses" (H.D. 23). Dorothy Richardson seconded H.D., and extended her support for the moviegoer to the space outside the theatre: "The cinema . . . is now a part of our lives," she joyously proclaimed that same year, embracing cinema and cityscape alike. "We go. No longer in secret and in taxis and alone, but openly in parties in the car" (Richardson 61–62).

Lowry, like his elders, draws on cinema's production of a heightened self-consciousness about the effects of cinema spaces on the role of the body. Movies, and their architectural surround, provide him with a setting for understanding the individual through a reading of the sensorium. Further, he suggests that movies as mechanized narrative invite completion by the collaborating body or, more likely, resistance by the protesting body. His view of the performance of the movie-going body anticipates Marshall McLuhan's; Lowry was interested in sense ratios, finding in the sense of sight, as well as the sense of sound, the dynamics that play—even prey—upon the sense of touch, thus altering the body's capacities and limitations. He anticipates, too, later work of film theorists such as Vivian Sobchack, who is interested in the "lived body as, at once, both an objective subject and a subjective object: a sentient, sensual, and sensible ensemble of materialized capacities and agency" (Sobchack 2). This recent theory redresses the long-standing tendency in film practice and criticism to ignore what Mary Ann Doane describes as the "progressive despatialization and disembodiment of the spectatorial position" (Doane 543).

Without producing a dogma out of what he understood or observed, Lowry dramatizes varieties of the spectatorial body, from disembodiment to bodily renewal. Yet patterns do emerge. Like McLuhan (whose exploration of the body, complexly examined by Richard Cavell in *McLuhan in Space*, also extends literary modernists' late-1920s evaluative categories), Lowry at times registered a Lewisian world of the overwhelmingly subjugated body betrayed by the eye. Occasionally, his tone and temper move closer to the spirit of H.D.'s mockery that the spectatorial body is put at risk in the cinema. In a short essay that he published in a Vancouver newspaper in 1939, Lowry offers a light gloss of modernist anxieties about the loss of the body, drawing attention to ways in which the eye, the ear, and the hand are brought into contradictory play in the modernist discourse. Having just travelled from Hollywood to Vancouver, he describes the insubstantiality of movie actors' bodies loosed from space and place in a mediatized world where cinema, as well as radio, turns "real" space into "ultimate Unreality": "Somewhere in Hollywood a soldier leaned against a radio. Round his head was a bloodstained bandage. In his muddy uniform he seemed rigid with listening," Lowry writes; "This man, an extra, despite his unlikelihood, was real. So was what he heard from Warsaw. His look, as of one who sees into hell but doesn't believe it, was real too." But in a town where "unreal" fragments of history are the norm, where NBC and CBS loudspeakers cause pandemonium in 1939, an observer is "forced to wonder whether or not our extra . . . was convinced that the war was real at all. Did it not seem, perhaps, on the contrary, an ultimate Unreality?" (Lowry, "Hollywood" 4–5)

In Lowry's fiction, the body, whether extended or truncated, is a function both of the camera and projector, and of spaces surrounding the theatre: lobby, side-walk, street, city. In a fleeting moment one evening in his second novel, In Ballast to the White Sea, Lowry's protagonist, Sigbjørn Tarnmoor, on board a ship on the River Ribble, gliding past Preston, Lancashire, sees in the distance an alluring space shaped by "an apron of lights [that] flashed on over the cinema fronts." Occupying one such space, a man "lingered as though haunting," seemingly on the verge of entering the cinema. Sigbjørn imagines the man going inside to "take refuge." He imagines, too, the man, seated in the theatre, granted some kind of mirror of his inner being, if only "a caricature of his most private passions." Meanwhile, says the narrator in a gentle observation, poor lovers wander nearby. With "no rooms to go to and no money for the cinema," they must content themselves with watch-ing Sigbjørn's location as watcher, "strain[ing] their eyes towards the lights and shadows of the ship" (Lowry, Ballast 218). The subjectivity of Lowry's spectatorial bodies is constituted both on the street and in front of the screen. He easily would have concurred with Maggie Valentine's argument, in The Show Starts on the Sidewalk, that "the experience of the film—that is, the reality for the observer—was largely influenced by the surroundings. The experience of 'going to the movies' equaled, and often surpassed, what was seen on the screen" (Valentine xii).

That unknown figure in Preston, like the "soldier" in Hollywood, intro-duces us to other moviegoers in three of Lowry's major works: his first novel, Ultramarine, from 1933; the 1936 draft of his recently published In Ballast to the White Sea; and his masterwork, Under the Volcano, 1947. It introduces us also to filmgoers in the film script that Lowry wrote in 1949/50, an adaptation of F. Scott Fitzgerald's Tender Is the Night, in which Lowry turns the modernist tropes about cinema, space, and the body into a practical experiment that imagines "us" as actual moviegoers.

◆

In Ultramarine, Dana Hilliott carries his upper-middle-class self-consciousness into the theatre, where he can perform, however clumsily, an awkward and embarrassed resistance to a movie's obviously vulgar appeal to cheap emotion. He puts on an act of challenging the presupposition that moviegoers will bow to commercial cinema's rigidly mechanized storytelling. With loud bravado, he acts out the autonomy of the moviegoer against the taunts of movie technology, and also strikes a blow on behalf of himself as a manly lad.

The prelude to Dana's movie-going occurs when Dana and the friendly German sailor Hans Popplereuter totter drunkenly along a sidewalk, stumbling on the curb in front of a cinema, brightly lit like other of Lowry's cinemas: "We paused, swaying on our heels, before the snowy theatre front. A sailor was reeling round in front of the box office" (*Ultramarine* 103). They and the other sailor move as if in single lockstep through space: from the curb to the ticket office and into the pink glow inside the auditorium (104). Here, in the face of a tawdry picture show (no title given), Dana tries to find the rhythm, not of the film but of the crowd, leading and simultaneously defying it with his screams and clapping. Against the disembodiment of the hapless audience by the cinema machine he asserts a raucous animal protest, claiming the space for the audience.

This visit to the cinema—described in detail (103–107)—ends on an indeterminate note, with the audience clapping mindlessly, its action (stamping, roaring, spitting, belching) finally losing any shape or function. Dana, who has pushed his mates into joining him at the movie, now, assuming he has won a bit of moral high ground in trying to become one "hell of a fellow" (79) in his riotous behaviour in front of the audience and the apparatus, tries to maintain his spot within their drunken momentum. In his ever-deferred womanizing, he is determined not to be "beaten tonight" (109). "We edged out into the alley and staggered down the steps into the street" (107). The street resumes its position, narratively contiguous with the space and the meaning of the spectacle in the movie theatre. Street and audience and screen in this comic-burlesque atmosphere possess an overlapping sensory rawness, a visual surrealism uninformed by civilized conversation with (to take examples we shall come upon) a moviehouse manager or a member of the audience.

❧

In chapter 5 of *In Ballast to the White Sea*, the protagonist, Sigbjørn, and his father, the operator of a shipping line, go on a circuitous walk through the Liverpool Exchange district, a walk that might recall Dana's and Hans's pre-cinema walk in *Ultramarine* and anticipates Laruelle's pre-cinema walk in chapter 1 of *Under the Volcano* (just as it contrasts with Yvonne's in chapter 9). They are probing, deeply and guiltily, the tragedies in their lives: the suicide of Sigbjørn's brother at Cambridge University and the loss at sea of one of his father's ships, with all its crew. As friendly companions who bring philosophical and personal conversation to the movie house, father and son partially recall Dana and Hans, and anticipate aspects of Laruelle and his successive companions, first Vigil, then Bustamente, in *Under the Volcano*. Crucially, other of Lowry's characters—Yvonne in *Under the Volcano*; then, in Lowry's unproduced screenplay of Fitzgerald's "Tender Is the Night," Dick Diver on one occasion, Nicole Diver on another—inhabit cinemas in various modes of extreme isolation, socially and inwardly, marginal or alone.

Sigbjørn and his father's dialogue occurs within the afternoon hubbub of familiar city streets and the sudden eruption of social unrest—"shouts, the ringing of hooves, chaos"—with workers and police clashing (*Ballast* 64–65). Swept by three mounted policemen away from the workers' demonstration, they arrive at Mount Pleasant, where the "signs of a cinema, . . . built on an incline" like Bustamente's in *Under the Volcano*, "attracted their attention" (66). Here, at the *"Century Theatre, the Home of Unusual Films,"* they are met by advertisements for a 1927 film that has obvious thematic and dramatic resonances with the labour strife on the streets of Liverpool: Pudovkin's *The End of St. Petersburg*.

No interlude separates exterior vistas from the safe harbour of interior space; the theatre simply becomes the still, fixed, even intended, centre of their walk: "They entered unhesitatingly as if they had been making all along for this place of refuge." At the same time, its environment reflects their conversational groping for meaning in their lives: "once inside they were almost lost. Like blind men they felt their way to a seat" (66–67). The cinema offers respite to the aesthete in Sigbjørn and stirs only mild discomfort within his barely-awake political side. Its agenda of hope and courage, its posters with the peasant's visionary look to the future, confirm for Sigbjørn, and for us, his feeling of political/spiritual malaise.

On the screen, the story is well under way (as it is with other of Lowry's moviegoers who enter cinemas, film in progress); people are marching against Kerensky's Russian Provisional Government. But Lowry's focus once again is on the body. His two moviegoers feel the palpable texture of the space: its darkness, the handful of others whose personal burdens—more political than aesthetic—are unlike theirs. Varying subjectivities inhabit a single theatrical space. Quiet conversation between two students about the status of workers in the film—though even such speaking is nearly hushed by an older moviegoer—penetrates the mechanized atmosphere as though even here asserting an irreducibly human presence determined to emancipate a space otherwise dominated by cinema's machine-driven images (67).

The film ends without warning, the next screening scheduled for later that evening. The sudden and intrusive brightness assaults Sigbjørn's body, as clock time intrudes on his emotional time and on the warm pleasure of film images flooding his eye in the darkened room. Rising to leave, he sees the three people who make up the interactive collectivity in the back of the theatre (67). The narrator, seeming to lament the loss of this provisional community, says poignantly that Sigbjørn will not see the others again (68): something filled with the pulse of shared life at the movies will dissolve once they leave the theatre. In much of

Lowry's work it is more salutary to attend a movie in the context of the corrective, consoling, and empathetic eyes of a small group than alone.

The dynamics of community in this instance are expanded to include the cinema manager. Father and son enjoy a brief encounter at the doorway—a temporary but productive social space—that separates theatre and street. The manager apologizes for the termination of the custom of continuous performance and comments, not without a bit of wry satire in the presence of these two well-heeled men, that this specialty house in Liverpool, even when it showcases films about workers' revolutions, does not, given its emphasis on high artistry, appeal to the masses but to "high-class audiences" (68). Lowry is making a light joke at the expense of the pretensions of patrons of modernist art cinemas that favour directors like Pudovkin. Later, in *Under the Volcano*, he pokes fun at the more obtuse pretentiousness of Laruelle and his one-time attempt at an avant-garde reputation with his laughable film version of Shelley's *Alastor*. In an earlier version of *Under the Volcano*, an arrogant Laruelle even claims his film as a forerunner to Jean Cocteau's 1930 film *Le sang d'un poète* (Lowry, 1940 *Volcano* 132).

❦

In *Under the Volcano*, Jacques Laruelle's visit to the cinema balances and objectifies Yvonne's. Through the worldly, if pompous, film director, Lowry explores a masculinist counter to Yvonne's persona (and, as we shall see, to Nicole Diver's and also Dick Diver's). The architectonics of space in and around a movie house serve in each instance as an organizing site for plumbing something of the tenor and tone of the inner life of each character.

The "one cinema" of Quauhnahuac is visible to Laruelle and Arturo Vigil from the Hotel Casino de la Selva, just outside the town; it is, as noted above, "built on an incline and stand[s] out sharply" (Lowry, *Volcano* 11). Laruelle makes it his destination in his "circuitous" orbit. Lowry again calls it—in his letter to Jonathan Cape—a place of "refuge" (Lowry, *Sursum* 1:510). He describes Laruelle's arrival there in terms of the people who have gathered to wait for the restoration of electrical power. Laruelle, realizing he has already seen *Las Manos de Orlac* (*Volcano* 31), decides against taking any of it in again (should there actually be a screening, given the troubles with the wiring).

In an earlier version of the text, Laruelle does go in to see again this "bloody story ... grotesquely fumbled" and "fuddled" (1940 *Volcano* 20, 22), with its "bloodthirsty theme" so popular with "Mexican audiences" (13). Though distinguishing his own from the tastes of the local spectators, he wanders in with them, once it seems the electricity might be operating. Lowry lavishes attention on the rituals of entry, on the texture of the theatrical space, on the presence of a courteous manager: "[Laruelle] looked around him, uncertain where to sit in the theatre, which in the gloom itself resembled a huge cemetery. The manager, fussing about, caught sight of him and apologizing . . . for the delay, showed him, with a torch, into a box for the *Autoridades*" (18). Laruelle promptly falls asleep and dreams, his dream corrupted by images from the film.

In the final manuscript, published in 1947, Laruelle is also a consumer of images, though not of any screened narrative nor of any dream. Rather, he observes the moviegoers who fill the spaces around him. After a polite exchange of pleasantries with the gracious and urbane cinema manager, Señor Bustamente (who, as Rick Asals [382] points out, remains unnamed in the 1940 draft), Laruelle is alone in the cantina. He sits in a visually privileged position relative to the interior of the movie theatre, voyeuristically gazing into it through a side partition where a curtain has been drawn back. Within this camera obscura he cannot be seen by others.

Watching this private show, while flickering shadows cross the movie screen, he sees children bawling, hawkers selling fried potatoes, pariah dogs prowling among the stalls. And, in a moment that is deeply affecting for the reader who follows the development of Lowry's moviegoers, he sees, set apart, a row of "men along the right-hand balcony, who hadn't bothered to move or come downstairs, a solid frieze carved into the wall, serious, moustachioed men, warriors waiting for the show to begin, for a glimpse of the murderer's bloodstained hands" (*Volcano* 34). These men—covertly observed by Laruelle, who in his position of silent surveillance recalls Sigbjørn from the ship imagining the identity of a distant moviegoer—comprise one of Lowry's most stunning portraits of moviegoers. We do not enter their experience, except to understand that they are altogether unlike Laruelle, who is their uninvited witness. Patient and impassive, they cast into relief the impatient or agitated or burdened European/American audience members whom Lowry explores in the fraught spaces of his cinema environments.

Lowry presents Yvonne—Laruelle's one-time fellow denizen of Hollywood, perhaps a little better as an actress than he as a director (18)—as an emotionally fragile young woman, haunted by dark spaces of city and cinema alike. The reader, taken into a desolate period in New York that precedes the main action of the novel, is enwrapped in a tale of Yvonne's earlier self. She is alone, lonely, and vulnerable after failures in relationships and two tries at a career in Hollywood, where she was commodified in tawdry public-relations gimmickry. One night, among advertisements that include those for *Romeo and Juliet* and *Dead End* (films released in 1936 and 1937, respectively), she walks from the Astor Hotel just above

42nd Street through a remorselessly unforgiving "numb brilliant jittering city" all the way down to 14th Street (267). Fearing that she is being followed but finding herself in front of a "little cinema," she enters. The program, we learn, includes *Le Destin de Yvonne Griffaton* (a fictitious title) plus a newsreel, an animated cartoon, a documentary about the African lungfish, and a revival of Howard Hawks's 1932 *Scarface*. The stills pasted on the outside of the theatre—recalling those that Laruelle has shown her of his pretentious "old French films"—depict a solitary figure surrounded by the advertisements of a city, a figure not unlike Yvonne herself, but one haunting and haunted by another urban space, Paris (267).

For Yvonne, this New York cinema space might seem a "sanctuary" (to borrow from the idea of the church that the Yvonne of the film enters to pray). But it offers her no bodily or psychic distance from her terror, only an ambiguous invitation to some kind of reprieve. With Lowry's narrator withholding narrative succour, as it were—that is, without his offering the mediating and humanizing presence of as much as a ticket seller—Yvonne is inside the cinema. She seems transported from outside to inside as if through thin air. With Lowry defining the subjective by the material, she felt "as if she had walked straight out of that world outside into this dark world on the screen, without taking breath." She hears a voice from the screen call "'Yvonne, Yvonne!'" and a shadowy statue of a horse seems to leap at her from the screen through three-dimensional space (268).

The arbitrary randomness of Yvonne's cinema experience contrasts with the conventional experiences of other moviegoers. They comprise a typically constructed movie audience at a theatre specializing (like the Liverpool theatre of *In Ballast to the White Sea*) in "revivals and foreign films" (267). These polite moviegoers objectify Yvonne's raw encounter with image and sound, though they pay her no attention. They are a "sophisticated audience" that "laughed, or coughed, or murmured" during the screening (269). Having arrived earlier than Yvonne (who, like the protagonists in *Ultramarine* and *In Ballast to the White Sea*, arrives in medias res), they have seen what was "buried back in the earlier episodes of the film" (269); in any case, they know how to read this movie. Their amusement stems from their recognition of the film's unintentional self-parody, "satire, almost, of itself" (268): for example, English-language subtitles that are too literal and reductive (269), and the redundant application of Ravel's *Bolero* (269).

That Yvonne sees only a part of the film—broken up even further by her stepping out for a cigarette—is not, for Lowry, itself a problem. In fact, it may be an opportunity, because film experiences for him were often a matter of parts rather than wholes. Having "arrived in the middle" (268)—a playing out of a *sortes cinematographica*—Yvonne feels that this might be "the best film" she has ever seen. It is "so extraordinarily complete in its realism" (whatever we might take that complicated term, realism, to mean here) that Yvonne, as though freed of her body, feels she is the Yvonne on the screen, hunted and haunted, "groping for something" that will let her overcome her problem-filled past (268). But alas, the self-parodying phantoms on the screen signal to us that Yvonne's capacity for reading the image, or herself, as text founders. Further, that Yvonne does not share an emotionally sedate space with the relaxed community of the other moviegoers gives Lowry a means to reveal a woman lost within the solipsism of her mutually isolated eye, ear, hand, and body. Her social and bodily marginalizations are markers of her precarious inner condition. Lowry explores through Yvonne as moviegoer a crisis of perception that, rooted in the inherent contradictoriness (from cliché to self-parodying effect to apparent "realism") of the photographed image.

∾

Lowry (in tandem with Margerie Bonner Lowry, his wife and co-writer on this 1949/50 script) drew on his treatment of Yvonne when he wrote the twenty-three-page New York portion of his "Tender Is the Night" (Lowry, Cinema 147–69). In keeping with his source in Fitzgerald, he sets it in 1927, about a decade prior to Yvonne's New York. In passages heavily laden with "poetic and visual and aural *drang*" (*Sursum* 2:218), Lowry has his protagonist wander along city streets that, like Yvonne's, echo the spaces of German expressionist cinema of the 1920s, and allude to the streets of 1940s film noir.

Lowry's protagonist is a version of Fitzgerald's Dick Diver. Isolated and alone, filled with despair over his disintegrating life, Dick spends kinaesthetically complicated nights in and around cinemas and live theatres along the Great White Way or 42nd Street. Interpenetrating planes of streetscapes and screen worlds are barely separated by permeable membranes: doorways open in one direction on vistas of the city, in the other, on movie screens. Clusters of movie images from one theatre dissolve into those next door (*Cinema* 165). One evening, Dick follows Yvonne's route from the Astor Hotel in the Times Square area down to 14th Street (149, 153–54), past cinema marquees "mingling," as Lowry puts it, "the thematically significant with the insignificant" (147).

Moreover, with his "Tender Is the Night," working with a screenplay rather than a novel, Lowry uses his cinema-space tropes to incorporate us, his audience, into his space experiments. To take one example from the New York section, with its apron of lights recalling the Preston cinemas of *In Ballast to the White Sea*:

Cut into a head on shot of the apron lights of a cinema: it is playing de Mille's *King of Kings*. The screen slides by and we see the film playing next

door: it is Eisenstein's *Battleship Potemkin* . . . then a confused noisy super-
imposed shot of electric lights merges into Dick entering a cinema—again
a head-on shot of its electric lighted apron front—playing Rex Ingram's
Mare Nostrum: immediately on the screen in this cinema a man is seen
drowning beneath the sea: the scene of drowning now fills our screen so
that we feel ourselves almost to be drowning in this sea through which
now appear other electric apron fronts of other theatres which we feel
Dick still walking into. (*Cinema* 165–66)

Lowry is in search of the historical 1949–1950 moviegoer here, one for whom he
is determined to create a subjective experience that is as contradictory, volatile,
and raw as it is for his character. We and Dick become "like Alice going through
the looking glass" and dissolve (recalling here Lowry's 1939 reference to "ultimate Unreality") into a zone of "unreality and phantasmagoria" (163). Or, to take
note of McLuhan's reading of *Alice in Wonderland*, we enter "a fantasia of discontinuous space-and-time" like those of Kafka, Joyce, and Eliot (McLuhan 220).

For Lowry, a stage within the film, like a screen within the film, commingles
with the street in vividly articulated passages. Moments before an anguished
walk along the Great White Way, Dick stands at the back of a live performance
of *Antigone* and drinks from his flask. "On the stage we see the Chorus," and we
hear the words, "Wonders are many," right through to "But from baffling maladies, hath he devised escapes" (*Cinema* 162). The enclosed space of the theatre
is pierced by the fluid space of the street: "Cut [from the theatre] to Dick going
down into the street . . . pursued by the voices of the Chorus endlessly repeating
the first and last lines, so that it sounds above the traffic, as he walks . . . down
Broadway." Meantime, we, as audience, our own subject position thus all the
more made to overlap with Dick's, continue to hear the words, "Wonders are
many and none is more wonderful than man . . ./But from baffling maladies
hath he devised escapes . . ./as if they were pursuing Dick in relentless counterpoint" (162). The diegetic words of the chorus and their non-diegetic afterlife,
the "acoustical" and the "visual" intensity: these produce for Dick a surrealism
of warring impressions, as they do for Lowry's audience, whom Lowry dazzles
and buffets with phantasmagoric fury. The street, in turn, is filled with advertisements and announcements, captions and headings; subtitles, as it were, functioning both materially and symbolically. This overloaded sequence is Lowry's
spatial rendering of the first epigraph for *Under the Volcano*—from Sophocles'
Antigone. Like Yvonne, Dick is given no recourse to rituals of language or pleasantries of social discourse as a buttress against and mediator for excesses of
unruly perception uncontrollably assailing eye and ear in enclosed spaces. The

cinema and its contiguous spaces take over Dick's mind and senses, H.D.'s sarcastic quip notwithstanding.

Earlier in his "Tender Is the Night," Lowry explores what begins as a sedate movie-within-the-movie experience, but escalates to something again frightening, at least for one participant. Five Americans in Paris, including Rosemary Hoyt, attend a private screening in 1926 of a new Hollywood film that stars Rosemary. It is called—with recognizable irony—Daddy's Girl.

Lowry's space for his fictional audience in this instance becomes, again, coextensive with "our" space. We, along with the fictional audience, absorb the shock of a sudden shift in the activity of our sensorium when Lowry withdraws music from the film within the film's diegetic performativity: "we hear the flickering noise of the projector . . . we have become aware that the silence—the sudden total absence of music, with nothing to be heard save the whining projector—constitutes a dramatic element in itself" (72). Lowry sets us into something like the position of the "sophisticated audience" at the Griffaton movie. Nicole Diver, suffering the severe illness of a schizophrenic patient driven into guilt and madness after having caused a horrific car accident, occupies an emotional position more tenuous even than that of Yvonne upon entering the 14th Street cinema. Indeed, all five viewers—including one snoring—are locked into separate viewing positions, examined separately by Lowry, with no one offering the other much of a corrective vision. A car in Daddy's Girl, with Rosemary and her daddy, is speeding ever faster: "We," Lowry's audience, still (though ironically, now) clinging to some degree of objective distance from the image, "begin to feel that this part of Daddy's Girl is rather good. . . . We get a tremendous horrendous sensation of increasing speed and the exhilaration of being on the road ourselves, which ever recedes beneath our very chairs" (72). Nicole's reaction to the scene—her hysterical, sobbing laughter—breaks the stillness when the film carries us "down that rushing road until beyond the breaking point of exhilaration and excitement" (72–73; cf. 91). For her, the force of the moment exceeds the safety of a movie's genre conventions, and it destroys her.

In an unexpected gesture at the very end of his "Tender Is the Night" experiment, Lowry again speaks explicitly to "us" as audience, but this time suggesting—in images that might recall the conclusion of chapter 11 of Under the Volcano—that he can bring renewal to the contradictory terrains that we bodily occupy in his cinema. With the help of his camera, he draws us from a spatial world where sense and subjectivity run amok among "shocks" delivered to the body, to a space more serene. He proposes to alter bodily experience, infusing it with a healing spirituality that transforms the physical into the metaphysical. In two short paragraphs that follow Dick Diver's life-giving sacrifice at sea and that start with our glimpse of a bright sailing moon, Lowry first points to our shared space with the screen "in the theatre." But he spirits us out of that space, closing the film with "the shot of the night sky and the stars blazing with which the picture opened," with music shaping that space: "the music does two things; all at once it rises to a dissonant scream, a paean of dreadful pain: then, as all the planes upon which the film has progressed are resolved, and while the stars themselves remain on the screen, it strides forth in triumphant harmony" (242). Here—in a multiplication of the layers of acoustical and visual space—Lowry imagines sweeping his moviegoers into a oneness of sense and sensibility, sweeping them beyond their corporeality within a terrestrial cinema space so that we are "borne straight upwards into the night sky and the stars" (241–42).

❧

For Lowry, a human presence, typically male, engaged in pleasant (or even, as with Dana, rude) dialogue, marks a protagonist's mastery of cinema spaces, a protest against the tyranny of the wayward and flickering image that threatens to disembody the moviegoer. Lowry's cinema manager in *Under the Volcano* stylishly contributes to marking safe social space around a cinema. Even during the thunder storm he stands as an elegant figure, "impeccably dressed in striped trousers and a black coat, inflexibly *muy correcto . . .* despite earthquake and thunderstorm. . . . 'Come and have a drink,' he said [to Laruelle]" (*Volcano* 31). He is a smart commentator observing local and international affairs, simultaneously overseeing the details of his movie business. He responds philosophically and practically to the demands of film distributors and audiences alike. On a small scale, he is anticipated by the theatre manager in *In Ballast to the White Sea*.

With his film script, Lowry himself becomes a "meta" cinema manager, meticulously attentive to the screen and its relationships to the spectatorial body. Lowry as "explicator" (Mota 132) provides a vivid reading of sensorial meaning in a space defined by the sights and sounds of a movie. He is interested not simply in the screen image but in the social body as it moves about in the gaps between screen and curb, between seat and street. He directs the corporeal traffic in and around cinema's array of spaces. And—even in his treatment of the body in space in the transfigurative final moments of his script—he proposes approaches to "seeing" as a shared and collaborative act, one that overcomes the arrogance or limitations of solitary or isolated insight by the corrective embodiment of "seeing" as a social act, of "seeing" in conversation, as it were.

Lowry's brother Russell has described an encounter that includes Lowry and a cinema manager. His recollection goes back to his and Malcolm's visits to little cinemas when they were schoolboys with easy access to a motorbike. On one occasion, they enjoyed the humanizing interaction afforded by the presence of a cinema manager, and afforded, too, by their capacity to determine the sonic texture of the space of a silent-movie theatre. With sounds they generated from their own spectatorial bodies, they helped straighten the balance between the mechanized phantom image and the flesh-and-blood moviegoer: "Malcolm & I were the only customers at an afternoon cinema. They wanted to give us our money back. No, we'd come a long way at considerable effort to see the show so . . . Well they couldn't afford the pianist. All right we'll do our own sound effects. We did. The manager came & sat with us & joined in"! (R. Lowry, personal communication).

ACKNOWLEDGEMENTS

I am grateful to the late Russell Lowry for his description, in a 1980 letter to me, of his brother's visits to the movies in the days of "silent" cinema; the ellipses and ampersands in the quotation are his. I am grateful to the Social Sciences and Humanities Research Council of Canada for supporting research related to this essay.

WORKS CITED

Asals, Frederick. *The Making of Malcolm Lowry's Under the Volcano*. Athens: U of Georgia P, 1997.

Cavell, Richard. *McLuhan in Space: A Cultural Geography*. Toronto: U of Toronto P, 2003.

Doane, Mary Ann. "Technology's Body: Cinematic Vision in Modernity." *A Feminist Reader in Early Cinema*, edited by Jennifer M. Bean and Diane Negra, Durham: Duke UP, 2002, pp. 530–551.

H.D. "The Cinema and the Classics—I—Beauty." *Close Up*, vol. 1, no. 1, July 1927, pp. 22–23.

Lewis, Wyndham. *The Childermass*. London: Methuen, 1928.

Lowry, Malcolm. *The 1940 Under the Volcano: A Critical Edition*. Edited by Paul Tiessen and Miguel Mota, annotations by Chris Ackerley and David Large, Ottawa: U of Ottawa P, 2015.

——. *The Cinema of Malcolm Lowry: A Scholarly Edition of Lowry's "Tender Is the Night."* Edited by Miguel Mota and Paul Tiessen, Vancouver: U of British Columbia P, 1990.

——. "Hollywood and the War." *Malcolm Lowry Newsletter* 11, Fall 1982, pp. 4–6.

——. *In Ballast to the White Sea.* Edited by Patrick A. McCarthy, annotations by Chris Ackerley, Ottawa: U of Ottawa P, 2014.

——. *The Letters of Malcolm Lowry and Gerald Noxon, 1940–1952.* Edited by Paul Tiessen, Vancouver: U of British Columbia P, 1988.

——. *Sursum Corda! The Collected Letters of Malcolm Lowry.* Edited by Sherrill E. Grace, vol. I: 1926–1946; vol. II: 1947–1957, Toronto: U of Toronto P, 1995 and 1996.

——. *Ultramarine.* London: Jonathan Cape, 1963.

——. *Under the Volcano.* Harmondsworth, UK: Penguin Books, 1963.

Lowry, Russell. Personal communication. August 10, 1980.

McLuhan, Marshall. *Understanding Media: The Extensions of Man.* Corte Madera, CA: Gingko P, 2003.

Mota, Miguel. "'We Simply Made One Up': The Hybrid Text of 'Tender Is the Night'." *A Darkness That Murmured: Essays on Malcolm Lowry and the Twentieth Century,* edited by Frederick Asals and Paul Tiessen, Toronto: U of Toronto P, 2000, pp. 530–551.

Richardson, Dorothy. "Continuous Performance, VI: The Increasing Congregation." *Close Up,* vol. 1, no. 6, Dec. 1927, pp. 61–65.

Sobchack, Vivian. *Carnal Thoughts: Embodiment and Moving Image Culture.* Berkeley: U of California P, 2004.

Valentine, Maggie. *The Show Starts on the Sidewalk: An Architectural History of the Movie Theatre, Starring S. Charles Lee.* New Haven and London: Yale UP, 1994.

Woolf, Virginia. "The Movies and Reality." *New Republic* XLVII, no. 609, Aug. 4, 1926, pp. 308–310.

7

Projecting the Volcano: The Possibilities of Margerie Bonner Lowry's Film Proposal

W. M. HAGEN

Early film theory emphasized the medium's success in its "redemption of physical reality" (Kracauer). It compelled our gaze: "the clouds or the tree acquired meaning because someone had put a frame around them" (O'Brien 125). Every technical improvement, from sound and colour to wide screens and multitrack Dolby, intensified and expanded the perceptual field. Directors such as F. W. Murnau, G. W. Pabst, René Clair, and Robert Wiene may have crossed the threshold from the objectively dramatic to the subjective or psychological in silent pictures, but the advent of sound, a primacy of dialogue in the 1930s and 1940s, restored the hegemony of realist cinema, hardening into the assumptions and formulas embodied in many Hollywood films.

Some directors were able to adapt the psychological or expressionistic elements of silent film into mainstream talkies: Alfred Hitchcock in *Suspicion* (1941), *Shadow of a Doubt* (1943), and especially *Spellbound* (1945); Luis Buñuel in *L'Age d'Or* (1932) and *Los Olvidados* (1951); Billy Wilder in *The Lost Weekend* (1945). It was with the expectation that subjective or psychological states could be redeemed through physical imagery that Malcolm Lowry and Margerie Bonner Lowry proposed a screenplay of F. Scott Fitzgerald's *Tender is the Night*, and later Margerie proposed making a film of Lowry's masterwork, *Under the Volcano*.

It is the latter I wish to consider: the possibilities of filming *Under the Volcano*, as proposed by Margerie. In sending her fifty-page film proposal to Luis Buñuel in 1962, she certainly thought that he could capture the psychological and symbolic richness of the novel. That *Under the Volcano* had been compared to James Joyce's fiction in rendering character psychology seemed a worthwhile challenge for a director who extolled film as "the superlative medium through which to express the world of thought, feeling and instinct. . . . The Cinema seems to have been invented to express the life of the subconscious" (Edwards 34).

In her proposal, it is clear that Margerie thought the subjective and symbolic dimensions she had adapted from the novel were quite accessible. Her credits in the film world included the Lowrys' script "Tender is the Night," a text that presented a character's mental states, as well as her own acting career. By the same token, even with the psychological elements included, husband and wife had wanted any film treatment of *Under the Volcano* to reach a mainstream audience (Tiessen 162).

Apparently, Buñuel expressed some interest in doing the novel. Not entirely clear are the reasons the project was dropped, although finances were always uncertain for his less-commercial properties. Later, Buñuel defended his decision not to proceed, claiming that the internal or subjective dimensions of the novel made it impossible to film (Boyum 207). Since Margerie had helped edit the manuscript of *Under the Volcano* in the first place, and was a fierce advocate for Lowry's legacy, Buñuel may have decided to avoid the hassle that negotiating a script with her could have involved.

There is no evidence that John Huston, his scriptwriter, or his producer based their film *Under the Volcano* (1984) on any part of Margerie's outlined proposal. As I have previously documented, while the mainstream press praised the film for some fine acting and vivid cinematography, those familiar with the novel recognized a severely reduced vision in Huston (Hagen, "Under"). That reduction actually made it harder to understand the plot: it must have seemed to mainstream audiences quite stupid for a sensitive and intelligent man not to welcome his beloved, beautiful wife with at least a measure of attempted sobriety when she returned to their home in scenic and festive Mexico, for example.

In researching Huston's production, I kept coming back to an article by Wieland Schulz-Keil, the producer who surveyed over sixty scripts and proposals of *Under the Volcano* in choosing one that would interest Huston. Among them were a script by Cuban novelist Guillermo Cabrera Infante and a proposal or treatment by Columbian novelist Gabriel García Márquez. Out of all those, he chose Guy Gallo's screenplay, written while he was still a student at Yale. What became evident in reading other accounts of the pre-production process was that Schulz-Keil was quite aware that Huston favoured strong, realistic storylines, and had a corollary tendency to objectify action and omit character subjectivity. So while reading the novel may have helped the lead actor, Albert Finney, method-act the Consul with needed subtext, Gallo worked with Huston in the opposite direction to eliminate what Schulz-Keil termed "Flashback orgies and flashback visions" (qtd. in Gold 66). Even diegetic images that might carry larger meaning were scaled back for fear that they might be too symbolic: Gallo remembers Huston constantly asking of an image: "What does it mean in terms of *present tense*? What does it mean for our *character*? And our *situation*?" (qtd. in Hamill 61). So fans of the novel looked in vain for Laruelle, for the garden sign, for the omnipresent *barranca*, even for much of the volcanoes in the resulting film.

In defending what the film was to become during the production process, Gallo, Huston, and Schulz-Keil raised the same issue Buñuel did: whether mainstream film can successfully incorporate or translate the techniques of modernist psychological fiction or expressionistic theatre. Although advances in what can be done today in the laboratory seem to have overcome material or location limitations, the question may still arise. A number of reviews of Huston's film in the popular press indeed raised that very matter, some with an obvious animus toward the novel itself.

Margerie's film proposal offers an opportunity to reconsider what might have been done and what might be done with her husband's novel. Equally, it offers an opportunity to reconsider the larger issue raised about a film based on such a densely textured novel—the adaptation of which would need enough of the density, enough of the subjectivity, to be reasonably congruent, to have some of the resonance of the fiction.

Let us acknowledge that to even speak of a film called *Under the Volcano* based upon a fifty-page proposal made over fifty years ago is to speak of something that neither exists nor likely ever will. The hypothetical film of this chapter, based on that proposal, will be imagined through scenes in films that were released prior to or during the 1960s, when Margerie wrote her proposal. Since Bonner Lowry addressed her proposal to Luis Buñuel, certainly his films from that period will be included. In addition, it seems fair to estimate the success of some of her sequences in comparison with what was done by the Huston production team—particularly the scenes where flashbacks and subjective imagery take on a life of their own.

Bonner Lowry's proposal attempted to conform to mainstream or classical narration, not art-film narration as defined by David Bordwell and others. As she saw it, "Malcolm was an English Writer, in the great classical tradition of English literature. The plot of the book is as tightly and expertly constructed as a Shakespearian plot" (Lowry 113). However, that did not, for her, rule out adopting some techniques of art films: "Malcolm was also a great experimenter, and on this solid foundation of plot we can experiment with our camera to replace his magnificent flights of language" (113). On her side of it, the history of modernist and postmodernist fiction and film certainly demonstrates how both mediums can incorporate and naturalize what was once considered avant-garde.

Film historian David Bordwell quotes a critic from the 1960s to the effect that "new cinema deals with the reality of the imagination as well, but treats this as if it were as objective as the world before us" (Bordwell 206). Alf Sjöberg, Ingmar Bergman, Orson Welles, and Billy Wilder, in different films from the 1940s and 1950s (*Miss Julie, Wild Strawberries, Citizen Kane, The Lost Weekend*), had included realistic dreams, flashbacks, and hallucinations. There might or might not be a transition for the viewer, in the form of narration or remembered voices, a dissolve that might include some effects, accompanied, perhaps, by a theremin, but realism was preserved within the mental scene itself, without the warped scenery, split screens, or blurry imagery of earlier expressionistic films. So it seemed possible in the early 1960s to show something of the Consul's state of mind. As she prepared to set up the climax of the film, Margerie certainly felt that "much of its incomparable richness can be retained in the final script, and the film itself" (Lowry 112). Further, she hoped larger themes could be implied as well:

> This book is, actually, about Original Sin and the Fall of Man. The Consul is of course a Faustian character . . . and he embodies the destructiveness and the self-destructiveness of Man, from Adam down to "Do you like this garden that is yours?" (112)

So Margerie included many elements of the novel that would be scrupulously ignored by Gallo and Huston twenty years later: a flashback framework, significant (symbolic) use of the setting, and auditory and visual hallucinations and projections. Furthermore, although she is deferential to Buñuel and whomever the cinematographer might be, she has some definite ideas as to what from the novel should be included and, in some cases, how the shots might be set up.

She sought to portray some of the sudden associative or metaphoric imagery that occurs in the consciousness of a character, or that might occur, so to speak, to the consciousness of the camera (non-diegetic). She wanted the voices that bedevil Geoffrey, the alcoholic Consul, his "familiars." Her proposal consists of twenty-one sequences, in just over fifty pages, some of which involve changes of scene (the bus ride, the climactic deaths of Geoffrey and Yvonne); frequently she suggests going to the novel to fill out dialogue. She has all of the sections from the novel that would be included in Huston's film, but significantly retains Laruelle, both in the first chapter prologue, set one year later (1939), and in the scene in his house. She includes Yvonne and Hugh's horse ride and the scene at the Salon Ofélia, when Geoffrey rejects Yvonne (and Hugh). On the other hand, she does not create new scenes, unlike Huston in his film, in which a walk-through of Day of the Dead activities or a drunken political speech at the Red Cross Ball the night before Yvonne arrives are probably intended to define the Consul's character, build a context for his condition, and foreshadow his death.

Hallucinations, voices, and metaphoric imagery confront the question of filming psychological states quite directly. The many scenes from the novel raise concerns about length as well. In the remainder of this chapter, I want to consider how well such subjective auditory and visual elements could be rendered by Buñuel, who, by the 1960s, had developed a direct style (Edwards 165), a style in which continuity of narration is preserved for the sake of a larger audience. I will then turn to Margerie's management of the plot, particularly the framing prologue, set a year later, and the handling of two climactic events that occur almost simultaneously.

The Voices: Having an off-screen voice linked to imagery or even a voice that is not linked or supported by imagery seems logical within the conventions of narrative voice-over or non-diegetic soundtracks in general. Voice-over can be used to express thoughts within a character, demonstrated theatrically by the interior monologues in Eugene O'Neill's *Strange Interlude* (1928) and in film by Laurence Olivier in his handling of the soliloquies in *Hamlet* (1948). Both might seem to be special cases, and perhaps not entirely successful ones. But Buñuel had successfully used voice-over with imagery in his most famous Mexican film, the neo-realistic *Los Olvidados*, when a dying murderer hears a voice telling him a mangy dog is coming for him, and then when his own inner voice cries out: "I'm falling into a black pit. I'm alone" (Edwards 107). Ironically, so did Huston after he made *Volcano*, in the conclusion of his 1987 adaptation of James Joyce's *The Dead*. So having an inner voice for the Consul, in Margerie's proposal, when Yvonne and the Consul are first entering their house, could be made a natural feature of his character. Nor, to my mind, would a series of voices overlapping, the Consul's familiars, a kind of sound montage, push too far, since the visual montages of Hollywood pictures were often accompanied by a mix of sounds and music. Buñuel successfully sets up a montage of character-motivated voices and projections in *The Exterminating Angel* (1962). But such montages are usually contained, transitions to some change in scene or character behaviour. In the sound Karl Freund remake of the *Hands of Orlac* (aka *Mad Love*)—a film often mentioned in the novel—the appearance of different selves in mirrors, speaking to Dr. Golgol, leads to his transformation. Though mirrors are a bit too stagey to be used more than once, their use indicates that there are in-scene means of accessing voices and images.

On the other hand, one would have to question Margerie's proposal to integrate several discrete voices and/or images of the Consul's familiars on a regular basis. They are strange enough in a modernist novel, even as hallucinations induced by alcohol. As a kind of montage, they would work. But she adheres to the novel in having voices speak directly to the Consul, as if present in the scene (Sequence 4). Done often, it would thrust one back to allegorical drama, such as "Everyman" or Marlowe's "Dr. Faustus." While modern psychology has split the unicameral mind, the variously defined parts are not personified as such in most stream-of-consciousness fiction. (Bergson, rather than Freud, has influenced narrative technique.) To listen to frequent extended dialogues with unseen voices would be too theatrical in a film that seeks a large audience.

Taking his cue from Stephen Spender's introduction to the novel, Tony Kilgallin argues that Lowry's juxtapositions of past and present, real and imaginary, and the fragmented diegetic images owe more to the films of Sergei Eisenstein than the fiction of James Joyce (Kilgallin 139). But the filmmaker in the novel, Jacques Laruelle, represents the European sensibility that has accepted Hollywood principles of narrative continuity. Nor does Margerie propose a montage of conflicting planes, images, and camera angles, although she suggests metaphoric imagery in places. Eisenstein had used such montage in early films, such as *Strike* (1924), where the shooting down of workers is intercut with a bull being butchered in a slaughterhouse (Burch 316).

Certainly jump cuts to particular images within a scene (an insect on the wall) or even insertion of transitory, non-diegetic images would seem natural to the inebriated Consul, such as when he sees a dead man beside a pool (Lowry 84) or imagines a cantina when he unsuccessfully attempts to make love to Yvonne (83). These are motivated images. But when Margerie inserts a series of non-diegetic metaphoric images—"horse half stopped over the hurdle, the diver, the guillotine . . . poise" (84)—all to simply express Hugh's surprise at meeting Yvonne, the effect would seem mechanical rather than poetic in a mainstream film, and possibly provoke laughter. It is worth recalling that Eisenstein later moved toward metaphoric imagery from within the scene itself. In the narrative sequences of *Que Viva Mexico!* (1931), continuity is preserved within a scene—whether a wedding, a bullfight, a gunfight—even though the editing follows dialectic principles. Margerie's proposal was addressed to Buñuel, who had incorporated hallucination and dream sequences in *Los Olvidados* and *The Exterminating Angel*, and used close-ups within the scenes to reveal the preoccupations of characters in *Viridiana* (1961).

Margerie suggests some effective thematic set-ups, using in-scene imagery: as Huston did, she suggests keeping a bottle in frame when the Consul is drawn to his wife or to her suggestion of escape to a northern paradise. But projecting images of such a paradise, though motivated, would have to be handled very carefully. An early association of her description of the northern paradise with the green and snow-capped volcanoes frequently seen in the background would provide metaphoric means to evoke her dream; otherwise, any projected visualization would more naturally come from the Consul's prolific imagination, and could be juxtaposed or merge into his opposed image thoughts of bottles or a cantina. Unless the film is to follow the novel's practice of switching point of view, sectioning the plot similar to the flashback sequences of *Citizen Kane*,

Margerie's depiction of Yvonne projecting a woman hysterically beating the ground in the middle of her vision of a desired life with her husband in paradise (108) would overload things, assuming the director would even want her to have such a vision in the first place.

The Plot: Although she doesn't frame the picture with Day of the Dead imagery, as Huston did, Margerie uses the letter Laruelle discovers in an anthology of Elizabethan plays quite effectively to bridge to the past events of 1938. Shot from behind, he reads the letter while the voice of the Consul articulates it; Laruelle's image dissolves to the figure of the Consul "half-staggering" up the street to his house as his voice-over of the letter continues. This is a significant transition because the voice that Lauruelle "hears" is so affecting that burning the letter becomes a natural catharsis for him. In the language of the novel, he is trying to "throw away his mind." When the image dissolves to the Consul unsteadily walking up his street to his house, the disjuncture of voice-over words and the Consul's action accomplishes two effects: when he speaks of his hallucinations, we put such thoughts inside the man walking; we are prepared for the haunted and projecting mind. The other effect is quite elemental, but essential in the novel: even while he is speaking in voice-over, Geoffrey is doing something else, setting up a theme of disjuncture, a split in the self. In fact, to continue this imagery, I would amend Margerie's directions once he goes into the house: when his voice locates the writing of the letter in the cantina, the Farolito, why not show him writing in his house? Let the split be more dramatic; it need not, I think, communicate the drunk who does not know where he is, or, more negatively, the character of a self-dramatizing liar. (Though I recognize both as possibilities.) This technique was used in Robert Altman's movie adaptation of Sam Shepard's play *Fool for Love* (1986). Interestingly, it seemed to add mystery, rather than deception, when a character's words describing the past were directly contradicted by what was shown. The character spoke with conviction, so one could not determine what the truth was. In a strange way, both were true. And we do have Laruelle's judgment that the Consul's life had become "a quixotic oral fiction" (60).

When the voiced-over letter refers to the dream of a northern paradise in the same scene, Margerie suggests the projection of a cottage between forest and sea to the side of the Consul, writing, with a bottle in the foreground. Duality is emphasized, and such a projection is certainly in keeping with expressionistic "mindscreening," as seen in Murnau's *Sunrise* (1927) or Eugene O'Neill's play *The Emperor Jones* (1920), produced as a film in 1933. Given its removal from Laruelle in 1939, a more realistic way of imaging his thoughts might be preferred: have him glance up, in the midst of writing and drinking, and see (in close-up) a calendar picture of just such a scene—using here what occurs later in the novel.

However it might be filmed, Margerie created a superb opening sequence. The image of the Ferris wheel turning backward—taken from the novel—as the transition back to 1938 works well, perhaps an echo of the use of the cradle endlessly rocking that D. W. Griffith used to move from one storyline to another in his multi-plotted *Intolerance* (1918). Given Lowry's suggestion that the events of 1938 could be viewed as Laruelle's mindscreen movie—a position that Sherrill Grace has developed (see Grace)—a director might even conclude with Laruelle, using the Ferris wheel and/or the burning from the Consul's last visions to Laruelle's burning of the letter. The risk here would be the implication that Laruelle himself knows the details of the last day, even though he was largely not present. But such questions of reliability are more likely to occur to readers than viewers who, after all, have *seen* the events taking place. Given Margerie's decision to use the Laruelle frame in the beginning, it is a conclusion at least to be considered.

As was the case with Huston's version, Margerie does not attempt to deliver the action through different characters' points of view. The focus is very much on the Consul. She, like Huston, gives Yvonne and Hugh their early scene together, when their past relationship, their pleasure at seeing each other, and their discussion of the Consul are featured. Their walk and then ride are full of good humour and natural beauty, portraying what might be possible between humans if there were no watchtowers, inebriation, or bad memories. Importantly, both the actual and proposed films include here the first full articulation of the northern retreat where Yvonne and Geoffrey could mend their marriage and he could resume his writing. That they are riding in the countryside would also offer an opportunity to show and associate the volcano with the northern paradise. In the interests of economy, however, Gallo/Huston eliminated the pleasant ride as a separate scene, placing the conversation on the back veranda, while Geoffrey lay semi-conscious in the middle of the street. In so doing, they eliminated enforcing the theme with significant features of the landscape—notably the garden sign, the *barranca*, the volcano, the Indian with the seven-branded horse, the watch towers and target practice, all hints of a sinister police/militia presence. Margerie especially urges that the camera show the *barranca* "in all its appalling depth," and that the conversation about the northern paradise, enhanced by the beauty of the Mexican landscape, be included to set up the sought-for pastoral Edenic existence and to set it *against* the garden sign warning those in the public park to respect it or be evicted (as it is mistranslated). These images add significance to the fact that it is the Chief of Gardens who is in charge and assents to the murder of Geoffrey in the end. One of the last things the audience sees after the Consul has been thrown into the *barranca*, in Margerie's script, is a similar garden sign as the camera cranes out of the *barranca* to a shot of the volcanoes, "their peaks pure and clear in the evening light above the storm," an image associated with the paradise that has been lost.

Another of Huston's later excisions that Margerie retains in her script is the visit to Laruelle's house, which interrupts the walk into town, preparatory to taking the bus to Tomalín. Here is a question of economy: Is the scene itself necessary? The same might be asked of the Salon Ofélia scene, occurring between the upbeat bull throwing in Tomalin and the fatal climax at the Farolito. The scene is an important turning point: under the influence of mescal and the voices it brings, remembering his own past in a vision of broken bottles and remembering his wife's past infidelity with Hugh, the Consul turns against Yvonne, their future, and, significantly, against himself. After an invective against Hugh and Yvonne, he "chooses hell" and takes off for Parián and the Farolito. Given its function in the plot, one can agree with Margerie that this is a "long and important sequence" (108). Still, in the interest of economy—the film length—would this turning point work if its key elements were consolidated with the happier Tomalín sequence? That is exactly what Huston did—to great effect.

Margerie sought to preserve the simultaneity of the last two chapters, even while realizing the risks of actually trying to make the two separate character plots simultaneous through cross-cutting in the Griffith manner (as in *Birth of a Nation*) (112). Margerie sets up a rhythm of cross-cuts that is lengthy, then quickens (1 for 1) in the middle and ends with emphasis on the Farolito action. The horse flees before the murder of the Consul, so that Yvonne is shown dying before in discourse, but at the same time in the story, as was the case in the novel. Contrary to the Huston film, Margerie's preferred conclusion keeps the focus on the Consul and the significance of his death.

Would such cross-cutting work, as Margerie has it? She apparently had doubts or wished to maintain control in case someone in the production process should have doubts. So Margerie included an alternative ending (about which she was also ambivalent), in which the Farolito action is carried straight through, after the release of the horse and Yvonne's death.

This essay has imagined what might have been, presenting an assemblage of pieces of text, a concentration of chapters into scenes, and materializing certain images in the hopes that they would not deflect overmuch from the textual subjective (and symbolic) import of the novel. Insofar as my efforts value Margerie's proposal, they only support the scenes separately, without necessarily insuring a narrative wholeness—or its success as a film. Furthermore, in hypothesizing, the already displaced novel has been placed at the wrong end of the telescope, distant from Margerie's lengthy proposal, further reduced and distant from the scenes of other films used to test and support her work. Indeed, to imagine Margerie's film I have had to project other films.

Margerie's 1962 film proposal certainly captures more of the significant subjectivity and thematic structure of Malcolm Lowry's novel than was the case with John Huston's film. Much of her proposal, I argue, would have filmed well in the 1960s, or later. Through careful inclusion of the natural features that serve thematic purposes and some of the Consul's hallucinated imagery in the novel, it magnifies the battle between alcoholism and love, the rejection of paradise sought, really a rejection of hope, and all that that can imply. She strengthens the motives for killing the Consul by including the anti-fascist telegram that is found in his pocket.

There would be limits to what her film or any film might do: references to Faust or Dante, or to William Blackstone, for that matter, would probably be lost on mainstream audiences. The real tragic theme of *Under the Volcano* is similar to Eliot's in *The Waste Land*: that we have lost the traditional stories that once gave meaning to life; in such a world, any way you die becomes, in the words of the Consul, "dingy." Margerie Bonner Lowry's proposal would be a good place to begin if a director or producer wanted to offer more of the vital depths that keep readers coming back to *Under the Volcano*.

WORKS CITED

Bordwell, David. *Narration in the Fiction Film*. Madison: U of Wisconsin P, 1985.

Boyum, Joy Gould. *Double Exposure: Fiction Into Film*. New York and Scarborough, Ontario: New American Library, 1985.

Burch, Noel. "Sergei M. Eisenstein." *Cinema: A Critical Dictionary: The Major Film-Makers*, edited by Richard Roud, vol. I, London: Nationwide Book Services by arrangement with Martin Secker & Warburg Limited, 1980, pp. 314–328.

Edwards, Gwynne. *The Discreet Art of Luis Buñuel*. London and Boston: Marion Boyars, 1982.

Eisenstein, Sergei. Supplemental. "*Que Viva Mexico!* An Outline." *Que Viva Mexico!* 1931. DVD. King Video, 2001.

Gold, Herbert. "Huston Films a Cult Classic." *The New York Times Magazine*, 11 Dec. 1983, pp. 60–70.

Grace, Sherrill E. "'Do you remember?': War and the Landscape of Memory in *Under the Volcano*." Malcolm Lowry: A Centenary Celebration, U of British Columbia, Vancouver. 25 July 2009.

Hagen, W. M. "Under Huston's Volcano." *Literature/Film Quarterly*, vol. 19, no: 3, 1991, pp. 138–149.

Hamill, Pete. "Against All Odds." *American Film*, July-August 1984, pp. 19–28, 61.

Kilgallin, Tony. *Lowry*. Erin, ON: P Porcepic, 1973.

Kracauer, Siegfried. *Theory of Film: The Redemption of Physical Reality*. New York: Oxford UP, 1960.

Lowry, Margerie Bonner. "*Under the Volcano*: A Film Proposal." *Malcolm Lowry and Conrad Aiken Adapted: Three Radio Dramas and a Film Proposal*, edited by Paul Tiessen, Waterloo, ON: Malcolm Lowry Review, 1992.

O'Brien, Geoffrey. *The Phantom Empire: Movies in the Mind of the 20th Century*. New York and London: W. W. Norton, 1993.

Schulz-Keil, Wieland. "The Sixty-Seventh Reading: Malcolm Lowry's Novel *Under the Volcano* and its Screenplays." *Proceedings of the London Conference on Malcolm Lowry: 1984*, edited by Gordon Bowker and Paul Tiessen, London and Waterloo, ON: Goldsmiths' College and The Malcolm Lowry Review, 1985.

Tiessen, Paul. "Literary Modernism and Cinema: Two Approaches." *Joyce/Lowry: Critical Perspectives*, edited by Patrick A. McCarthy and Paul Tiessen, Lexington: U of Kentucky P, 1997, 159–176.

8

Soundscapes in Lunar Caustic

AILSA COX

I nspired by his brief sojourn in a psychiatric ward at Bellevue Hospital, New York, in 1936, and revised throughout his lifetime under several different titles, Malcolm Lowry's long story—or novelette or embryonic novel—that has come to be known as *Lunar Caustic* is destined to remain a work in progress. The final draft, which Lowry was working toward at the time of his death in 1957, remains an irrecoverable ideal. A French translation of a version known as "Swinging the Maelstrom" was published in 1956, ten years after he had declared his intention to expand this material within the context of his larger life's project, the multipart novel "The Voyage That Never Ends." The 2013 critical edition of *Swinging the Maelstrom*, edited by Vik Doyen with copious supporting material from other leading scholars, has yielded fresh insights into its various ur-texts and provides a version that is as close to definitive as humanly possible.[1] It may supplant the text that most readers know and that is the subject of this chapter, the posthumous version, "spliced" from Lowry's surviving fragment by Margerie Bonner Lowry and Earle Birney.[2] Here, I shall be interpreting *Lunar Caustic* as a valid text in its own right, disregarding the complex issues of authorial intention and editorial interventions, so skilfully addressed by Doyen and his peers.

The term "spliced" suggests film restoration, and the cinematic is indeed deeply implicated in *Lunar Caustic*, as in so much of Lowry's fiction. He himself claimed that the first hour of F. W. Murnau's *Sunrise* (1927) influenced him "almost as much as any book I ever read."[3] The pared down, present-tense section in the opening prologue—"A man leaves a dockside tavern . . . Soon he is running . . ." (*Lunar Caustic* 9)—resembles the treatment for a script in its swift rendition of external actions. The title itself is another term for silver nitrate, which was used in early film stock, but also served as a disinfectant against and a treatment for syphilis—a disease much feared by Lowry. Scopic elements—views of the river and the sky seen from the asylum; hallucinations; images of the eye and the gaze—are strongly invoked throughout the text. However, the cinematic is not only predicated on the visual, and these images are all placed in dialogue with a range of auditory effects. Lowry's own choice of words in describing his

later plans for "a much amplified *Lunar Caustic*"[4] provides a clue to the importance of sound in this text. His protagonist, Bill Plantagenet, is a jazz musician,
driven to distraction by the pandemonium both inside and outside his head.
Graham Collier has already likened the "freewheeling language" in *Lunar Caustic*
to, in Lowry's own words, the "odd but splendid din" of the improvised solo
(Collier 28). The alternative title, "Swinging the Maelstrom," confirms the parallel between Lowry's prose composition and musicianship. (The story's first title,
"The Last Address," is the least memorable.)

Taking her cue from an essay by Mathieu Duplay on the "operatic paradigm"
in Lowry's fiction, Sherrill Grace also draws attention to "the continuous musical
textures of Lowry's metaleptic prose narration" (Grace, "Lowry" 181–88). One of
the many pleasures of reading Lowry derives from an immersion in the purely
rhythmic and sensory aspects of language, which Julia Kristeva has conceptual-
ized as the "semiotic," but which the ordinary reader might call its musicality.
But the operatic aspects of Lowry's fiction also extend to the primacy of voice,
and the integration of direct discourse into the descriptive or narrative elements,
just as words and music are synthesized in operatic composition.

In an earlier essay on the posthumously collected short stories in *Hear Us O
Lord From Heaven Thy Dwelling Place*, Grace applies Bakhtinian theory to Lowry's
polyphonic narratives, showing how the text is constructed through the juxtaposition and interaction of multiple voices, undermining any centralizing authorial
consciousness, and resisting unitary meaning (Grace, "Sound" 91–102). As we
shall see, these strategies are also in play in *Lunar Caustic*. As Grace suggests, the
symphonic terms used metaphorically in Bakhtin's analysis of dialogic discourse
in the novel ("polyphony," "orchestration," "counterpoint") can be understood
almost literally in relation to the "continuous musical texture" she identifies in
Lowry's work. In this chapter, I shall be especially interested in the cinematic
qualities of *Lunar Caustic*'s soundscapes, especially the analogies with the early
talking pictures and with silent film.

When Lowry began his first draft, in 1936, the sound era in film was, if not in
its infancy, still relatively new; his love of cinema was grounded in the silent days,
especially the work of the German expressionists, including, as well as Murnau's
Sunrise, Robert Wiene's *The Cabinet of Dr. Caligari* (1920). The surrealistic nightmare that is *Dr. Caligari* has much in common with the world of *Lunar Caustic*.
In *Dr. Caligari*, the narrative is framed as the reminiscence of an intradiegetic
narrator, who in the final sequences is revealed to be a lunatic; focalized mostly
through the man allegedly called Plantagenet, *Lunar Caustic* is also framed as
largely delusional, although both narratives invite the reader to question our ability to distinguish madness from sanity. Both deploy carnival imagery. *Dr. Caligari*

travels the fairgrounds exhibiting a somnambulist, who is under the sway of the title character's hypnotic powers. In *Lunar Caustic*, carnival is evoked through song and dance and honky-tonk piano playing, by oral storytelling (all elements I discuss later), and most explicitly through the puppet show mounted for the patients. Bakhtin argued that heterogeneity and ambivalence is generated still further in texts that incorporate the carnivalesque, which may also be introduced through parody, broad humour, intertexuality, and the grotesque, especially the grotesque body. All of these are present so extensively in *Lunar Caustic* that one or two examples must suffice. One of the most striking of these is the "hand of the blind giant" (36) that manipulates the puppets. The nonsensical patter between the black "Judy" puppet and the New Yorker "Punch" plays around with the dual concepts of a cannibalistic giant "eating all our tribe up" and the New York Giants baseball team (35). The grotesque image of the giant hand also recalls Plantagenet's earlier feelings when observing the operating theatres from the distant vantage point of his own ward:

> Plantagenet suddenly caught sight, through the bars, of four operations being performed simultaneously in the wing opposite in high sunlit rooms of glass, so that it seemed as though the front of that part of the hospital had suddenly become open, revealing, as in the cabin plans of the "Cunard" or in charts of the human anatomy itself, the activities behind the wraith of iron or brick or shin: and it was strange to watch these white-masked figures working behind the glass that now glittered like a mirage. At the same time the whole scene that lay before them suddenly, like the looming swift hand of a traffic policeman, reeled towards him; he felt he had only to stretch out his fingers to touch the doctor working on the right side of the table sewing up the incision, or the nurse plastering and binding the patient or placing the blanket over the body; and it seemed to him that all these dressings and redressings in these hours of north light were at the same time being placed, torn away and replaced, on a laceration of his own mind. (25–26)

The "looming swift hand ... reeled towards him" suggests the camera's eye, zooming in for a close-up, and the dizzying perspectives of expressionist cinema. The grotesque body is evoked not only by this gigantism, but also by the image of the anatomy chart. The sleight of hand that turns the observer simultaneously into the observed, and subject into object—a "laceration of his own mind"—adds to the prevailing sense of bodily dismemberment and metamorphosis.

According to Bakhtin, carnival suspends social hierarchies and defies authority. In both Dr. *Caligari* and *Lunar Caustic*, the lunatics' antics parody the sane, and the social hierarchy of the asylum mimics the social divisions of the outside world. In Dr. *Caligari*, the carnival tradition of the "boy bishop" or "king for a day" is replicated through role reversal. The second-level narration, not yet revealed as the tale of a madman, closes with the image of Caligari bound by a straitjacket and incarcerated in the madhouse. Returning to the first narrative, we find the situation inverted, and the narrator himself in the straitjacket. The man he thinks is Caligari is the director of the asylum. Such a drastic role reversal is merely hinted at in *Lunar Caustic*—"that paranoid Head Nurse" compared by Plantagenet to his old nanny who "ended up in an asylum too" (49). But, like the inmate in Dr. *Caligari* who screams helplessly, "He is Caligari!,"[5] Plantagenet is at times convinced that Kalowsky and Garry are unjustly detained, and that it is up to him to make the authorities see reason. Throughout the lengthy exchange between Plantagenet and Doctor Claggart in section IX, the patient appropriates the dominant role, lecturing the psychiatrist on this topic. Plantagenet considers himself not properly mad, "only a drunk" (21), but he is less preoccupied with that distinction than with bigger issues. "Many who are supposed to be mad here," he declares, "are simply people who perhaps once saw, however confusedly, the necessity for change in themselves, for rebirth, that's the word" (52).

Rebirth is the word, even though the hyperbolic language of Plantagenet's diatribe parodies his naive idealism: "You've been the only star above his life, for months and months his only possible hope" (54). The utopian or salvationist rhetoric of liberation recurs throughout the text, often making hubristic references to Christ's sacrifice on the cross. When in the story's closing section, or epilogue, Plantagenet has been discharged, it is a church painting of the tormented Christ being offered vinegar to drink that finally induces him to take a swig of whisky. Drunk, in a tavern, he imagines "some heroic sacrifice" that will not only liberate Garry and Kalowsky but will free all mankind (75). Parody, in a "carnivalized" text, does not entail negation; it is the free interplay of many voices, none of them the final word. Carnival ambivalence engages with time as change and self-renewal—with the constant metamorphosis we see (and hear) in Lowry's work.

SUNRISE, PUDOVKIN, AND THE SOUND OF SILENCE

The Cabinet of Dr. Caligari provides some interesting comparisons with *Lunar Caustic*, especially in terms of carnival ambivalence and the chronotopic space of the asylum, a subject that deserves lengthier analysis in its own right. Wiene's film also illustrates Lowry's affinity with expressionist techniques in the visual and other arts. However, it is that other favourite, *Sunrise*, which provides a point of reference when considering the impact of sound technology on the aesthetics of film and the analogies between the soundscapes of *Lunar Caustic* and the interaction of the visual and the auditory in film narrative.

Released in 1927, the same year as the first all-talking picture, *The Jazz Singer*, Murnau's epic was commissioned by the American producer William Fox as a silent film, but was released with a Movietone soundtrack in the United States. Lowry saw the film in Germany—without, one assumes, the soundtrack. In any case, *Sunrise* was shot as silent and cannot be disguised as anything else. The soundtrack added consists of an orchestral score with naturalistic sound effects, such as train whistles and thunderbolts; essentially, it is not so very different from the various forms of live music that accompanied silent films. The subtitle of *Sunrise*, "A Song of Two Humans," highlights the lyrical, symbolic, and poetic properties conferred on Murnau's film, intended by its makers to represent the acme of cinematic art. The train whistles and thunderbolts interpolated into the Movietone score disrupt the poetic synthesis of sound and image by introducing a crude literalism. Paradoxically, the naturalistic intrusions draw attention to their actual separation from the visual image.

Highly sophisticated, with fluid camerawork and bold visual composition, *Sunrise* marks the sudden extinction of silent film at the height of its potential. If *Lunar Caustic* is set around 1936, the year of Lowry's spell in Bellevue, the version of *Broken Blossoms* showing at the picture palace (74) is probably the inferior British talking version released in that year, and not D. W. Griffith's silent masterpiece, from 1919. Today's audiences take synchronized sound for granted, experiencing sound and vision as a unified whole; in the early to mid-1930s, sound on film was still a novelty, and intelligent filmgoers like Lowry were still aware that sound was an extraneous element, tacked onto film to maintain an illusion of simultaneity. Whether or not Lowry shared the view that the coming of sound on film was a detrimental step, the disjunction between sound and image in *Lunar Caustic* may be related to this awareness of a separation between the visual and auditory channels. While I am not suggesting that, in any of the stages of its protracted composition, Lowry necessarily intended *Lunar Caustic* to mimic cinematic effects, there is, to adopt the model used by David Trotter in his analysis of modernist technique, a "parallelism" between Lowry's soundscapes and the acoustics of the talkies (Trotter 3). In a close reading of the opening prologue, I shall look specifically at the fissure between sound and image, before going on to analyze this fissure with the help of Soviet film theory.

In Section I of *Lunar Caustic*, Lowry attributes a voice to the city itself, collapsing the boundaries between the animate and inanimate; the human, the bestial and the mechanical: "The heat rises up from the pavements, a mighty force, New York groans and roars above, around, below him" (9). (The word "roar" recurs throughout the text, accumulating further meanings, which I discuss later.) When the as-yet-unnamed protagonist finally speaks—he is silent until the end of the section, his lips "moving in something like prayer" (10), but no sound issuing from them—his voice is also described as a "roar." The human subject is identified with the urban environment, which is itself a living organism; the double "roar" undermines the distinction between the self and the external world. Kristeva's claim that "all literature is probably a version of the apocalypse that seems to me rooted . . . on this fragile border (borderline cases) where identities (subject/object, etc.) do not exist or only barely so—double, fuzzy, heterogeneous, animal, metamorphosed, abject" (207)—could scarcely be better illustrated. The protean central consciousness absorbs and is also engulfed by the city itself. From the beginning, carnival ambivalence is strongly pronounced, in the "animal, metamorphosed, object" and the grotesque (the aged crone posting a letter), as well as through numerous intertextual references.

The words the protagonist finally delivers form a kind of soliloquy, mingling quotation from Rimbaud's *A Season in Hell*, a possible reference to "negro" music (i.e., jazz), and a third voice, introducing messianic zeal:

> I want to hear the sound of the Negroes," he roars. "*Veut-on que je disparaisse, que je plonge, à la recherche de l'annéa . . .* I am sent to save my father, to find my son, to heal the eternal horror of three, to resolve the immedicable horror of opposites! (*Lunar Caustic* 11)

With the addition of the bestial "roars" and the clinical "immedicable," this amounts to at least five different voices clashing against one another—voices which recur with further references to Rimbaud and more heroic speeches of the kind I discussed earlier. These histrionics are punctuated by the elaborate metaphor which follows, describing the character's entrance into the fictionalized Bellevue: "With the dithering crack of a ship going on the rocks the door shuts behind him" (11). The wrecked-ship metaphor is attached to a specific sense impression—the sound of the door—but also applies to the protagonist himself, who in the story's first sentence was "gliding over the cobbles lightly as a ship leaving harbour" (9). Between this first sentence and the prologue's hyperbolic ending, the volume has gradually increased, from near silence to an explosion of noise. Plantagenet's over-sensitive hearing is symptomatic of his dementia. Once he enters the asylum, the intense level of noise aggravates his condition. "The noise, the noise," he complains in the psychiatrist's office, to the accompaniment of an electric fan and rattling typewriter (54).

Coming at the end of the opening prologue, the double-voiced sound—ship/door—serves as a kind of dramatic underlining, punctuating a decisive moment, the point of no return. Acoustically, it is analogous to the amplified sound effects we find in cinema, whether in the supposedly "natural" sounds of the diegesis or through the clanging chords of a musical score. The door itself is heard but not seen; it shuts behind the protagonist. The ship metaphor ruptures the text even further. Metaphor always describes an object through an absence; one thing is perceived as another, which is not physically present. The absent ship, evoked so vividly in the prologue, haunts the whole of the subsequent narrative.

In his 1929 essay "Asynchronism as a Principle of Sound Film," the Soviet filmmaker V. L. Pudovkin argues that sound and image are not truly synchronized, but work in counterpoint, reflecting the fragmentary nature of subjective experience:

> The world is a whole rhythm, while man receives only partial impressions of this world through his eyes and ears and to a lesser extent through his very skin. The tempo of his impressions varies with the rousing and calming of his emotions, while the rhythm of the objective world he perceives continues in unchanged tempo. (186)

The function of sound is not to enhance a supposed naturalism in the cinematic image, but to construct meanings in dialogue with that image:

> A primitive example of the use of sound to reveal an inner content can be cited in the expression of the stranding of a townbred man in the midst of the desert. In silent film we should have had to cut in a shot of the town; now in sound film we can carry town associated sounds into the desert and edit them there in place of the natural desert sounds. (184–85)[6]

For Pudovkin, reality consists of a boundless flow or Bergsonian duration, grasped intermittently through sensory perception. (Bergson argues that all perceptions are laced with memory, and Pudovkin's description of the interplay between remembered sounds and immediate surroundings might be placed within the context of a more widespread modernist aesthetic, shaped by his philosophy of time.) The technological disjunction between sight and sound enables film, as Pudovkin describes it, to represent a dialogue between memory and perception.

In *Lunar Caustic*, the fluctuating "tempo" of mental instability is represented by the amplification of sound and by a clash of visual and aural images. "The man who now gave the name of Bill Plantagenet" (13) has introduced himself as "the s.s. Lawhill" and confuses the cacophony of noise in the asylum—keys, buzzers, shuffling feet, the babble of speech—with sounds on board a ship. In the hallucinatory passage that follows, distorted sounds and disembodied voices resonate against disjointed and grotesque visual imagery.

> Horrid shapes plunged out of the blackness, gibbering, rubbing their bristles against his face, but he couldn't move. Something had got under his bed too, a bear that kept trying to get up. Voices, a prosopopoeia of voices, murmured in his ears, ebbed away, murmured again, cackled, shrieked, cajoled; voices pleading with him to stop drinking, to die and be damned. A cataract of water was pouring through the wall, filling the room. (14)

There are several other examples of the disassociation between sound and image. They include the puppet show, mounted for the patients in the semi-darkness. The puppets are voiced backstage by the "blind giant" (36), who for the most part is invisible, though the giant hand intervenes, snatching the figures away like some malign deity. The tap-dancing negro, Battle—"Dat guy talks wif his feet" (21)—provides another instance of "prosopopoeia" (the rhetorical device whereby a speaker communicates through another person or object). When Plantagenet observes the surgical procedures in the opposite wing, they appear to be speechless, a silent pantomime. All of these instances contribute to the dizzy atmosphere of sensory distortion.

With its intense noise and frenetic activity, the hospital stands, in a metonymic relationship, for New York and a chronotope predicated on random collisions, contingency, atomization, speed, and density. However, the hospital soundscape does include quantities of silence and speechlessness, woven into the "almost continual unebbing surf of noise" (24). The dumbshow Plantagenet observes in the operating theatres is one of these, and so is the passage a little later in section V, where Lowry describes:

> the old men considered too jittery or too obscene to eat with the others ... bent over their stew in a grey, trembling despair, some seeming not to know they were eating at all, the food perhaps tasteless to them as they cuffed it slowly and sleepily with their harmless spoons, others not even attempting to eat but wearing a fixed smile, as though the thought even of misery afforded them some perverse comfort. (26–27)

The image of slow, silent feeding is repeated further down the page when another inmate, Mr. Kalowsky, watches Battle being restrained by the attendants, "his spoon poised, his gaze passing mechanically, like a slowed fan, from them to Battle and to the attendants and back again" (27). These evocations of silence in section V are juxtaposed with a reference to semaphore, which translates speech into voiceless gesture. The boy Garry's attempt to teach Battle semaphore is in itself far from silent, but the concept of semaphore itself underlines the significance of silent actions and wordless communication in this section of the narrative.

Plantagenet's acute sense of hearing accentuates silence and makes it palpable. In any dialogic context, silence plays an active role, juxtaposed with sounds and voices. If, as Plantagenet claims, death is a "function of life" (27), perhaps silence is a function of sound, rather than its negation. In chapter 2 of *Under the Volcano*, an awkward silence between Geoffrey and Yvonne restates the connection between sensitivity to noise and the symptoms of madness, which is also made in *Lunar Caustic*:

> the Consul imagined he still heard the music of the ball, which must have long since ceased, so that his silence was pervaded as with a stale thudding of drums . . . It was doubtless the almost tactile absence of the music however, that made it so peculiar the trees should be apparently shaking to it, an illusion investing not only the garden but the plains beyond, the whole scene before his eyes, with horror, the horror of an intolerable unreality. This must be not unlike, he told himself, what some insane person suffers at those moments when, sitting benignly in the asylum grounds, madness suddenly ceases to be a refuge and becomes incarnate in the shattering sky and all his surroundings in the presence of which reason, already struck dumb, can only bow the head. Does the madman find solace at such moments, as his thoughts like cannonballs crash through his brain, in the exquisite beauty of the madhouse garden or the neighbouring hills beyond the terrible chimney? (*Volcano* 80)

Here it is silence which first induces thoughts of the asylum, even though madness itself is "made incarnate" in a "shattering" sky (alluding, perhaps, to the storm described in *Lunar Caustic*), and "his thoughts like cannonballs crash through his brain." "The almost tactile absence of the music" creates an antinomy, turning absence into substance.

Bergson argues that we cannot truly experience such a thing as the present moment, since every perception is pervaded by memory, and the instant vanishes into the past as soon it arises. If that is the case, we might argue that pure silence cannot exist either; mediated by consciousness, silence is imprinted by memories of sound, like those drums thudding inside the mind of the Consul. Physiologically speaking, it is almost impossible to encounter absolute silence. The composer John Cage's "silent" composition, "4'33"," demonstrates this point, conceived after he experienced the sound of his own nervous system and his blood circulating on a visit to an anechoic chamber at Harvard, designed to expel all exterior noise.[7] In other words, silence generates its own antithesis; the lull in the storm accentuates the sound of rain (Lunar Caustic 68).

Silence in Lunar Caustic does, however, slow down what Pudovkin might term the "tempo" of Plantagenet's impressions, sometimes introducing a more reflective mood, sometimes building up dramatic tension or contributing to a sense of the uncanny. The passage in section X, describing the prelude to the storm, brings some relief from the logorrhea of Plantagenet's interview with the psychiatrist in the previous section. As he stands outside Dr. Claggart's office, looking out over the park, human voices—"the cries of children" (63) and the lovers laughing as they run for shelter from the rain—are harmonized with the natural sounds of leaves, wind, and rain. These subdued natural sounds form a contrast to the industrialized noises heard from inside the ward—the familiar rattling of keys, ringing of bells, and mechanical shuffling of feet; and even when he returns to the ward, as the storm begins, there is a "perplexing silence." Another kind of silence is also invoked in an analeptic passage describing the sea voyage into New York, on the paddle steamer *Providence* with his former wife, Ruth:

> From the muffled corridor they saw the firemen shovelling down below.
> They had listened together to that pulse of the ship he could hear now. (68)

The "pulse of the ship," like the Consul's "thudding of drums," seems almost to come from the body, like the sound of Cage's nervous system in the anechoic chamber. It is especially significant that the couple seem able to communicate wordlessly. Speech does not often make sense in Lunar Caustic. Battle's maniacal signalling at a seaplane that, in a phrase that reprises the ship metaphor in the very first sentence,[8] is "gliding whitely past" might be seen as a parodic allusion to the futility of the signifying process.

MUSIC, VOICE, AND THE ROAR OF THUNDER

When, halfway through Lunar Caustic, Plantagenet improvises "Sweet and Low" on the hospital piano, "he was harrowed to think how obliquely perfect an expression his rendition was of the tortured memories it might have evoked had he been playing it straight" (39). The tune he is approximating is, most probably, George Gershwin's "Sweet and Low-Down," a somewhat misleading title for a ragtime melody. The sentence is itself scarcely "playing it straight," doubling back on itself, and unravelling its own meanings. The other patients are unable to recognize the tune, and remain underappreciative of this expression of emotional dissonance, playing cards and keeping up a conversation that, like much of the direct speech in *Lunar Caustic*, is mostly a series of monologues. The patients exchange well-rehearsed anecdotes and what the elderly Mr. Kalowsky calls "humoristic stories" (38), shifting effortlessly into songs and rhymes. "I can tell you a better song that that," insists Garry, the child killer (42), "I can tell you a better sea poem" (43), "I'll tell you a better story about an iceberg" (43).

In his first interview with the psychiatrist, Plantagenet gives an account of his time as a pianist with "Bill Plantagenet and his Seven Hot Cantabs" (18), an undergraduate jazz band that failed to make the transition to a professional career in the United States:

> "But it's my hands, my hands, look"—he held them out, shaking. "They're not big enough for a real pianist. I can't stretch over an octave on a piano." (19)

The shaking is, of course, a symptom of Bill's alcoholism, and the anxiety about the size of his hands an avoidance of the real issue. The images of the giant hand in sections V and VII form a counterpoint to his continuing preoccupation with these hands, and with their trembling.

As he himself acknowledges, his expectations when he sits down to play "Sweet and Low-Down" are absurdly inflated. The inmates are trying their best—Kalowsky is even nodding along—but, whatever the standard of Plantagenet's playing, they are incapable of forming a passive audience, watching a performance from the outside. (Bakhtin tells us that the whole community participates in carnival, without distinguishing between audience and spectacle.) Recognizing this, Plantagenet starts to provide a piano accompaniment to the voices of the inmates, responding to the changing riffs with what he believes to be virtuosic brio, covering everything from a ragtime version of Grieg to the Dixieland showstopper, "Clarinet Marmalade." This is the man who told the psychiatrist his hands are too small to stretch an octave ("Perhaps," the doctor suggests, "it was your heart you couldn't make stretch an octave" [19]).

Plantagenet orchestrates voices and music, just as the author orchestrates the diverse voices of the text, translating cacophony into polyphony; as a jazz musician he imposes coherence on the seemingly random and dissonant, but also resists smooth harmonic patterns. When he tells Doctor Claggart, "it's funny how people want to create, and do, in spite of everything—order and chaos both" (56), he is alluding to the stories told by another patient, Garry, but the concept applies equally to a dynamic tension between cohesion and dissolution in a fragmented and paradoxical text that always seems balanced on the verge of chaos.

Meaning is generated through the constant recontextualizing of voices and imagery in shifting relationship to one another. These voices interact across the text, forming a non-linear network of allusions. The "roar" that in section I is the sound of the city and Plantagenet's primal outpouring is simultaneously the sound of a cargo of zoo animals, trapped in a ship's hold during a storm, which he recalls much later in the text, during the storm he experiences from the asylum:

> The panthers died, in the Indian Ocean at night the lions roared, the elephants trumped and vomited so that none save the carpenter dared go forward: when they smashed into the hurricane the jaguars moaned in terror so that none save the carpenter dared go forward. . . . No forest had ever plunged so deeply in the long bending winds as that ship, while "Let us out, let us be free," was the meaning of that wailing during those bitter hours. He had thought, "Let us be free to suffer like animals." And that cry was perhaps more human than the one he heard now. (69)

The cry he now hears is initiated by three black inmates who, in imagery which echoes Platagenet's fancy that he might reach out a giant hand to the operating theatres, seem to feel a thwarted desire to reach out and touch a paddle steamer caught out in the storm. It is quickly taken up by the other inmates:

> three gesticulating Negro sailors rushed to the bars: climbing up within the steel meshes they started a roaring which was instantly taken up by almost everyone in the ward. Was the ship the Providence herself? The roaring had become an uncontrollable yell by now, the Negroes were beating on the bars, shaking the windows. (69)

Plantagenet has indeed heard "the song of the negroes" (11), though not in the form that he anticipated. The overlapping imagery of the zoo and of human incarceration is self-evident; and the rhetoric of "Let us be free " also elides the human and the animal, re-introducing the discourse of political or spiritual liberation. It is striking, and slightly incongruous, that the only human being who dares approach the trapped animals is, like Christ, a carpenter.

Thunder itself is often described as a "roar," and in this passage the storm is reaching its climax. At the height of the storm, memories and perceptions, past and present, are tightly fused, the paddle steamer out on the river fusing not only with the *Providence*, which carried Bill and Ruth into New York, but also the freighter with its doomed cargo. Perhaps that freighter is the ship in which Bill believed himself to be sailing when he awoke in the asylum, and also the *s.s. Lawhill*, the name he gave himself on his arrival there (13). In this accelerated passage, both sound and vision are used to collapse past and present, engaging with time as Bersgonian duration, and representing a heightened subjectivity with synaesthetic force:

> his dream of New York crystallised there for an instant, glittering, illuminated, by a celestial brilliance, only to be reclaimed by the dark, by the pandemonium of an avalanche of falling coal which, mingling with the cries of the insane speeding the Providence on her way, coalesced in his brain with what it conjured of the whole mechanic calamity of the rocking city, with the screaming of suicides, of girls tortured in hotels for transients, of people burning to death in vice dens, through all of which a thousand ambulances were screeching like trumpets. (69–70)

The hospital has become a ship again, and so has the "rocking city." With the momentary fading of the storm and the disappearance of the steamer, the roaring on the ward, and in Plantagenet's mind, subsides. But when the thunder returns, the metaphoric process restates itself. The white seaplane, which Battle is signalling to, and which in Plantagenet's consciousness has been transformed into a Melvillean whale, generates another synoptic vision, which once again evokes an explosion of noise, associated with the image of the ship which also stands for subjectivity:

> But while that part of him only a moment before in possession of the whole, the ship, was turning over with a disunion of hull and masts uprooted, falling across her decks, another faction of his soul, relative to the ship but aware of these fantasies and simultanities [sic] as it were from above, knew him to be screaming against the renewed thunder. (72)

Following the climactic section X, and the thunderstorm, the narrative in section XI leaves the asylum as Plantagenet is discharged back onto the street.

Here too sound retains its significance as an indicator of his mental state. He feels "no sense of release, only inquietude" (73); he hears "strange voices" (73), including the words "womb" and "tomb" in the "roar of the train" (74). Lowry's phrase "the darkness was full of vibrations" (76) might suggest, once again, the image of the ship. The vibrations are synaesthetic, in that they refer not only to inescapable voices but to indelible visual impressions—the old woman posting the letter, or a vision of Garry committing the murder for which he has been incarcerated. Darkness is to light as silence is to sound, permeated by echoes and imprinted images.

There are many differences between *Lunar Caustic* and the version now available in *Swinging the Maelstrom: A Critical Edition*. One of the most significant of these, as Vik Doyen and Miguel Mota suggest in their introduction, is a change in narrative viewpoint. In this version, events are clearly focalized through Bill's internal consciousness: "Through the open door he was still aware of the hospital, towering up above the river. He thought he had been looking for something else, though he couldn't recall what" (Lowry, *Swinging* 3). The narrative centres around the human subject, and events are mediated through perceptions that are clearly ascribed to its protagonist.

In the ceaseless dialogue between self and other at the heart of *Lunar Caustic*, Plantagenet both absorbs the world and is consumed by it. He becomes the ship he once sailed on, but its sounds are also externalized, rising to a crescendo in the climactic section X. The "spliced" *Lunar Caustic* evokes heightened subjective states, often represented through a disjunction between the auditory and the visual channels, analogous to the "asynchrony" of sound film. Yet the fracturing of boundaries between the self and the external world and the interpenetration of the organic with the inorganic are also signs of the modernist "will-to-automatism," discussed by David Trotter (Trotter 113 ff). The human subject is, to some extent, displaced. The central consciousness is that which records, which is a medium for sound and for visual impressions. Plantagenet is the instrument through which we see and hear. Whatever its weaknesses, or the advantages of other versions, *Lunar Caustic* remains a fascinating and largely successful experiment in modernist technique.

NOTES

1. See Lowry, *Swinging the Maelstrom*.
2. See Conrad Knickerbocker's foreword, "Malcolm Lowry and the Outer Circle of Hell," in *Lunar Caustic*.
3. Letter to Clemens ten Holder (*Selected Letters* 239).
4. Letter to Jonathan Cape (*Selected Letters* 63).
5. *The Cabinet of Dr. Caligari*, dir. Robert Wiene. Decla-Bioscop, 1920. Mayer was also the writer of Murnau's *Sunrise*, adapting a short story by Hermann Sudermann.
6. Lowry had seen Pudovkin's *The End of St. Petersburg*. See *Sursum* 1:354 and 1:355 n7.
7. See Larry J. Solomon, "The Sounds of Silence: John Cage and 4'33"," available on www.solomonsmusic.net/4min33se.htm. Accessed 11 October 2015.
8. "A man . . . gliding over the cobbles lightly as a ship leaving harbour" (*Lunar Caustic* 9).

WORKS CITED

Collier, Graham. "Lowry, Jazz and 'The Day of the Dead.'" *Swinging the Maelstrom: New Perspectives on Malcolm Lowry*, edited by Sherill E. Grace, Montreal and Kingston: McGill-Queen's UP, 1992, pp. 243–248.

Grace, Sherrill E. "'A Sound of Singing': Polyphony and Narrative Decentring in Malcolm Lowry's *Hear us O Lord*." *Strange Comfort: Essays on the Work of Malcolm Lowry*, Vancouver: Talonbooks, 2009, pp. 91–102.

———. "Lowry, Debussy and *Under the Volcano*." *Strange Comfort: Essays on the Work of Malcolm Lowry*, Vancouver: Talonbooks, 2009, pp. 181–188.

Kristeva, Julia. *Powers of Horror: An Essay on Abjection*. Translated by Léon S. Roudiez, New York: Columbia UP, 1982.

Lowry, Malcolm. *Sursum Corda!: The Collected Letters of Malcolm Lowry*. Edited by Sherrill E. Grace, vol. 1: 1926–1946, London: Jonathan Cape, 1995.

———. *Lunar Caustic*. London: Jonathan Cape, 1977.

———. *Selected Letters of Malcolm Lowry*. Edited by Harvey Breit and Margerie Bonner Lowry, New York: Capricorn Books, 1969.

———. *Swinging the Maelstrom: A Critical Edition*. Edited by Vik Doyen, introduction by Vik Doyen and Miguel Mota, annotations by Chris Ackerley, Ottawa: U of Ottawa P, 2013.

———. *Under the Volcano*. Harmondsworth, UK: Penguin, 1968.

Pudovkin, V. I. "Asynchronism as a Principle of Sound Film." *Film Technique and Film Acting*. Translated by and edited by Ivor Montagu, London: Vision P, 1958, pp. 183–193.

Trotter, David. *Cinema and Modernism*. Oxford: Blackwell, 2007.

9

Dwelling In-Between: Rituals and Jazz as Reconcilable Opposites in "The Forest Path to the Spring"

CATHERINE DELESALLE

"At dusk, every evening, I used to go through the forest to the spring for water": the very opening sentence of Malcolm Lowry's "The Forest Path to the Spring," comprising its own separate paragraph, clearly makes time and space central to the daily ritual that is at the core of Lowry's short story. The sentence is indeed programmatic, and the entire text revolves around this everyday and vital chore, which, far from being mechanical, is endowed with religious solemnity. And indeed, "The Forest Path" has been greeted as Lowry's most appeased work, the paradise facing the infernal *Volcano*. In the liminal space of Eridanus, Lowry's fictional name for that paradisal place between land and sea embodied for him by Dollarton, British Columbia, the fire of the *Volcano* has been subdued into an oil refinery, which stands on the opposite bank of the inlet, "with the red votive candle of the burning oil wastes flickering ceaselessly all night before the gleaming open cathedral of the oil refinery" (Lowry 227); "Borda's horrible-beautiful cathedral"[1] has been turned into an open cathedral, the death-dealing mescal replaced by life-giving water. The very rhythm of the first sentence confirms this evolution as the first two feet, made up of words stressed on the first syllable, and separated by commas, create a solemn rhythm, while the three occlusives, t, d and k, seem to work as protective ramparts. Within these safe bounds, a repetition can be instituted that will allow for a more dynamic ternary rhythm, supported by the three prepositions, to emerge. Likewise, the ritual is what provides a safe organization of time and space and enables the protagonists to live peacefully, in harmony with the regular rhythm of the seasons and tides.

Yet, the rhythm in the second part of the sentence already proves slightly irregular, from four-syllable foot to three-syllable feet with a different stress pattern in the last one. Acceleration is created and emphasizes the dynamic quality of the sentence. Therefore, a kind of subtle, hardly perceptible, rhythmical tension is at play within this very first line, which is emblematic of what is staged in the text as a whole. Playing with rhythm is a recurring feature in the short story, which is hardly surprising considering the narrator is a jazz musician who eventually composes an opera entitled "The Forest Path to the Spring." We may therefore surmise that what we are reading is the literary transposition of this musical piece, the narrator's everyday pilgrimage to the spring having eventually released his creative powers. And it is precisely the influence of jazz on the writing, working both with and against ritual repetition, which prevents the rigidity and fossilization inherent in performing the same task in the very same place. Indeed the ritual can be seen as a fixed pattern mapping out time and space, and meant to try and suggest the infinite through a complex system of symbols:

> A rite is always the formalization of a gesture, of an act; it therefore naturally belongs to the realm of aesthetics, of that of forms. . . . By formalizing an archetypal act of which it is the concrete expression, the religious rite aims at revealing its supernatural meaning. . . . The religious rite does not rely on imitation but on symbolization, symbols being considered as the concrete signs of invisible realities.[2] (Souriau 1237)

However, thanks to jazz, it can open up to the unexpected, which is but another manifestation of infinity. Thus, both rituals and jazz acknowledge the existence of something boundless, a space that lies beyond the scope of human comprehension, but while rituals try to propitiate the secret powers of the infinite, jazz embraces their unpredictable emergence. Taking up the narrator's own words, we might say that "Hear Us O Lord," the Manx hymn that serves as the title of the collection of stories that contains "The Forest Path," is turned, as shall be seen in the first two parts, from "an appeal to God's mercy" to "a poem of God's mercy." Eventually, "The Forest Path" achieves a fluidity of form that celebrates creation as both chaos and order, repetition and difference, eternity and impermanence. The aesthetic space foregrounded in the novella is therefore one of "in-betweenness," best expressed in the metaphor of the interlocked circles made by the rain falling on the ocean. Swinging in the rain: such could be another name for this celebration fated to be but an ephemeral moment of equilibrium.

CHARTING THE INFINITE: AN APPEAL TO GOD'S MERCY

"Ritual" is defined as "a series of actions that are always carried out in the same way, especially as part of a religious ceremony" (*Oxford Advanced Learner's*

Dictionary) It therefore appears as a form in which repetition and regularity are essential, whether the ritual be religious or secular, and it is usually meant to bring some kind of order to a changeable reality and make it endurable. Reality is indeed threatening for the protagonists of "The Forest Path," who seek refuge in a secluded place, away from civilization, away from the impersonality of city buildings and the unfeeling cruelty of its citizens, away from the violence of the war that has just been declared. Besides, the protagonist, a jazz musician, has had to leave behind his nightlife existence and its excesses to save his health and his marriage. As they arrive on a beach for their honeymoon, the narrator first dismisses any possibility of staying longer than a summer vacation, for "it would be almost tantamount . . . to renouncing the world altogether," (Lowry 233) and he compares the backhouses of the little beach shacks to "monastic cells of anchorites or saints" (217). The narrator's efforts at making the place sacred are therefore a means to keep it separate from the rest of the world: he invites the reader to an imaginary visit of the place that clearly defines its boundaries, and intersperses his text with religious metaphors (cathedral, Shinto temple, votive lights, miracle, shrines), comparing the narrator on his path to the spring to "a poverty-stricken priest pacing the aisles of a great cathedral at dusk, who counting his beads and reciting his paternoster is yet continually possessed by the uprush of his extraneous thoughts" (253).

And indeed, this sacred place offers no haven of peace. What security there is has to be earned and worked for "with clawbar and hammer" (238), and it is no coincidence that the protagonists arrive on the beach on Labour Day. Fetching water at the spring partakes both of a ritual and a chore that have to be performed dutifully to secure peaceful living. Indeed, danger is always lurking outside the bounds of the small paradise, ready to overthrow its fragile balance; ironically, the narrator's improved health now makes him liable for enrolment in the army and thus to being separated from his young wife; and the shoreline squatters in Eridanus are under permanent threat of eviction, their beach always at the mercy of an impending oil slick caused by the oil tankers that come to anchor at the refinery wharf. Besides, the frail and brave little shacks suffer the onslaught of the elements, especially in winter, when "the house itself could be in jeopardy . . . from the huge timbers or uprooted trees racing downstream" (235), and the ocean's wrath is always likely to take its toll among the fishermen. Other rituals then need to be carried out: singing together the old Manx fishermen's hymn in Quaggan's shack, sharing tea or whisky when the tempest is raging outside, or again swimming every morning in the invigorating waters of the ocean to be baptized afresh. The narrator is indeed well aware that he also needs to propitiate the dark powers that lie within him:

One night . . . I saw my shadow, gigantic, the logs of wood as big as a
coffin, and this shadow seemed for a moment the glowering embodiment of all that threatened us; yes, even a projection of that dark chaotic
side of myself, my ferocious destructive ignorance. (234)

The lovers even manage to keep the dangers at bay by turning them into loving
catchphrases that become their private ritual:

"None of this nonsense about love in a cottage?"
  I was lighting the oil lamp as I said this, smiling as I reflected how this
unprophetic and loveless remark had become a loving catchphrase . . . or
a monstrance.
  "But now it's night, and the Chinese Hats are on the move!" (243)

The humorous reference to the teeming nightlife outside, just under the shack,
may be read, in these times of war, as a creeping fear of an Asian invasion on the
Pacific coast.

  Thus the rituals aim at protecting the paradisiacal community from any
kind of invasion. Like any ritual, it is also an attempt at denying the passing of
time: repeating the very same gestures or words creates the illusion that nothing changes. Past, present, and future are fused in a kind of eternity, which
Quaggan's son's Celtic use of tenses expresses amusingly: "It's blowing real
hard. I'm just dashing madly to see how things were" (267). Mircea Eliade writes:

The repetition of archetypes betrays the paradoxical desire to achieve an
ideal form within the very human condition, to find oneself in lasting time
without having to bear its burden, that is its irreversibility. (Eliade 341)

The short story, which depicts the protagonists' everyday life with the same
rituals performed over the seasons and over the years, succeeds in creating an
impression of eternity as cyclical return.

  With its eight self-contained sections, "The Forest Path" is also given a clear
form, based on repetition, which in itself may act as a ritual. Textual space is
visibly subdivided and textual borders are firmly delineated. Time also seems to
be under control. Indeed, though it is narrated in the past, implying that the protagonists' life in Eridanus is over, the first section, which introduces the reader
to Eridanus, contributes to creating a feeling of timelessness since it presents us
with images that will recur throughout the short story: the gulls, the lighthouse,
the wild roses, the deer, the "Frère Jacques" canon to represent the engines of

the freighters passing by, and so on. After this first section, each section is built according to the same pattern, ending on the resolution of a crisis, and six of them are centred on the narrator's ritual to the spring (the second section stages the protagonists' first discovery of the beach and their decision to stay). Ritual repetition is furthermore enhanced by the opening sentence's essential reappearance throughout the various sections. Its first occurrence is mirrored in the last, with the introduction of a chiasmus, which seems to create the sacred, self-enclosed space ritual aims at:

> At dusk, every evening, I used to go through the forest to the spring for water. (216)
> And I remembered how every evening I used to go down this path through the forest to get water from the spring at dusk. (287)

Yet, the suspension points after the word "dusk" and the slightly different phrasing indicate an opening, confirmed by the fact that these are not the last words of the story, the narrator "looking over his wife's shoulder . . . to see a deer swimming toward the lighthouse" (287). Not only does the sentence foreground signs of hope (deer, lighthouse) but, with its two "-ing" forms and the preposition "toward," it underlines dynamic movement and process. And indeed, each time the introductory sentence is taken up, it appears with slight variations that develop one feature or another.[3] If the ritual affords a pattern, the latter in "The Forest Path" is never strictly identical: it allows for variation that may be seen as an influence of jazz on the composition. No simple ritual prayer, an *appeal to* God's mercy imploring his protection from any kind of change, it actually is a work of art, a *poem of* God's mercy, celebrating infinity in its everyday manifestations.

CELEBRATING INFINITY: A POEM OF GOD'S MERCY

Although the rituals are meant to keep dark forces away, the narrator experiences a series of crises on the return path from the spring. Each section stages the sudden irruption of an event or a feeling, which the end of the section eventually resolves, proving that what has been excluded inexorably returns. The first of these crises occurs in the third section, when the protagonists discover that the access to the first spring has been barred, the creek where they used to get fresh water having become private property overnight, and their barrel breaks in their hurried flight from the angry owner. Thus the fear of eviction, of the shacks being replaced by "autocamps of the better class" (277), is enacted on a minor scale. In the fourth section, the narrator, for no apparent reason, is overwhelmed by an all-consuming hatred against mankind, which, like a forest fire, eventually turns back on himself. This time, it is both the raging war and elemental wrath that resurface in the narrator's mind, as he himself realizes:

> One day, after I had been turned down again for the army, it occurred to me that in some mysterious way I had access to the fearful wrath that was sweeping the world, or that I stood at the mercy of the wild forces of nature . . . or something that was like the dreadful Wendigo, the avenging man-hating spirit of the wilderness. (245)

The next section, taking place in winter, does not so much present a particular moment of crisis as apprehension about the violence of the winds and ocean as well as about the risk of losing their hard-won paradise. Section six confronts the narrator with two unexpected encounters: the sight of a rope on the path conjures up suicidal thoughts, while his finding himself face-to-face with a cougar revives deep-seated anxieties about being the prey of an Other intent on devouring and destroying him to punish him for some inexpiable fault:

> Half conscious I told myself that it was as though I had actually been on the lookout for something on the path that had seemed ready, on every side, to spring out of our paradise at us, that was nothing so much as the embodiment in some frightful animal form of those nameless somnambulisms, guilts, ghouls of past delirium, wounds to other souls and lives, ghosts of actions approximating to murder, even if not my own actions in this life, betrayals of self and I know not what, ready to leap out and destroy me, to destroy us and our happiness.[4] (266)

In section seven, after being under the impression that the path is shrinking at both ends, the narrator and his wife make up a story of the path's getting so short that it eventually absorbs him, thereby enacting the separation that might have happened had the narrator been enlisted in the army. The ritual, whose pattern is supposedly meant to order and channel reality and prevent any intrusion from the Other, opens up each time to the unexpected, a reminder that the Real cannot be so easily dismissed. As the incomplete sign on the refinery reveals, the shell cannot protect from the hell that coils inside.

Yet this opening up of the ritual to the unexpected does not preclude it from working miracles. Indeed each crisis is somehow miraculously solved: the narrator providentially discovers a canister on the beach and Kristbjorg, a neighbour met on the path, indicates another "wand," the Danish or Norwegian word for spring, clearly expressing the touch of magic brought to this particular resolution; the narrator's hatred subsides when he is reminded of his neighbours' solidarity and his fellow musicians' generous gift of a piano, the section ending on artistic creation regained; in section five, language offers the comfort of its startling polysemy; next, in a scene that almost reads as a parody of St. Francis of Assisi, the cougar listens to the narrator's quiet voice and departs; ultimately, thanks to the conscious repetition of a parting scene, the narrator and his wife manage to overcome their fear, and even to bear the loss of their first shack and of the narrator's symphony in a fire. The final section sounds like a coda: the narrator reviews all the epiphanies that have been experienced and marvels at their having miraculously survived so many hardships, like the little boat of the first short story in the collection, at their having become different yet having remained the same. While bringing closure, the coda is a reminder of those miracles that resist conclusiveness.

The very structure of the short story testifies to this variability within a set pattern, infinity being reinterpreted as unexpectedness rather than incommensurability. The eight sections do provide a form but are of unequal length, and the crisis followed by a resolution supplies a frame within which something that cannot be predicted nor reproduced occurs. This is what happens with jazz, whose basic rhythm is based on a succession of tension and release:

> There is a tendency in jazz to create a tension and immediately bring it to a resolution before creating another which, in its turn, is resolved. . . . The emphasis is no longer laid on great overarching tensions, as in European music, but on a diversity of elements generating tensions that keep rising and falling. (Berendt 486)

With this basic rhythm, the jazz musician is at liberty to improvise, as Graham Collier emphasizes: "Taken overall, the blues form simply provides a basic structure for improvising, and it is on the repetition of such structures that jazz is traditionally based" (244). And those improvisations are not reproduced, each performance being different from the next. The narrator is made to realize this as, despite his secret wish, he never meets the cougar again. A jazz musician, he learns to respond to the unknown infinite and to turn it into art. Besides, some of the narrator's very poetical descriptions—that of the seething life in the mud flats (Lowry 237), for instance—may be seen as solos where verbal inventiveness, play with rhythm and sounds, without being essential to the narrative line, are important for the colour of the whole:

But then we went out to a morning of wild ducks doing sixty downwind and golden crowned kinglets feeding in swift jingling multitudinous flight through the leafless bushes, and another day of winter companionship would draw down to an evening of wind . . . our conscious knowledge. (256)

Being but one long sentence, the paragraph bears out the comparison with a soloist improvisation, the beginning of which is a virtuoso arrangement of sounds that develop, some being taken up and dropped (*d*, *i*, and next *g*, *ow*, *ing*, then *f* and *s*). With these linguistic games, some jouissance transpires within a structure that yet prevents it from spilling over, jeopardizing meaning. The narrator thus reflects:

Nonetheless those thoughts, and they were abysmal, not happy as I would have wished, made me happy in that, though they were in motion they were in order too: an inlet does not overflow its banks, however high the tide, nor does it dry up, the tide goes out, but it comes again, in fact as Quaggan has observed, it can do both at once. (268)

Not only sounds, but words are taken up throughout the short story and create a feeling of unity without uniformity, since each time they develop with variations (my italics throughout):

It was a *whitewashed* concrete structure . . . like a magic lighthouse . . . but oddly like a human being itself . . . with its generator *strapped to its back like a pack; wild roses* in early summer *blew* in the bank beside it. (219)

When the *wild roses* began to *blow* . . . these fishermen went away, . . . like proud *white* giraffes their *newly painted* fishing boats with tall gear would be seen going round the point. (223)

Gulls slept like doves on its *samson posts* . . . and in early *spring* pecked their old feathers off to make room for their new shiny *plumage like fresh white paint.* (226)

Then I turned right so that now I was facing north toward the mountains, *white plumaged as gulls themselves with a fresh paint of snow; or rose* and indigo. (244)

The further mountains grew nearer and nearer until they looked like the precipitous rocky cliff-face of an island *gashed with guano.* . . . A *gull* whose wings seemed almost a *maniacal white* suddenly was drawn up. (267)

The landmarks that punctuate the aesthetic space and give it coherence are subject to change and variation. As in jazz, the same motifs appear with different combinations, nothing is fixed:

> Jazz consists in such models, fragments—such as the falling lines in old blues or in modern "funk"—which sometimes are endowed with the aura associated with the opening words in fairy-tales: "once upon a time . . ." These constitute a model element. And jazz is like fairy-tales where elements-become-symbols become the contents: the wicked witch casts a spell on the noble prince and the king's stone-heart melts before the lovely shepherdess, and lastly the young prince meets the lovely shepherdess who turns out to be a princess under a spell—witch and prince, magic and stone-heartedness, king and shepherdess . . . so many elements likely to be united in infinite combinations. (Berendt 492)

This jazz-like process could also refer to the inter- and intra-textual practices present in all of Lowry's works, even though they are quite toned down in "The Forest Path," as if the omnipresent music had partly silenced others' voices, which elsewhere assail the author.

Those infinite combinations are a key to the fluidity and impermanence of the form, the eternity which the rituals try to generate being reinterpreted as recycling, which is already present both in the narrator's concrete salvaging of the canister, the ladder, and such, and in his composing his opera, "built, like our new house, on the charred foundations and fragments of the old work and our old life" (Lowry 274). Eternity encompasses impermanence, as the sunken canoe, intermezzo, reminds the lovers soon after their arrival in Eridanus; space encompasses infinity. As the protagonists experience with the shrinking path, time and space are closely interrelated and can be elastic, both being highly subjective, depending on one's perception of them:

> There is not on the one hand hearing, a time-related sense, and on the other hand sight, a space-related sense. Rhythm inserts sight into hearing, creating a continuum between categories in its subjective, and transsubjective working. (Meschonnic 299)

Understanding the continuity of time beyond its discontinuities, the boundlessness of space beyond its limits, seeing difference at the heart of repetition: these are some of the things the narrator's wife, through her closeness to nature and its rhythm, initiates him to:

and I thought that perhaps she was herself the eidolon of everything we loved in Eridanus, of all its shifting moods and tides and darks and suns and stars. Nor could the forest itself have longed for spring more than she. She longed for it like a Christian for heaven, and through her I myself became susceptible to these moods and changes and currents of nature, as to its ceaseless rotting into humus of its fallen leaves and buds—nothing in nature suggested you died yourself more than that, I began to think—and burgeoning toward life. (Lowry 249)

In Lowry's paradise Eve gives Adam the fruit from the tree of knowledge, so that, in an inversion of the original myth, he may be reborn. She educates his gaze, restores his capacity to wonder and to see the world with new eyes. Thus the Manx hymn, which the protagonists sing "to the tune of Peel Castle with its booming minor chords," is introduced as "less an appeal to, than a poem of God's mercy" (223). "The Forest Path" is less an attempt at creating a sacred place than an attempt at the sanctification of man:

The separation between the profane and the sacred originates in a distinction between the human and the extra-human. But the Biblical tradition insists on the coming of God in this world—His Incarnation, according to the Gospels. Thus the distinction between what is prophetic or provisional, what is pure or impure, what is allowed or prohibited in the ritual, is abolished. God's will is that man should sanctify his whole life instead of separating it into two antithetic sectors. (Cazeneuve 461)

Celebrating God through His creation rather than appealing to His authority to protect man, celebrating the redeeming elements present everywhere in the world rather than appealing for redemption, such is the achievement of "The Forest Path." "Hear us O Lord" is an address to an Other that cannot be located, like the spring's original source, which recedes in the forest and the mountains. The last page of "The Forest Path" indeed points to another path: not the one the protagonist walked on to go to the spring, but that of the spring itself: "Feeling its way underground it must have had its dark moments. But here, in springtime, on its last lap to the sea, it was as at its source a happy joyous little stream" (Lowry 287). No awe-inspiring source, the little stream, like the protagonists, has survived several ordeals, and is in itself a joyous celebration of life where the profane and the sacred merge. This is the feeling conveyed by the last sentence of the story, where the reverent attitude of humility combines with sheer joy: "Laughing we stooped down to the stream and drank" (287). The double origin of jazz, profane for blues and sacred for the gospel, makes it an apt instrument to translate such feelings. "Swinging the Maelstrom," Lowry's title for an early version of *Lunar Caustic*, has become, in such an appeased short story as "The Forest Path," "swinging in the rain": a celebration of life's manifold and contradictory facets.

DWELLING IN-BETWEEN: SWINGING IN THE RAIN

With its combination of spirituality and sensuality, which can be traced back to its origins, jazz affords Lowry a means to reconcile man's mystical aspirations with his earthly reality, his infinity with his finiteness. As Mason and Bellest write: "[The African tradition] was the permanent concern with tempo, in a ritualistic perspective which did not separate music from dance and from singing, always very rhythmical" (6). A spontaneous form of music, whose lyrics are often concerned with everyday life, blues or jazz is an ideal expression for everyday epiphanies such as those experienced by the narrator. Related to the work of slaves, it is the perfect accompaniment to the protagonists' labour:

> the jobs begat the songs, so that it was as if we had discovered the primitive beginnings of music again for ourselves; we began to make up our own songs, and I began to write them down. (Lowry 250)

Indeed, the short story is interspersed with songs and mini dialogues between the protagonist and his wife, which could be likened to call and response in jazz. In these poetical exchanges, coherence is no major concern; what matters is the creation of a mood, which again is a recurrent feature in some blues lyrics:

> "Moonrise of the dying moon."
> "Sunrise of the dying moon, in a green sky."
> "White frost on the porch and all the roofs ... I wonder if it's killed poor Mr McNab's nasturtiums. It's the first heavy frost of the year. And the first clear sunrise in a month."
> "There's a little flotilla of golden eyes under the window."
> "The tide is high." (234)

These little rituals, which create a specific mood, are immediately recognized by the reader, as are the voices of the various inhabitants in Eridanus, either because of their recurrent motifs or their particular accents or idiomatic phrases. In "The Forest Path," the forbidding voice of the Other has been replaced by the interlaced melodic lines of others, which compose a richly textured score where each voice, easily recognizable, brings its own colouring to the whole. Thus, we may hear Quaggan's hymn, Kristbjorg's bawdy songs, Sam's poetic prose with its particular twang ("–And soon the crabs will bring the spring. . . . But crabs . . . I had a friend, a diver—thief he was in private life, never come home without somethink. . . . Well this time he goes down, down, down, you know, deep. Then he get scairt . . . And soon the crabs, my dearies, and soon the birds will bring the spring" [254]), Mauger's song and Scottish accent, to which are added the boats and trains' engines singing "Frère Jacques," the sounds of the ocean and the wind, the peal of bells (cf. 280). Those various lines cross, mingle, are taken up at various moments, each one keeping its specificity and yet making up a whole, again something which is very much in tune with jazz. As the jazz pianist and composer Dave Brubeck said, "Today, jazz is probably the only artistic form which preserves individual freedom without jeopardizing the group's cohesion" (qtd. in Berendt 79). "The Forest Path" is indeed the literary transposition of the narrator's heterogeneous, polyphonic jazz opera, an artistic form which tries to encompass the multitudinous infinity of the whole creation:

> I composed this opera. . . . It was partly in the whole tone-scale, like *Wozzeck*, partly jazz, partly folksongs or songs my wife sang, even old Hymns, such as Hear Us O Lord from Heaven Thy Dwelling Place. I even used canons like Frère Jacques to express the ships' engines or the rhythms of eternity; Kristbjorg, Quaggan, my wife and myself, the other inhabitants of Eridanus, my jazz friends, were all characters, or exuberant instruments on the stage or in the pit. The fire was a dramatic incident and our own life, with its withdrawals and returns, what I had learned of nature, and the tides and the sunrises I tried to express. (Lowry 274)

Another metaphor for this particular composition is also to be found in the image of the raindrops falling on the sea, the importance of which is signalled by its appearing twice in the short story: first in the third section when this sight comforts the narrator's wife after they have lost their access to the spring and she opens her husband's eyes to the beauty of it, and then, far more developed in the last pages of the short story where this time, under the moon, the circles on the water become circles of light:

> Each drop falling into the sea is like a life, I thought, each producing a circle in the ocean, or the medium of life itself, and widening into infinity, though it seems to melt into the sea, and become invisible, or disappear

entirely, and be lost. Each is interlocked with other circles falling about it, some are larger circles expanding widely, others are weaker, smaller circles that only seem to last a short while. [. . .] They were perfect expanding circles of light [. . .] each raindrop expanded into a ripple that was translated into light. And the rain itself was water from the sea, as my wife first taught me, raised to heaven by the sun, transformed into clouds and falling again into the sea. While within the inlet itself the tides and currents in that sea returned, became remote, and becoming remote, like that which is called the Tao, returned again as we ourselves had done. (286)

Each of the voices could be one of those circles, each with its own tempo, its separate life, against the background of the wider rhythms of the rain, the tides, and currents. This combination of individual and universal rhythms is characteristic of jazz, with what is known to jazz musicians as "swing"—the interplay between a fundamental rhythm, the beat, and counter-rhythms; the swing that is an inner rhythm, a pulse that must be felt, for it cannot be explained or decomposed. When asked what jazz/swing was, Louis Armstrong allegedly replied, "If you have to ask, you'll never know." Swinging in the rain: this is the path the short story points to, a means for rational man to cope and make do with his worst anxieties: randomness, paradox, impermanence, and infinity. Like the spring and its "faint tang of mushrooms, earth, dead leaves, pine needles, mud and snow" (287), man is humus, and belongs to the earth, but his varied experiences can be cleansed and turned into a work of art, raised to heaven to trace a rainbow, a mingling of water, air and fire (light), a beautiful and ephemeral celebration of the world's wonders, almost a music manuscript; indeed, the rainbow's arched shape reminds us of the suspension bridge the lovers in "The Bravest Boat" see in the distance "much as a piece of jazz music mounts towards a break" (16). Under the three rainbows which "[go up] like rockets across the bay" (286), bridging here and there, the earthly and the spiritual, the reader is invited to swing in the rain, adding his voice to the chorus.

An appeased short story in Lowry's long line of anxiety-ridden works, "The Forest Path to the Spring" is yet no simple recipe for happiness. If Eridanus is the name of a specific place, the protagonists' personal heaven on earth, it is also that of a "starry constellation . . . known both as the River of Death and the River of Life" (227); the specific place opens up onto ambiguous boundless space that will not be assigned any fixed meaning. In the uncertainty of infinity, not only do rituals, with the rigidity of their form, and jazz, with the liberty it affords, work together to create a soothing mood, but they also coalesce in that most people performing a ritual cannot explain the reason for it, although they know every detail of its performance. As Fats Waller said, "Jazz is not *what* you do but *how* you do it" (qtd. in Berendt 205). What matters is not invention but execution. Thus the reader of "The Forest Path" is left free to interpret this jazz opera as he or she wishes, remaining open to the unpredictable, which forbids any stable meaning; dwelling in-between, one may find, however momentarily, in the infinity of possibilities, one's own way to the spring.

NOTES

1. Cf. Lowry's famous letter to Jonathan Cape, who had tentatively agreed to publish *Under the Volcano*, in defence of the work. The letter is published in the 1985 Penguin edition of *Volcano*.

2. All translations in the chapter are the author's own.

3. "Nor shall I ever forget the first time I went down that path to the spring for water" (Lowry 243).

    "Thereafter at dusk, when the gulls came floating home over the trees, I used to take this cannister to the spring" (244).

    "In the evening, when I went for water, which I always liked to time to coincide with the seagulls' evening return over the trees and down the inlet" (256).

    "And then, before I had time to think, I would seem to be getting water again, walking as if eternally through a series of dissolving dusks down the path" (258).

    "In early spring, we had not yet moved to our second house and this is the time I am really thinking of when I say that each evening at dusk I used to go down the path for water" (262).

    "We climbed the steps . . . and began to walk into the mist and down the path to the spring" (279).

4. The expanding nature of the sentence, with its accumulative pattern, is a clear index of the impossibility to circumscribe any secure space, the latter being indeed threatened "on every side."

WORKS CITED

Berendt, Joachim-Ernst. *Le grand livre du jazz*. 1986. Paris: éditions du rocher, 1994.

Cazeneuve, Jean. *Encyclopaedia Universalis*. Vol. 20. Paris: Encyclopaedia Universalis, 2005.

Collier, Graham. "Lowry, Jazz and 'The Day of the Dead'." *Swinging the Maelstrom*, edited by Sherrill E. Grace, Montreal and Kingston: McGill-Queen's UP, 1992, pp. 243–248.

Eliade, Mircea. *Traité d'histoire des religions*. Paris: Payot, 1991.

Lowry, Malcolm. *Hear Us O Lord from Heaven Thy Dwelling Place*. 1961. New York: Carroll & Graf, 1986.

Malson L., and C. Bellest. *Le Jazz*. Paris: PUF, 1987.

Meschonnic, Henri. *Critique du rythme*. Paris: Verdier, 1982.

Souriau, Etienne. *Vocabulaire d'esthétique*. 1990. Paris: PUF, 2004.

10

The Expressionist Gaze in the Psychic Space of Under the Volcano

JOSIANE PACCAUD-HUGUET

In the first chapter of *Under the Volcano*, Jacques Laruelle, a French film director, recalls the spell of Chartres and a café "where he could gaze at the
Cathedral eternally sailing against the clouds" (Lowry 12). A director is an
impersonal camera eye, and it is significant that Laruelle should be the focal-
izing mind opening a novel whose cast of characters are rather poorly equipped
for intersubjective looking. As amply shown by the work of Sherrill Grace and
Paul Tiessen, *Volcano* swarms with references to expressionism, an art form foregrounding the expressionless gaze, whose emergence in painting and film was
simultaneous with the rise of fascism in Europe.[1] The Consul, who wanted to be a
voyant like Arthur Rimbaud, has become a gaze himself—"Hounded by eyes and
thronged terrors / Now the lens of a glaring world" (Lowry 330). His symptom,
Stephen Spender observes, has become "diagnosis, not just of himself but of a
phase of history" (Spender xii), as if some transfer from the individual to the collective had taken place. It will be assumed here that the forms of looking/gazing
within the novel's socio-symbolic space cannot be separated from the forms of
looking/gazing involved in the reading process, where the visual and the acoustic constantly interact. Lowry's book, far from being mad, is ultimately a "most
lucid novel" (Spender xii)—a sort of *voyant* too, but this time in the sense of a
warning signal, in response to the rise of the totalitarian gaze in Europe.

THE REIFYING GAZE

The psychoanalytical notions of gaze and voice may be of some help in understanding the structuring of space and time in *Volcano*. Voice and gaze are the two
objects added by Jacques Lacan to the list of Freudian "partial objects": they are not
on the side of who sees or hears, but of *what* the subject hears or sees. For example, we may feel that a blind gaze is being returned by a window, a lighthouse, or
a star; or that a voice floating in space betrays the presence of an impersonal gaze
watching us. Dealing with the photographic image, Roland Barthes has given the

name of *punctum* to such an odd element sticking out of the composition/*studium*,[2] likely to leap out of the picture, to point at you, even to sting you. Trouble begins when this point, which should remain enigmatic, evanescent, begins, as it were, to swell out, as if it were loaded with intentionality: it is no longer an object, it is "subjectivized"—as in the case of the "Big Brother is watching you" motif.[3]

Conversely, when we say that there is always "more than meets the eye" in what we see or understand, we admit that the view under our eyes or under the mind's eye cannot be complete. For example, when we look at ourselves on a reflecting surface, we cannot see the point from which we are gazing at ourselves: what does not appear in the mirror precisely deserves the name of the subject-less gaze, "abstracted" from the mirror image. In *Volcano*, Yvonne experiences that very schism as she stands looking at the printer's shop window on the square in Quanahuac:

> From the mirror within the window an ocean creature so drenched and coppered by sun and winnowed by sea-wind and spray looked back at her. . . . In the window itself, on either side of this abstracted gaze of her mirrored face, the same brave wedding invitations she remembered were ranged. (Lowry 54)

More generally, the self-conscious illusion of *seeing itself in the process of seeing* can never coincide with the invisible gaze from which the world looks at us—the Other's gaze cleft from the eye, and which cannot be pinpointed to any specific agent.[4]

The classic example of the antinomy between gaze and view is Holbein's famous painting, *The Ambassadors*, a vanity built according to the technique of anamorphosis. The scientific and musical instruments displayed by the richly dressed ambassadors are emblematic of the semblances of knowledge and power that composed the reality of the West at the time. Yet the image gravitates around a shapeless spot, a disharmonious blot, which, looked at from a certain perspective, turns out to be a skull gazing at you without seeing you. The point of the anamorphosis is that you see first the view, and then the gaze—you cannot see them simultaneously: the spectral "vanishing point" lies both within and without the depicted view, its *elision/evacuation* from the field of the visible is necessary for the construction of reality which, however, never fully covers it. The gaze contained/constrained by the painter's art is, like Barthes's *punctum*, a blind spot pointing to some unpleasant truth, in this case the knowledge of death, our ultimate Other; one of the lessons of anamorphosis is that an unbridgeable gap thus separates what we call reality with its spatial and temporal coordinates, from the shapeless underlying substance—the real which can never be fully covered by the veil of semblances.[5]

In "normally" constituted reality, this gap is less a frontier zone than an elusive point of contact; at the other end of the spectrum, in the case of hallucinations, the gaze is no longer the abstracted, empty object it should be—it becomes an effective part of visible/audible reality, it is subjectivized: we know that we are being observed by someone out there, the distinction subject/object is lost—which is often the case in the psychotic landscape of *Volcano*. The Consul goes through such moments, for example in the bathroom scene where the mosquito stains and the cracks on the wall swell out into a Kafkaesque army of insects wriggling their way toward him:

> Now a scorpion was moving slowly across to him. Suddenly, the Consul rose, trembling in every limb. But it wasn't the scorpion he cared about. It was that, all at once, the thin shadows of isolated nails, the stains of murdered mosquitoes, the very scars and cracks of the wall, had begun to swarm, so that, wherever he looked, another insect was born, wriggling instantly toward his heart. (Lowry 148)

This, however, is not a simple case of psychotic dissolution: the Consul's symptom points to the derailing of relations in the private and public spheres, it brings forth the malignant forces of persecution at work on the whole political body: the picture of the Western world with its spatial coordinates can no longer be that of *The Ambassadors*, the internal abyss of the *barranca* seems to be waiting round the corner wherever one turns—and, Laruelle reflects, "Quaunahuac was like the times in this respect" (15).

There are indeed moments in *Volcano* when the gaze does seem to leap forth, for example when Yvonne, Hugh, and the Consul glimpse the cruel hole in the dying Indian's head (243), a vision foreshadowed by the Consul's own hallucination of an "object shaped like a dead man . . . with a large sombrero over its face" (91). The brief moment of vision is surely reminiscent of Marlow's encounter of the dying helmsman's gaze in Conrad's *Heart of Darkness*, a work much admired by Lowry. But we are no longer in the context of the modernist flash of insight, where the gaze ultimately recedes in the background of reality. In the paranoid space of Lowry's novel, many topographical details stick out like visual protuberances: of all details, "old Popeye" (75) pops into view now and again, more threateningly toward the end:

> Popocatepetl slid in and out of view continually, never appearing the same twice, now far away, then vastly near at hand, incalculably distant at one moment, at the next looming round the corner. (252)

On the morning of Yvonne's arrival, the sunlight on the town square blazes on the ambulance, whose headlights are "transformed into a blinding magnifying glass," itself glazing on the volcanoes (53). And the *barranca* is "chock full" with the dead journalists spying through keyholes that keep tormenting Hugh's consciousness (100).

The Other's gaze can also be felt through uncanny voice effects loaded with malevolent jouissance—manifestations of what film theory calls the acousmatic voice.[6] The tossing trees tell the Consul he is a liar, the plantain leaves rattle that he is a traitor (151), his familiars gabble in his ear as if he were constantly being regarded. Hugh and Yvonne overhear a sharp, pistol-like report from somewhere ahead, the signal of target practice—and of the presence of the fascist gaze (333). The writing on the wall motif returns in many variants, whether as texts or pictures (posters, boards, signs) traversing diegetic space. And, of course, there is the technological gaze of the cinema, whose theatre in Quanahuac looks like "some gloomy bazaar," possibly reminiscent of the place where the narrator in Joyce's "Araby" goes through a brief epiphanic moment:

> At the box office, momentarily vacated, the door left half open, a frantic hen sought admission. Everywhere people were flashing torches or striking matches. . . . *Las Manos de Orlac*, said a poster; 6 y 8:30. *Las Manos de Orlac, con Peter Lorre.* (24)

But here again we are far from the matches struck unexpectedly in the dark of the modernist epiphany. The cinema's poster seems to tell "a complicated tale of tyranny and sanctuary" (25), confirmed by the uncanny presence of authorities in the box where "three cigarettes were lit on one match" (26)—three telltale *punctum*-like details.

The enjoyment associated with the object gaze ranges from innocent visual pleasures to the fantasy of the invisible Master watching you. The first thing Laruelle offers his visitors is not a drink but a pair of binoculars; Yvonne sits gazing from a parapet, "with every semblance of interested enjoyment" (70). Two policemen peer east and west from a watchtower (13), spies and spiders in dark glasses are posted everywhere around the town (56):

> The Consul regarded her without expression as she stared up into the sun at the bizarre house opposite them near the head of their street, with two towers and a connecting catwalk over the ridgepole, at which someone else, a peon with his back turned, was also gazing curiously. (57)

Even though the Consul is seldom without the pair of dark glasses he found out-side a cantina, his naked eyes look to Yvonne like streetlamps betraying a curious, vaguely threatening glare "turned inward" (49). In short, the spectral, inhuman gaze is omnipresent, *de-localized* to the point that the shapeless substance of the real oozing from the abyss seems to be devouring the loosening fabric of reality:

> He was in a room, and suddenly in this room, matter was disjunct: a door-knob was standing a little way out from the door. A curtain floated in by itself, unfastened, unattached to anything. The idea struck him it had come in to strangle him. (314)

After which the Consul makes his own declaration of affiliation to unbridled sin: "I love hell. I can't wait to get back there" (314). The knowledge of books which can't "show you how to look at an ox-eye daisy" (207)—that is, how to confront the gaze—will be of no help.

THE SUBLIME *PUNCTUM* AND THE MELANCHOLY VOICE

Whenever the gaze as object is no longer the elusive blind spot in the field of the visible but is included in this field, one meets one's own death:[7] the two tragic deaths of *Volcano* occur in the shadow of old Popeye, the Popocatépetl volcano, itself the dwelling place of Typhœus, the fire daemon with flashing eyes and boiling mouth, which seems to claim them. The *Borrachones* poster in Laruelle's house, with its representation of space divided according to the traditional dichotomy of good vs. evil, seems to provide a first built-in "moralising" reading for Yvonne's and the Consul's deaths in the shadow of the volcanoes: while the saintly woman goes up to heaven, the drunken husband goes to hell, not without relief (199). Yet, as the Consul wonders, "Mightn't it have another meaning, that picture, unintentional as its humour, beyond the symbolically obvious?" (361). It may indeed be rewarding to look beyond the symbolically obvious, precisely in terms of an economy of the gaze—economy being taken here in its sense of the circulation and regulation of energies. For if the over-intrusive gaze mortifies, its evacuation by a process of hollowing out will be the condition for the advent of a vivifying voice-in-the-void effect, in the place of the threateningly popping eye.

For Yvonne, whose character is still inscribed in the post-Romantic para-digm, the two volcanoes are first the symbols of a mythical reunion of both sexes in eternal sleep. Yet, as she moves closer, the feminine Ixtaccihuatl tends to slip out of sight from her mirror, eclipsed by the summit of Popocatépetl (256). In the thunderous forest, as she loses sight of her beacon and gets closer to the boiling daemon, she hears the fateful horse's neigh, "a scream almost human in its panic" (334). Then she hears herself scream as the horse turns upon her before she feels herself borne upward and rejoins the Pleiades, where she becomes by a process of poetic sublimation, a gazing star. In other words, Yvonne's death is the moment when the gaze is at last elided from the picture, kept at bay, to become a *punctum* in the peaceful *studium* of the picture: Yvonne has been meta-morphosed into a sublime radiating object, marking out the point of contact between the visible and the invisible: she is part of the harmony of planets whose universe is still symbolically ordered by a naming process. Like Medusa after her death, she is now inscribed in the ethereal body of the constellations.[8]

The Consul's own downfall is more emblematic of acedia, "the spiritual apathy of the religious" (Spender xxviii), itself a form of melancholia; here the resolution will be more vocal than visual. From a clinical point of view, melan-cholic subjects often tend to see themselves as unworthy of the Other's regard, whose gaze may even become persecutory to them. In the novel's last scenes, the ex-Consul, who has stepped out of the field of symbolic reality, is increasingly identified to an abject object, disregarded by everyone, a piece of litter to be ulti-mately sucked in by the abysmal eye:

> Strong hands lifted him. Opening his eyes, he looked down, expecting to see, below him, the magnificent jungle, the heights. ... But there was nothing there: no peaks, no life, no climb. Nor was this summit a summit exactly: it had no substance, no firm base. It was crumbling too, whatever it was, collapsing, while he was falling, falling into the volcano. (Lowry 375)

The Consul, then, rejoins the crack in the wall, the blot in the picture, the *barranca* of the world: there is no sublime constellation here. A truly cathartic ending, however, might leave us to suppose that a bright world, a newly ordered space will emerge after the expulsion of the tragic hero, after the abyss has closed in upon itself—but it won't be so. Clearly, in a world where art itself has to become "a sort of defiant action" (Spender xxvii)—that is, where the issue is more ethical (involving an act) than moral (a question of obedience to established values)—the solution is no longer on the side of sublimation, which produces a faintly radiating object standing against the void: rather, it will be a question of containing and constraining the melancholy abyss, whose presence is still felt by an appealing, vibrant voice effect.

The Consul's fall is simultaneous with another vocal event, a scream, strongly reminiscent this time of Kurtz's cry in *Heart of Darkness*:

Suddenly he screamed, and it was as though this scream were being tossed from one tree to another, as its echoes returned, then, as though the trees themselves were crowding nearer, huddled together, closing over him, pitying. (Lowry 375)

In terms of resolution and of the construction of psychic space, the logic is not quite the same as what happens with Yvonne. Here the emphasis is more on the waves that keep hovering in the air, like an uncanny remainder of the scream, than on the sublime point of the silently gazing star. The first thing to be noted is that for a resonance to take place, there has to be a hollow space, a vacuity, which, as in Yvonne's case, is the result of the evacuation of the paranoid gaze, of the popping eye that recedes in the background. No visual sublime object, however, comes to fix the hole that remains a pulsing zone of instability—yet another kind of poetic transmutation has taken place. The voices of the tossing trees in the forest that so far accused the Consul of being a liar, no longer materialize the presence of the persecutory gaze. At the very moment of this death, the echoes tossing from tree to tree start travelling in space, like a conjuration, an anonymous vocal barrier reminiscent of the chorus of ancient tragedy, lamenting a sacrifice for nothing. The voice of lament—"*Dolente! . . . Dolore!*"—will continue to sound like a remainder of the Consul's passion, of his sin and glory, whose jouissance insists in the very fibre of Lowry's work.

SYMPTOM AND SINTHOM

The resonances between Lowry's voyage that never ends and James Joyce's work in progress have often been the object of critical attention.[9] I would like to consider them here in terms of the significance of the endless labour which was part of the lives of both novelists, like a working through of the symptom—which, however, does not mean coming to terms with it. As Slavoj Žižek observes, the symptom is what confers on the subject "its very ontological consistency, enabling it to structure its basic, constitutive relationship to enjoyment (jouissance)" (Žižek, *Enjoy* 155). It should therefore be less a question of evacuating/eradicating the sin of jouissance than of *making do* with it: the result of the operation will be the *sinthom*, a pun which Jacques Lacan coined after reading James Joyce—the word includes a reference to *sin* and to *Thomas* Aquinas, a major source for Joyce's aesthetics:

In contrast to symptom which is a cipher of some repressed meaning, *sinthom* has no determinate meaning: it just gives body, in its repetitive pattern, to some elementary matrix of *jouissance* of excessive enjoyment. Although sinthoms do not have sense they do radiate *jouissance*, *enjoy-meant*. (Žižek, *Enjoy* 199)[10]

Taking the example of Eisenstein's *Ivan the Terrible*, Žižek comments upon the motif of the thunderous explosion of rage which assumes different guises, ranging from the thunderstorm to the explosions of uncontrolled fury in the film's space:

> Although it may at first appear to be an expression of Ivan's psyche, its sound detaches itself from Ivan and starts to float around, passing from one to another person or to a state not attributable to any diegetic person. This motif should be interpreted not as an allegory with a fixed "deeper meaning" but as a pure "mechanic" intensity beyond meaning ... just floating as a provocation, as a challenge to find the meaning that could tame its sheer provocative power. (Žižek, *Organs* 5)

It is as if the fury had been unhooked from its origin in the phantasmatic frame (the person of the tyrant as the people's Other), dispersed in space where it continues to radiate with its own detached "provocative power." Eisenstein, perhaps the most direct influence on *Volcano*, according to Spender (xvii), called this process "naked transfer," which will certainly be apt for our reading of the novel. One year after the tragedy, Laruelle feels "as if somehow it had been transferred to these purple mountains all around him, so mysterious, with their secret mines of silver, so withdrawn, yet so close, so still, and from these mountains emanated a strange melancholy force that tried to hold him here bodily" (Lowry 13). We shall propose here that the strange force emanating from a novel like *Volcano* is a case of such "naked transfer" testifying to the creative passage from symptom to *sinthom*, by what Lowry called "a sort of mighty if preposterous moral deed of some sort"[11]—a form of heroism, certainly ethical, *meaning* to confront the truth enclosed in the symptom. Žižek also takes the example of the stains that "are" the yellow sky in Van Gogh: these are not sublime points marking out the division between the visible and the invisible in a symbolically ordered universe; rather, we are dealing with the level of material signs that just *relate* in a sort of pre-symbolic cross-resonance, a sort of meaningless network of correspondences. The "uncanny massiveness" of such enigmatic traces pertains to a kind of intermediate spectral domain, a "spiritual corporeality" (Žižek, *Organs* 199) ultimately endowed with an explosive dynamism of its own, certainly related to the rise of spatial form in modernist art.

The literary-expressionist *sinthom*, then, would be a subtle mix of gaze and voice, in-between the anamorphosis—it does produce a blot in the image—and the hallucination. The blot is loaded with enjoyment which, however, has to remain enigmatic: the hallucinatory quality remains, but without any intentionality being ascribed to the Other out there. In the face of the disruptive force of jouissance, the task for the artist will consist in cutting out a hole in a reality already saturated with meaning—the anger, the hatred, the fear of the day. Here, the cinematic technique of montage will be particularly apt to produce the *punctum*-like gaze, whose elusive presence will give some sort of consistency to the depicted reality/*studium*:

> Montage is usually conceived as a way of producing from fragments of the real—pieces of film, discontinuous individual shots—an effect of "cinematic space," i.e. a specific cinematic reality. . . . What is often overlooked, however, is the way in which this transformation of fragments of the real into cinematic reality produces, through a kind of structural necessity, a certain leftover, a surplus that is radically heterogeneous to cinematic reality but nonetheless implied by it, part of it. That this surplus of the real is, in the last resort, precisely the gaze *qua* object, is best exemplified by the work of Hitchcock. (Žižek, *Looking* 116)

We know that Laruelle himself has been an innovator in such techniques, in the film he made out of Shelley's *Alastor*, for example,

> which he shot in a bathtub, what he could of it, and apparently stuck the rest together with sequences of ruins cut out of old travelogues, and a jungle hoiked out of *In Dunkelste Afrika*, and a swan out of the end of some old Corinne Griffith . . . while all the time the poet was standing on the shore, and the orchestra was supposed to be doing its best with the *Sacre du Printemps*. (Lowry 202)

It is no great news to say that the technique of *Volcano* is kinetic, the invention of a new spatial form,[12] which, I would suggest, cannot be dissociated from Lowry's "moral deed." Examples of montage, of travelling shots interpolated by cuttings—forward or backward in space or time—are countless. The expressionless expressionist gaze, the voices without anchorage that traverse the novel's space, produce an aesthetics of *undecidability* whereby neither gaze nor voice can or should be pinpointed to a specific agent. In many cases, the gaze will be less a sublime object than an incongruous stain sticking out with an aura of anxiety and uneasiness—like the memory of the Samaritan supposed to have left the submarine "burning helplessly, a smoking cigar aglow on the vast surface of the

Pacific" (32), certainly a reminiscence from Conrad's short story "Youth." The almost surrealist object hovers in space and time, but it is not Abel's eye watching Cain from the grave: it is simply there, and the question of guilt remains suspended, complex, unresolved.

Sometimes, the image will simply make us hear a silence, it will emerge as "the placeholder for a sound that doesn't yet resonate but remains stuck in the throat" (Žižek, "I hear you" 93), thus pacifying the overwhelming flow of voices. For example, as Hugh and Yvonne watch from outside, the courteous exchange between the barman and the two Mexicans at the appropriately named cantina El Petate, beneath the roaring volcano:

> It stood, at a short distance from the clamorous falls, its lighted windows friendly against the twilight ... the barman and two Mexicans, shepherds or quince farmers, deep in conversation, and leaning against the bar—their mouths opened and shut soundlessly, their brown hands traced patterns in the air, courteously. (Lowry 319)

Clearly, the silence here is what contributes to the soothing effect of the "civilized" native scene, poles apart from the violence introduced by the Western world.

One year after the tragedy, the novel's "soundtrack" still brims with shreds of freely floating voices, autonomous yet human, sucked back by the luminous eye of the Ferris wheel that outlines a vacuity, a heart of darkness. Jacques Laruelle watches the town from a field:

> he thought he could distinguish the sound of human laughter rising from its bright gondola and, again, that faint intoxication of voices singing, diminishing, dying in the wind, inaudible finally. A despondent American tune, the St Louis Blues, or some such, was borne across the fields to him, at times a soft windblown surge of music from which skimmed a spray of gabbling, that seemed not so much to break against as to be thumping the walls and towers of the outskirts; then with a moan it would be sucked back into the distance. (10–11)

The fragments of human voices and music stand for the opaque inertia that cannot be recuperated by meaning, before it is sucked back into the silent hole. If the object voice is silence par excellence, it can be argued that music, which is primarily a matter of sound without meaning, of images without representation, is what comes closest to that object: we hear what we cannot see, the vibrating life force beyond the visual—in other words, we "see" the empty blind spot with our ears. The importance which Lowry granted to the "odd and splendid din" of his writing is, I believe, a result of his endeavour to both contain and constrain the over-intrusive gaze and voice.

If the novel's technique of shifting focalizers is crucial to fragment and to canalize the gaze, the point, however, is that the splitting up and traversing of the fantasy of the invisible Master watching does not mean getting rid of jouissance in the puritan or Romantic mode:

> "the distance towards fantasy means, rather, that I as it were unhook jou-issance from its phantasmatic frame and acknowledge it as that which is properly undecidable" (Žižek, *Looking* 115).

The Consul's own game of *sortes Shakespeareanae* and undecidable correspon-dences opens a space of *in-betweenness*, the possibility of playful interpretation, down to the absurd:

> "What had produced the illusion, the elusive flickering candlelight, or some correspondence, maybe, as Geoff liked to put it, between the sub-normal world and the abnormally suspicious?" (Lowry 34)

Clearly, the game of correspondences in *Under the Volcano* is important less for what they mean than for the way in which enigmatic details—like the horse with the number seven branded on its rump—punctuate the text rhythmically, giv-ing the novel its own specific temporality and space. Lowry playfully undercuts the fantasy of the Other that knows what you want, inviting the readers to won-der what *they* want. The ferocious gaze has ultimately been transmuted into the humorous voice: "¿Quiere vd.—a placard asked him in a shop window—*vestirse con elegancia y a la ultima moda de Europa y los Estados Unidos?*" (23)

If Lowry's ultra-modernity, then, is a truly psychotic landscape, the *sintho-matic* use the artist makes of the acoustic and graphic elements of language—of sound and letter—is certainly what gives the novel the translucent clairvoyance of a *témoin*, another meaning of *voyant*: not a person who sees, but a thing made of letters silently blinking from the page. On the morning of her arrival, as she stands on the square of Quanahuac, Yvonne has a glimpse of the wild gaze on the equestrian statue of Huerta—whose name means "garden" (14). The motif of the garden will recur throughout the novel: it will be as it were unhooked from the wildly gazing figure, until the uprooted public garden sign ultimately winks back at us from the last page, with its "oblong pallid face" (128). But this time it is not a figure on a horse heralding the catastrophe to come; it is a detached object gazing at us, inviting us to another form of enjoy-meant—meaning to awaken us to the *joy* of the properly human space, the garden of this world.

NOTES

1. See Grace, Tiessen.

2. The *studium* is what the image represents, what constitutes the view under the looker's scrutiny—the field of the image—unlike the *punctum*, an elusive point which is not really a detail of the composition, rather a little spot loaded with affect that *comes from* the picture: "A photograph's *punctum* is that accident which pricks me (but also bruises me, is poignant to me), . . . for *punctum* is also: sting, speck, cut, little hole—and also a cast of the dice" (Barthes 27).

3. As Slavoj Žižek explains: "Let us recall the archetypal scene from Hitchcock: a heroine (Lilah in *Psycho*, Melanie in *The Birds*) is approaching a mysterious, allegedly empty house; she is looking at it, yet what makes a scene so disturbing is that we, the spectators, cannot get rid of the impression that the object she is looking at is somehow returning the gaze. The crucial point, of course, is that this gaze should not be subjectivized: it's not simply that 'there is somebody in the house,' we are, rather, dealing with a kind of empty, a priori gaze that cannot be pinpointed as a determinate reality—she cannot see it all, she is looking at a blind spot, and the object returns the gaze from this blind spot. The situation is homologous at the level of voice: it is as if, when we're talking, whatever we say is an answer to a primordial address by the Other—we're always already addressed, but this address is blank, it cannot be pinpointed to a specific agent, but is a kind of empty a priori, the formal 'condition of possibility' of our speaking; so it is with the object returning the gaze, which is a kind of formal 'condition of possibility' of our seeing anything at all" (Žižek, "I hear you" 90).

4. "The gaze marks the point in the object (in the picture) from which the subject viewing it is already gazed at, i.e. it is the object that is gazing at me . . . the gaze functions as a stain, a spot in the picture disturbing its transparent visibility and introducing an irreducible split in my relation to the picture. I can never see the picture at the point from which it is gazing at me, i.e., the eye and the gaze are constitutively asymmetrical. . . . The gaze as object is a stain preventing me from looking at the picture from a safe, 'objective' distance, from enframing it as something that is at my grasping view's disposal" (Dolar 15).

5. "What we experience as reality cannot be the 'thing itself,' it is always already symbolized, constituted, structured by way of symbolic mechanisms—and the problem resides in the fact that symbolization ultimately always fails, that it never succeeds in fully 'covering' the real, that it always involves some unsettled, unredeemed symbolic debt" (Žižek, "I hear you" 110).

6. "The voice which transgresses the boundary outside/inside, since it belongs neither to diegetic reality nor to the external vocal accompaniment, but lurks in-between space,

like a mysterious foreign body which disintegrates from within the consistency of 'reality'" (Žižek, *Enjoy* 120).

7. A melancholy, poetic version of this meeting with the inhuman gaze, which is normally cleft from the eye, is Mrs. Ramsay's brief moment of being in *To the Lighthouse*, as she looks out to meet the stroke of the lighthouse that is both a caress and a blow: "this thing, the long steady stroke, was her stroke. Often she found herself sitting and looking, sitting and looking until she became the thing she looked at—that light for example . . . it seemed like her own eyes meeting her own eyes . . . if one was alone, one leant to things, inanimate things; trees, streams, flowers; felt they expressed one; felt they became one" (Woolf 71). After this "little death," Mrs. Ramsay returns to her social life—which is of course not the case for the protagonists in the tragic course of Lowry's novel.

8. The blood flowing from Medusa's head becomes a horse, Pegasus, who flies into the sky to become a group of stars.

9. See, for example, McCarthy and Tiessen's *Joyce/Lowry: Critical Perspectives*.

10. Let it also be recalled at this point that "jouissance" is a term that covers a whole range of affects: pain, suffering, but also, simply, joy, the joy of life.

11. Quoted in Spender, xxvii.

12. We may think, for example, of the incipit, with its close-up, narrowing the view from the mountain chains to the town of Quaunahuac, the walls of the town, the Hotel Casino de la Selva, two tennis courts, and then two men in white flannels (Lowry 4–5).

WORKS CITED

Barthes, Roland. *Camera Lucida: Reflections on Photography.* Translated by Richard Howard, New York: Hill & Wang, 1981.

Dolar, Mladen. "The object voice." *Gaze and Voice as Love Objects*, edited by Renata Salecl and Slavoj Žižek, Durham, NC: Duke UP, 1996, pp. 7–31.

Grace, Sherrill E. "Malcolm Lowry and the Expressionist Vision." *The Art of Malcolm Lowry*, edited by Anne Smith, London: Vision Press, 1978, pp. 93–111.

Joyce, James. *Dubliners.* New York: The Modern Library, 1969.

Lowry, Malcolm. *Under the Volcano.* Edited with an introduction by Stephen Spender. Harmondsworth, UK: Penguin, 1965.

McCarthy, Patrick A., and Paul Tiessen, editors. *Joyce/Lowry: Critical Perspectives.* Lexington: UP of Kentucky, 1997.

Spender, Stephen. "Introduction." *Under the Volcano.* Harmondsworth, UK: Penguin, 1965, pp. xi–xxx.

Tiessen, Paul. "Malcolm Lowry and the Cinema." *Malcolm Lowry: The Man and his Work*, edited by George Woodcock, Vancouver: U British Columbia P, 1971, pp. 133–143.

Woolf, Virginia. *To the Lighthouse.* 1927. London: Flamingo, 1997.

Žižek, Slavoj. *Enjoy Your Symptom*. 1992. London: Routledge, 2001.

——. "'I Hear You With My Eyes': or, The Invisible Master." *Gaze and Voice as Love Objects*, edited by Renata Salecl and Slavoj Žižek, Durham, NC: Duke UP, 1996, pp. 90–126.

——. *Looking Awry: An Introduction to Jacques Lacan through Popular Culture*. Cambridge, MA: MIT P, 1992.

——. *Organs Without Bodies: On Deleuze and Consequences*. London: Routledge, 2004.

III

Charting the Human Landscape

11

From Liverpool to Eridanus in the Twinkling of an Eye

ANNICK DRÖSDAL-LEVILLAIN

"We meet our destiny on the road we take to avoid it"[1]

Malcolm Lowry left Liverpool swearing never to return. Yet, though physically he never did return to the city of his birth, he did so repeatedly in his writing. Liverpool appears in most of Lowry's texts, as if he had been attempting to write himself back to the city, akin to Sigbjørn Wilderness in "Through the Panama": "But I never came back. Nevertheless I wrote, regularly, which was more than I did for myself very often" (Lowry, *Hear* 69).[2] Or was it Liverpool that kept returning to him? In this essay, I explore the extent to which Lowry's childhood Mersey, identified by Muriel Bradbrook as the *Maternal Eden* (Bradbrook 108), informs and haunts Lowry's fiction. After a topographic and historical survey, I offer a glimpse of Lowry's *soulscape* as it coalesces with the landscapes of his British Columbian paradise of Dollarton/Eridanus, with a special focus on the structural motifs marking Lowry's multilayered soulscape, where bells and stars guide the reader on the path through locks and dams, passing Bakhtinian whirlpools, where time and space flicker, slide, and overlap along the watery ways of Lowry's silted ex-centered oceanic northwestern prose.

FROM TOPOGRAPHY TO SOULSCAPE

The topographic resemblance between Liverpool and Vancouver[3] is the first striking element that must be considered with a few typically Lowryan scale arrangements: both are major port cities, ex-centered at the edge of a continent, situated by an ocean that provides a vital link with the rest of the world. Vancouver was put on the map in 1886, when it was chosen as the western terminus for the Canadian Pacific Railway, and thus got its place on the symbolic "All Red Line," a telegraph cable line linking London to the major ports of the British Empire. For its part, the Liverpool–Manchester railway, one of the first in Great Britain, was inaugurated in 1831, and Liverpool was a major British port on the Atlantic throughout the eighteenth and nineteenth centuries, serving the slave trade as well as several waves of European emigration to America. Both cities, then, have been connected with major national and global ventures, and have been deeply implicated with the history of the Atlantic slave trade and the exploitation of native Americans. Both were, in addition, centres of adventurous engineering if we consider the technical feats necessary to cross the peat bogs north of Liverpool and, even more dauntingly, cut through the Rocky Mountains to reach Vancouver. Vancouver and Liverpool, both dubbed "Empire City" at different times, have been historically important metropolitan centres, as they have also each been home to the most economically impoverished neighbourhoods in Canada and Europe, respectively. Lowry hints at the Liverpool–Vancouver connection when he refers to Vancouver as "Gaspool" ("The Bravest Boat," *Hear* 11)—in which we can hear the merging of Gastown, Vancouver's historic downtown, and Liverpool. As a Liverpudlian in self-exile, Lowry carried to Vancouver the memory of the city of his birth. I will focus here on how Lowry managed to transpose the Liverpool–Wirral topography to the Vancouver–Dollarton–Eridanus topoi.

Dollarton/Eridanus echoes in several ways the Wirral Peninsula, where Lowry grew up. Both places face an estuary with impressive tidal flats, and the majestic mountains north of Dollarton can be seen as a "transoceanic" magnified echo of the Welsh Clwydian Range to the south of the Wirrall Peninsula. Both places are ex-centered from the hellish "city Moloch" ("The Bravest Boat"), out of direct sight and at least partly separated from the mainland by sea. Rock Ferry station, Birkenhead, is where Wilderness remembers last seeing his mother in "Through the Panama" (*Hear* 69). This paradoxical edgy combination of ex-centeredness and connection to the world perfectly suited Lowry who, we may say, was an exile all his life, and perhaps never more acutely so than in England. The sight of ships coming and going on Burrard Inlet, "cargoed with obscenities toward death" ("Forest Path," *Hear* 231), while the Second World War raged elsewhere, is likely to have reminded Lowry of the intense traffic on the Mersey during the First World War—he was then between five and nine years old and Liverpool was heavily involved due to its port. That traffic also carried the threat of separation—"And would the war separate us?" ("Forest Path," *Hear* 231). This fear, initially of separation, later of eviction, would actually fuel much of Lowry's writing during his years in Dollarton and act as a sacred bond, not only between him and his wife, but also between him and the world; writing becoming Lowry's way of coping with his symptom,[4] of covering the rent, and coming to terms with the real. Lowry's eldest brother, Stuart, recalls him wishing he had a hook instead of a hand (Bowker 15); luckily, his wish came true in the form not of a hook but of a pen that would allow him to reach out to both the world and himself.

If, for Lowry, Vancouver is a hellish sight appropriately announced by the missing "S" of the Shell neon sign above the oil refinery across the inlet from the narrator's shack in "The Forest Path to the Spring," then Liverpool hosts a likewise infernal memory of the Museum of Anatomy, on Paradise Street, where Lowry caught sight of "the famous pickled testicles" (Bowker 40), acquiring the consequent fear of venereal disease that never quite left him. As so often with Lowry, the coincidence is striking when one considers his fear of syphilis in the context of the devastation it, a European disease, had caused among the Aboriginal population in British Columbia a century earlier.

ON THE BELL-PROTEUS PATH[5]

Liverpool functions like a beacon, signalling the author's origins, carefully inscribed in most stories of the collection *Hear Us O Lord from Heaven Thy Dwelling Place*, not unlike the inscription we read on the stern of the "wrecked steamer of the defunct Astra line that gave it its name . . . *Eridanus, Liverpool*" ("Forest Path," *Hear* 226). References to Liverpool in the collection are generally brief, cynical, and contrapuntal, as if the city could not be evoked or looked at directly, but must instead be glimpsed from an impersonal, derisive, twisted angle, pointing at the necessity for separation, a detachment that seems to have a tempering effect even on the hellish refinery, which is "softened and rendered beautiful by distance" (Lowry, *Volcano* 82). Liverpool turns out to be Lowry's archetypal city, that by which other cities are measured, and each evocation of Liverpool resounds in a deeply private vibration, revealing Lowry's love–hate relationship with his place of birth. His poem "Iron Cities" features the transformational process at work in the invisible, unspoken depths of human psyche: "Iron thoughts sail from the iron cities in the dust, / Yet soft as doves the thoughts that fly back home" (*Selected Poems* 15).

A discreet homage to Liverpool is paid in "Through the Panama" when the narrator points out the exception of Liverpool for its "enormous sense of sea and ships" ("Panama," *Hear* 68), as if Lowry were reticent to recognize his love for "that terrible city whose mainstreet is the ocean" ("Forest Path," *Hear* 226). Similarly, the dunes surrounding the canal remind him of the "dunes at Hoylake, only infinitely more desolate" ("Panama," *Hear* 68). Liverpool vacillates flickeringly between presence and absence, signalling in the dark like "that lamp of love" ("Forest Path," *Hear* 279) lighting the window of the shack in the night. Stars were all the more important for Lowry given that during his years in Dollarton/Eridanus, he lived, so to speak, under the stars he so much enjoyed watching and integrating into his prose. Indeed, stars (Greek: *astēr*) are omnipresent in "The Forest Path to the Spring"; they shimmer and glitter through a wide range of signifiers scattered throughout the text: wild *asters* growing near the shack; the name of the shipping line, *Astra*, itself based in Liverpool; *Astrid's* very name in "The Bravest Boat"; and numerous direct references to the constellations, not least of course Eridanus itself. Lowry's early biography reveals the emergence of the star motif that probably acted as a beacon for the three-year-old Lowry, fond of "Twinkle, Twinkle, Little Star." In a birthday letter to Lowry, his beloved nanny, Miss Bell, recalling his singing that song to her (Bowker 10), remembered the "dear little baby with a brown face and blue eyes [who sang] 'Twinkle, Twinkle Little Star'" (Bowker 40). This must have been all the more traumatic to the child, given that Miss Bell had left the family to seek employment on a cruise liner just a few short months prior to Lowry's third birthday.[6] That stars are associated with both happy times and separation from Miss Bell, the substitute for an inadequate mother, suggests that stars and bells had strong emotional resonance for Lowry. This hypothesis finds textual support first in an apparently passing remark concerning the name of one of the inhabitants of Eridanus in "The Forest Path to the Spring": "Bell's name had no meaning that I knew of" (258). Yet the reader may also hear a faint voice humming, "I miss Bell," as if Lowry were pointing toward something ever missing, the gap left by the loss of love and pleasure known in youth. Bells and stars might be considered as traces of what Lacan called *lalangue*, that little language made of the remnants of the subject's entrance into language, the emergence of which is often connected with nursery rhymes, but also puns, narrative breaks, and repetitions. Was "Frère Jacques" another of those happy-days songs? Emergences of *lalangue* point at the loss of an unattainable jouissance, and result in a blind spot signalled by linguistic, narrative, and lexical devices accommodating a special occurrence of a voice that transcends all other voices.

HAUNTING THE "GUTTED ARCADES OF THE PAST"

The final, equally painful separation from Miss Bell took place when Lowry went to school. He developed "chronic chilblains" (Bowker 19) and was given electrical treatment for his swollen fingers. He was then five, and this is also when he learnt to write. It is worth noting that from very early on writing was Lowry's way of making friendships, so that it became his passport to the school community and, later, as a published author, to the world. Could his swollen, cracked fingers be the unconscious response of the little boy trying to reach out toward the loved one but not succeeding for lack of big enough hands? Other physical symptoms such as constipation echo on a symbolic level with his difficulty to release the

object of desire, reverting to endless revisions of his manuscripts. Quite significantly, about a year before his death, Lowry was diagnosed with Hirschsprung
disease (Bowker 583), causing intestinal obstruction, which provided him with
a plausible explanation for his alcoholic drive. Lowry called this deformation of
the bowel "the great empty hall" (583). Indeed, the hall could never be filled,
and the object of desire would be ever missing, out of reach, out of sight, too,
hence the ulceration of the cornea. Incidentally, Lowry considered himself an
eyesore to his parents, his schoolmates, and, later, by identification with his
shack, to the residents of Vancouver threatening to pull down the "eyesores" on
the beach ("Forest Path," *Hear* 277). Although Hirschsprung disease is named
after its discoverer, its literal meaning—the deer's spring—can be added to the
eerie coincidences jotting Lowry's life and fiction, since it takes us back to the
end of "The Forest Path to the Spring." Could this be a "dirty trick" of the unconscious? Or what Lacan called a *trait d'esprit* carved out in the body of the writer and
his work?

It seems that Lowry's *bodyscape* cried out after the lost object all his life. No
wonder that Lowry could not finish or deliver his manuscripts. "Know thyself,"
said the sign at the Liverpool Museum of Anatomy, and Lowry took note of it
(Bowker 40); but that personal, singular knowledge has to be processed into something universal that not only makes sense for the artist, but rings with the community of readers, because we all walk around with our symptom and struggle with it
in our own singular way. Artists are both gifted with the ability and burdened with
the ordeal to pass their mysterious knowledge on to the world. The creative act of
writing enabled Lowry to "haunt the gutted arcades of the past" (Lowry, *Collected
Poetry* 185) and reach out to the "high forgotten shelf," which might figure the
unconscious. That s(h)elf is the radiating spot which, as soon as it is attained,
slides from the horizontal plane to the vertical of the "mast . . . where one sways
crucified twixt two of me" (185). In this movement from horizontality to vertical-
ity, the poem shifts from shelf to self and invites readers to explore the layers of
meaning of a stratified text unfolding in time and space.

MISSED ENCOUNTERS

Lowry knew something about missed encounters, the most striking one being
his father's death before he completed the publication manuscript of *Under the
Volcano*. This is made clear in "Elephant and Colosseum": "Ah, this was what
hurt, that his 'making good' *had come too late*; his father was dead, his mother
was dead" ("Elephant," *Hear* 141–42; emphasis added). Repeatedly missed
encounters point at what Lacan called "neurosis of destiny,"[7] which sounds

quite likely, considering Lowry's "disastar"-paved path.[8] This may be what the inscription on the mirror of the weighing machine in "The Bravest Boat" is hinting at: "*Your weight and your destiny*" (*Hear* 13). Is Lowry's destiny inscribed in the American writer's name—Sigbjørn Wilderness—in "Strange Comfort"? The following explodes the narration into free indirect discourse: "Sigbjørn Wilderness! The very sound of his name was like a bell-buoy—more euphoniously a light-ship—broken adrift, and washing in from the Atlantic on a reef" ("Strange Comfort," *Hear* 102)—as if signifiers were like bell buoys, both ringing to the ear and catching the eye with their glitter. Or could we also hear "bell boy," and by association the emblematic "Frère Jacques" rhythmic theme? This would then be another interesting occurrence of *lalangue* where the bell and star motives are intertwined among the debris of the past, which Lowry has woven into his prose to become part of his chiming, twinkling, ringing style, finally celebrating "some great spiritual victory of mankind" ("Forest Path," *Hear* 280) and echoing Lowry's own spiritual progress, however chaotic it may have been.

Lowry had undoubtedly found the right place to live, with Eridanus aptly located at the edge of a world he visited from time to time, like Roderick McGregor Fairhaven, "the visitor from Ultima Thule" ("Pompeii," *Hear* 200), touring Italy with his wife. Lowry's territory is the edge in all senses of the word, and his task is to explore its contours and depths at the risk of being engulfed. Eridanus functions as a remote twin far in the horizon of Liverpool, or to put it in Michel Foucault's term, a "heterotopia," questioning the places where we live. This is a place that can be likened to an attic, a children's hut in the backyard, or the "monastic cells" ("Forest Path," *Hear* 217) at the back of the fishermen's shacks. It is a place that enables the subject to both evade the outside world and explore it from within: "And that was where he should be now—not in Paris or Naples or Rome, in Eridanus, reading, correcting papers and taking notes in the long summer twilight . . . watching the constellations" ("Pompeii," *Hear* 179–80). Lowry had an intimate connection with the cosmos and the forces it exerts through natural phenomena such as the tides and volcanoes, which can be read as a figuration of his inner turmoil reflecting the chaos outside. In "The Forest Path," the narrator can "hear the very underlying beat of the universe itself," and concludes that "no matter how grotesque the manner in which my inspiration proposed to work through me, I had something original to express" (270).

IN A FLICKER AND A SLIDE

Watching the ruins is, for Roderick in "Pompeii," "as if you could hear your own real life plunging to its doom" (*Hear* 177), and one may say that Lowry knew how to plunge, both literally and figuratively, showing great coherence between life and style. Lowry had a cinematographic perception of reality that made him plunge through different layers of reality in a slide and a flicker as, for example, when Roderick indulges in a stream-of-consciousness-like excursion to the ruins of Pompeii. In the twinkling of an eye, Lowry takes us from the ruins of Pompeii to those of post-war Liverpool and to the imaginary ruins of Vancouver:

> There was no one else in the city of Pompeii (which at first sight had looked to him a bit like the ruins of Liverpool on a Sunday afternoon: or supposing it to have suffered another, latter-day catastrophe since the Great Fire of 1886,[9] Vancouver itself—a few stock exchange pillars, factory chimneys, the remnants of the Bank of Montreal), just the guide. (183–84)

The reader is made to shift from one space to the other as if he were actually looking through the Pompeii stereopticon Tansy remembers having belonged to her grandmother. Time having passed, the reader flicks and slides through time and space, from the delights of Pompeii to the ruins of modernity embodied by the two cities of the northwest Atlantic and Pacific, Liverpool and Vancouver. Then, at the sight of the "ruined brothels" (191) of Pompeii, doubled by the guide's insistence on "clap" (195), Roderick inwardly flies into a rage—"How he loathed Pompeii!"—before imaginarily flooding "some Pacific Northwestern city," Vancouver, to relish yet another ironic description of modern ruins, as if his watering mouth itself had provoked the flood:

> Nonetheless Roderick found himself suddenly hating this street with an inexplicable virulence. How he loathed Pompeii! His mouth positively watered with his hatred. Roderick was almost prancing. It seemed to him, now that it was as though, by some perverse grace, out of the total inundation of some Pacific northwestern city, had been preserved a bit of the station hotel, a section of the gasworks. (192)

The story could have ended in a click with Roderick taking a snapshot of the witty guide erected in a Roman salute; but the guide has the last word as he mentions Vesuvius' last eruption: "'yesterday she give-a the beeg-a shake!'" (201)

LOCKS, DOCKS, AND CLOCKS

Growing up in the Wirral, where waterways and engineering were so predominant, is likely to have left some trace on Lowry. In "Through the Panama,"

Wilderness declares himself "hereditarily disposed in favor of canals in general, while in short loving them—any child could figure one out, indeed it is the first piece of engineering a child does figure out" ("Panama," *Hear* 58). With this in mind, we may consider *Hear Us O Lord* as a system of locks, since in each story "you are *locked*, as Primrose says, as it were, in an experience" (57; emphasis added). Not only have canals and locks left an imprint in Lowry's silted prose, they have also woven themselves into his style and method of composition, which is characterized by a finely chiselled compilation of all sorts of debris of life and language, to be sifted to silt in the creative process of writing, as announced in the poem "Peter Gaunt and the canals" (*Collected Poetry* 191–92). Lowry reshapes Ibsen's famous hero Peer Gynt as "Peter Gaunt," who also dreams of cutting a canal—the "canal that lives in mankind's dream"—leading from "Liverpool to Canaan via Manchester" or "Liverpool to Manchester via Runcorn," and "If, remembering Panama, he says Mersey," the poem tells us, "The silted truth is also dredgeable, / It is this man's empowered to reclaim / For man. It is a canal in mind. And it is for himself" (*Collected Poetry* 52–53). These lines encapsulate Lowry's artistic gesture of cutting a canal through an ocean of stories linking up his original Mersey and the fictional Eridanus rivers.

The lock metaphor in Lowry's work at large may be more central than it seems at first sight. It lurks in the background, taking different forms. Nothing is fixed in Lowry's prose; all is subject to metamorphosis and anamorphosis combined with reminiscences verging on hallucination, as if poised between delirium tremens and "delirium Clemens" ("Panama" *Hear* 73). The transillumination scene in "The Forest Path" (*Hear* 272) might read as an instance of "delirium Clarence" if we follow Lowry's invitation to unchain the signified and enter the free play of the signifier. We are nearing poetry as the ever-renewed experience of all the senses of space, the permanent anamorphosis of "all the possible landscapes" (Loubier 55).

Locks also appear in *Under the Volcano* as Laruelle remembers "Saint Près, the sleepy French village of *backwaters and locks* [emphasis added] and grey disused watermills"—from where he caught his first "chronotopic" sight of Chartres:

> Rising slowly and wonderfully and with boundless beauty above the stubble fields blowing with wild flowers, slowly rising into the sunlight, as centuries before the pilgrims straying over those same fields had watched them rise, the twin spires of Chartres Cathedral. (Lowry, *Volcano* 58)

In a letter to Jan, Lowry wrote that he had found the perfect place for them to live, in the Hotel du Pont in Saint-Prest. If we half shut our eyes, as Lowry liked to do,[10] we can travel from Saint Près/Saint-Prest[11] to Dollarton, with the tides replacing the locks and the Shell refinery standing for the Chartres Cathedral, or even look back to the Liverpool canals and locks. Lowry's inherited disposition "in favor of canals in general" ("Panama," *Hear* 58)—possibly locks—is also alluded to in "Elephant and Colosseum":

> My great-great grandfather Cronkbane was not only a poet but a successful inventor and engineer. . . . He surveyed the Isthmus of Panama and submitted to the United States, in 1855, *a scheme for a canal without locks*, for he was first to assert that *the Atlantic and Pacific Oceans were on a level*. . . . Cronkbane's poetry is admittedly rugged, but it is vigorous. ("Elephant," *Hear* 151; emphasis added)

Sigbjørn Wilderness successively compares the Panama Canal lock system to a "ghastly image of the modern world," then to "—something like a novel" ("Panama," *Hear* 60), and finally to a "celestial meccano" (61), as if the reader were invited to scale up and down the metaphoric layers of interpretation. Indeed, the narrative structure of "Through the Panama" features a main text paralleled by marginalia. Due to this dual design, the reader has to glide from one narrative to the other, from one level to the other in a constant movement of adaptation, to bring the two narratives to level and link them up, *lockwise*, so that the reader himself is penetrated by the lock motif.

Devised to raise and lower boats between stretches of water of different levels, locks act as regulators of the tension between water masses, and if we extrapolate, we can read them as a metaphor of Lowry's artistic gesture, balancing the individual and the universal, as if Lowry were attempting to bring two dimensions, two oceans, to level through the "canal that lives in mankind's dream" (*Collected Poetry* 152). In this gesture, Lowry wrestles with the universal dimension embodied by the ocean, to bring it to the singular, individual level figured by the floor of the endangered shack: "In the great high tides of winter, with the Pacific almost level with our floor, the house itself could be in jeopardy" ("Forest Path," *Hear* 235). If we step back and look at the tides from a distance, they can read as cosmic locks activated by the attraction of the sun and the moon on all liquids. Likewise, volcanoes participate in this motif as regulating outlets for the telluric energy built up along the fire belt. More domestic and on a much smaller scale, but quite effective, is the basket being lowered from a window in Naples to fetch some wine, and figuring in Roderick's eyes what voyaging should be—"the spiritual nourishment of one's voyaging" ("Pompeii," *Hear* 188)—which is being "jerkingly" dredged from the ruins of the past: "And that was what travel was supposed to be, thought Roderick, like that basket that is lowered down into the past, and is brought back again, safely through one's window, filled with the spiritual nourishment of one's voyaging" (188).

Finally, the Pompeian guide's commentary points at the "Porta Marina," which is "built like a funnel, for a ventilation, to suck up fresh air from the sea, blowing up to the mountain and ventilate town" (201)—an Aeolian lock system based on the principles of levity and gravity forces, amidst which the poet/engineer has to find a point of equilibrium foreshadowed by one of those mythical fictional ancestors—Cosnahan's great-great grandfather—who designed a "canal without locks," and whose poetry is "rugged, but . . . vigorous" ("Elephant," *Hear* 151). If great-great grandfather Cronkbane's poetry is rugged and vigorous, Lowry's is "subaqueous and barnacly" (*Selected Letters* 172), like the poem he imagined his "Crazy Wonder" of a pier might have been reciting to itself, its "simplicity, lightness, and freedom from top to hamper" (*Selected Letters* 305), giving it the elasticity necessary to withstand the winter tides and storms.

The lock motif embodies Lowry's wrestling as a poet/engineer of the edge, testing the elasticity of language, for example, turning the slopes of Vesuvius into a gigantic lighter as Fairhaven lights a cigarette "by placing it into the earth . . . to bring him luck" ("Pompeii," *Hear* 186), or in a bang, transforming the Shell refinery into an erupting Vesuvius, rescued by a fire-boat first heard "neighing like a horse" (197), then sighted as a "urinating dinosaur" in Fairhaven's cartoon-like "medieval but supermodern fantasy." The narrator *springs* from one dimension to another, from reality to fable, sensing confusion:

> An *uneasy* feeling for a moment, like seeing one of those grotesque films in which they use animated cartoons with real figures, a *mixture of two forms.* . . . And yet did the *confusion* come from *pinning the labels of one dimension on another? Or were they inextricable?* ("Forest Path," *Hear* 258; emphasis added)

Dimensions tend to overlap and thus create a blurred zone, where both narrator and reader have to grope their way toward a "sensitive chaos."[12]

A SENSITIVE CHAOS

"Please help me to order [this chaos] or I am lost," exclaims the narrator of "The Forest Path to the Spring" (*Hear* 269). Water turns out to be the key to this "inextricable confusion" so that it can become a "sensitive chaos" (Novalis). For Lowry—or should we perhaps call him Proteus?—water was a cure in the form of a dive and a swim in the sea when he did not resort to its fiery version—alcohol. Even in the middle of February, a dive in ice-cold Burrard Inlet was Lowry's response to the news of his father's death,[13] as if it could make him whole again in a healing holy process of connection with a supra-individual centre defined by Jung as a paradoxical quintessence of the individual and the collective (Adler 184). The common etymology of *heal*, *holy*, and *whole* may be an instance of language embodying the underlying truth that when one is healed, one is whole again (Adler 183–84). Or perhaps it was Lowry's way of coming to terms with reality, of putting out the fire that was consuming him and pursuing him in the form of a repetition of disasters, which might have been his unconscious way of saying "Look father, can't you see, I'm burning!" (Lacan 83)—ever missing the encounter and quenching his burning thirst in a dive.

On several occasions in *Hear Us O Lord*, Lowry mentions his love of fountains, brooks, and springs and even the magic power of "holy water" ("Elephant" 130). If we consider Lowry's fascination for the movements of the tides, light reflecting on water, the dance of seabirds, wild flowers, the stars in connection with the idea that water functions as an intermezzo[14] between heaven and earth, between the earthly and the cosmic realm, it is possible to venture that he instinctively turned toward this healing element as he developed a liquid style emerging from his overlapping, whirlpool method of composition.

Lowry expressed a metaphysical if not mystic intuition that, as Wilderness says in "Through the Panama," "life draws . . . strength from the depths among the stars, from the great world!" ("Panama," *Hear* 35). The transillumination scene in "The Forest Path" (*Hear* 272), where the narrator becomes the inlet, is one instance of fusion between the elements, as air, light, and water merge in a spiritual rebirth following the vanishing of the subject. Water seems to flow into Lowry's prose, while the narrator/protagonist of "The Forest Path" gives us a bird's-eye view of his Woolfian *moment of being*:

> It is as if I saw those thoughts at a distance, as if below me. In one sense I did not see them but heard them, they flowed, they were like a river, an inlet, they comprised a whole project impossible to recapture or pin down. Nonetheless those thoughts, and they were abysmal, not happy as I would have wished, made me happy in that, though they were in motion, they were in order too. (268)

Water acts as the opener of eye and ear to the mysterious links between the living and the cosmos,[15] and Lowry was looking and listening through that window provided by the Dollarton/Eridanus topoi. After all, wasn't Cosnahan a "water-diviner," whose powers "since his book's publication . . . had been falling off" ("Elephant," *Hear* 127)? Wasn't Proteus a "prophetic sea-god in the service of Poseidon [who] when seized . . . would assume different shapes" ("Forest Path," *Hear* 258)? Wasn't Lowry a swinging singer, swimmer,[16] sinner, and writer poised on the edge of eternity?

NOTES

1. British film director Terence Davies quotes Carl Jung in *Of Time and the City* (*Of Time and the City*, dir. Terrence Davies, DVD, Hurricane Films, 2008). At the end of the documentary film, Davies adds that "We love the place we hate, then hate the place we love. We leave the place we love, then spend a lifetime trying to regain it." The film portrays Davies' Liverpool from 1945 to 1973. As such, it briefly overlaps with Lowry's time away from Liverpool and stages the filmmaker's paradoxical relationship to the city through the use of archival material and a voice invoking T.S. Eliot, Joyce, and a few others, but not Lowry, whose "voice," in my eyes, is cruelly missing.

2. Page references to "Through the Panama," "The Bravest Boat," "Strange Comfort Afforded by the Profession," "Elephant and Colosseum," "Present Estate of Pompeii," and "The Forest Path to the Spring" are cited from Lowry, *Hear Us O Lord from Heaven Thy Dwelling Place*.

3. "The great mountains of Indian Arm, closing the Canadian scene on the other side, are perhaps no grander than to a child's imagination had seemed the Clwyd range" (Bradbrook 35).

4. Jacques Lacan defines the symptom as that lost *enjoyment* that has created an unquenchable thirst for the lost object, and which comes back to us in a *cyphered message*.

5. The forest path was called "the Bell-Proteus path" after Bell, one of the inhabitants of Eridanus, who helped cut the path ("Forest Path," *Hear* 257–58).

6. "Trauma struck when the nanny, thinking to better herself, took a job as a stewardess on a cruise liner, and departed suddenly in April 1912, when Malcolm was three months short of his third birthday" (Bowker 10). Miss Bell's birthday letter in fact led to her being reemployed by the Lowrys.

7. Which, according to Lacan, is characterized by a pattern of failure, disaster, and decay resulting from an unconscious desire of self-punishment on the part of the subject. He also links this pattern to repeated failed encounter, or *tuché* (Lacan 81).

8. "I told my father in 1934 that there would be a war in the autumn of 1939, & he replied: 'What kind of a son are you to tell his father & mother that the world is hurling to disastar?'" Letter to Margerie, Vancouver, September 1939 (*Sursum* 1:233). That Lowry punned on his father's pronunciation of the word "disaster" and transcribed it may signal the importance of the disaster pattern and its connection with the father figure. For more on Lowry and disaster, see Drösdal-Levillain (113).

9. The fire, which destroyed much of the newly incorporated city of Vancouver, occurred two weeks after the creation of the Vancouver fire brigade.

10. Looking at the Lake-District scenery through half-shut eyes, "they could imagine they were back on Burrard Inlet" (Bowker 597).
11. Lowry spelled it "St Prést" (Sursum 1:152).
12. Sensitive chaos is central to Novalis'romantic view of a chaotic world order.
13. Upon the news, he "fell silent for a few minutes, then said, 'Let's go for a swim,' and promptly plunged into the ice-cold waters of Burrard Inlet" (Bowker 331–32).
14. The sunken canoe is named Intermezzo ("The Forest Path," Hear 231).
15. Schwenk on the movements of water and their relationship with the cosmos: "Through watching water and air with unprejudiced eyes, our way of thinking becomes changed and more suited to the understanding of what is alive" (Schwenk 11).
16. Lowry enjoyed the analogy between him and the salmon, a British Columbia emblematic figure celebrated by the local Haida Aboriginal people throughout the ages. What is striking in this analogy is that the salmon is a fish known to be deeply influenced by the cosmic events of the spring equinotical tides, which mark the precise moment when the salmon spawn on northwest pacific shores (see Schwenk 69). Keeping in mind Lowry's links with Norway, another salmon-producing country, and one bearing many resemblances with British Columbia, one can but wonder at the convergence of details linking Lowry to Dollarton/Eridanus, of all places on the Earth.

WORKS CITED

Adler, Gerhard. Études de Psychologie Jungienne. 1948. Genève: Librairie de l'Université, Georg & Cie, 1957.

Bowker, Gordon. Pursued by Furies: a life of Malcolm Lowry. New York: Saint Martin's P, 1993.

Bradbrook, Muriel. Malcolm Lowry, His Art and Early Life: A Study in Transformation. Cambridge: Cambridge UP, 1974.

Drösdal-Levillain, Annick. "'Eridanus, Liverpool': Echoes and Transformations at the Edge of Eternity." Malcolm Lowry: from the Mersey to the world, edited by Bryan Biggs and Helen Tookey, Liverpool: Liverpool UP, 2009.

Lacan, Jacques. Les Quatre Concepts Fondamentaux de la Psychanalyse. Paris: Seuil, 1973.

Loubier, Pierre. Le Poète au Labyrinthe. Ville, Errance, Écriture. Fontenay/Saint-Cloud: ENS Edition, 1998.

Lowry, Malcolm. The Collected Poetry of Malcolm Lowry. Edited by Kathleen Scherf, Vancouver: U of British Columbia P, 1992.

——. Hear Us O Lord from Heaven Thy Dwelling Place. New York: Carroll & Graf, 1961.

——. Selected Letters. Edited by Harvey Breit and Margerie Bonner Lowry, Philadelphia: Lippincot, 1965.

——. Selected Poems of Malcolm Lowry. Edited by Earle Birney, San Francisco: City Lights Books, 1962.

——. *Sursum Corda!: The Collected Letters of Malcolm Lowry*. Edited by Sherrill E. Grace, vol. 1, 1926–1946, Toronto: U of Toronto P, 1995.

——. *Under the Volcano*. 1947. London: Jonathan Cape, 1985.

Schwenk, Theodor. *Sensitive Chaos: the Creation of Flowing Forms in Water and Air*. 1962. East Sussex, UK: Rudolf Steiner P, 1996.

12

Outgrowing the Alienating Inscape?
The Voyage Out in October Ferry to Gabriola

PIERRE SCHAEFFER

Referring to his indomitable literary daemon, Malcolm Lowry wrote in a June 1953 letter to his editor, Albert Erskine, "In Gabriola he has turned out what set out to be an innocent & beautiful story of human longing into quite one of the most guilt-laden & in places quite Satanically horrendous documents it has ever been my unfortunate lot to read, let alone have to imagine I wrote" (Lowry, Sursum 2:664). Here, in a nutshell, Lowry delineated the evolution of his most ambitious work-in-progress since the publication of Under the Volcano in 1947, which would become his second posthumously published novel, October Ferry to Gabriola.[1] Somehow, his autobiographical story of a bus trip from Victoria to Nanaimo that he and his wife, Margerie, undertook in October 1946, in order to catch an outward bound ferry to the British Columbia Gulf Island of Gabriola, had got out of hand and was well on its way to becoming a formidable, autonomous behemoth, ill fitted for inclusion, as had initially been planned, in the Hear Us O Lord from Heaven Thy Dwelling Place collection of stories.[2]

The plot of the story seems straightforward: a semi-retired criminal lawyer, Ethan Llewelyn, and his wife, Jacqueline, have set out on the aforesaid bus trip with a view to catching a ferry to Gabriola while a threat of eviction from their little foreshore cabin in Eridanus on Burrard Inlet hangs over their heads. The quest for a new "paradise" is thus the main reason for the trip, and the skeleton of the story, which covers a single day, October 7, 1949, comprises three parts dealing, successively, with the bus trip to Nanaimo (chapters 1 to 27), the arrival in Nanaimo and the search for a ferry to Gabriola (chapters 28 to 32), and the sea crossing itself (the last five chapters). But this deceptively simple outline does not reflect the complexity of the novel.

The text becomes indeed truly "Satanic," to use Lowry's own coinage, on account of the overwhelming and paralyzing presence of the past manifesting itself through two major sources of torment coalescing in Ethan's mind: the recent threat of eviction from Eridanus and the constantly rekindled sense of personal and professional guilt caused, respectively, by his involvement in the suicide (by hanging) of a university friend in England[3] and by his hitherto non-interventionist attitude in a serious criminal case involving an adolescent sentenced to die by hanging. Thus, if on the one hand the narrative is expected to propel the characters forward toward the future and a new space, Gabriola, another force, the backward and inward pull of the past, as relived, slows down the completion of the initial quest, both literally (for the characters) and syntagmatically (for the reader).[4] The author sums up his characters' difficulties in the following terms:

> Thus the difficulty of the future taking any shape at all, as of the present having any meaning for the protagonists, is really the whole plot. They have more trouble getting to Gabriola than K to the castle though Gabriola is not a castellan symbol; it *is*, finally, the future. (*Sursum* 2:697)

It remains to be seen whether Ethan's nightmarish *inscape*[5] will finally be outgrown and whether the *landscape* of the future will materialise in a convincing way. In other words, will time and space past give way to a forward-looking dynamics in this unusual "road novel," this journey narrative? Prior to answering these questions, this chapter will re-examine the aetiology of Ethan Llewelyn's self-envisioned "damnation."

TYING THE KNOTS OF CULPABILITY AND DESPAIR

From the outset, the novel strikes a melancholic note. Although we have not yet been introduced to the filtering consciousness of the narrative, the first three italicized lines already impart a feeling of sadness and melancholy:

> *Farewell, Farewell, Farewell, Eight Bells, Wywurk, The Wicket Gate. The little house looked all right. So we love forever, taking leave.* (OFG 3)

What reads like a leap from "The Forest Path to the Spring," with its reference to the novella's place names,[6] to a *Great Gatsby*–like nostalgic conclusion[7] is also indicative of the general direction of at least the first part of the novel: we shall indeed be "borne back ceaselessly into the past." Another textual metaphor of this journey into memory appears a little further down in the description of the foliage reflected in the rear-view mirror of the Greyhound in which the Llewelyns are passengers:

At times, when the Greyhound overtook and passed another car, where the road was narrow, the branches of the trees brushed the left-hand windows, and behind, or *in the rearview mirror ahead reflecting the road endlessly enfilading in reverse*, the foliage could be seen tossing for a while in a troubled gale at their passage. (OFG 3; emphasis added)

The mirror motif inaugurated on the first page of the first chapter is seminal in the organization of the novel: a number of sequences from the text will feature mirror reflections as moments of dramatically acute self-awareness for Ethan. However, in the present case, it is the very nature of the narrative that is thus tangentially conveyed: a story repetitively "enfilading in reverse," which stubbornly seems to go every so often à *rebours*, that is, in the wrong direction, or at least in the opposite direction to the one taken by the bus and to that which is indicated by the title: *to Gabriola*.

The bus journey from Victoria to Nanaimo is only a few hours in length but accounts for two-thirds of the narrative. During that trip, Ethan travels into the past and takes stock of the various ordeals that he has had to undergo. These chapters are supposed to be read as Ethan's mostly silent and unshared reminiscences about the past, and are geared toward explaining the psychological frame of mind of the protagonist. By showing the vice-like grip of the guilt-laden past on Ethan's conscience, they are also meant to prepare the reader for the dramatic climax in the second part. Thus, during the bus trip, Ethan looks back upon the time when he first met Jacqueline (chapters 2 to 9), then upon his early married life (shortly interrupted by Ethan's intelligence-service posting in Europe during the Second World War) and his return to Niagara-on-the Lake, Ontario, where the accidental fire that causes the family house to go up in flames also kindles Ethan's paranoia and hastens, along with professional frustrations, the Llewelyns' departure for British Columbia (chapters 12 to 21). The last six chapters of part one (22 to 27) deal with the "Eridanus" pastoral, which is soon upset by the threats of eviction, followed by a short stay in Vancouver, where a "soul-destroying ugliness" betokening the ills of modern civilization prevails (OFG 177). The interest of these chapters lies not so much in the avalanche of events and disasters that bedevil the Llewelyns as in the way everything is shown to be diabolically interrelated. Ethan sees himself as being "actually damned" or "under a curse" or "even mad" (OFG 107). Now, damnation, persecution, or madness requires a certain pattern of inescapability, a tracery of fiendish signs or crazy coincidences. As a soul writhing in anguish and paranoia, Ethan is adept at providing such manifestations of the supernatural, subnormal, or uncanny in order to prove his point.

Interestingly, this dramatization of Ethan's life can be traced back to the way he describes his experience at the cinema with Jacqueline during the year or two preceding their marriage: it enhances reality for him and makes him see life differently.

> It was like *deducing the real from the unreal.* It was as though the moonlight falling through the trees on the screen inside the theatre, by the transpiercing beauty of the manner in which it was perceived and photographed, *gave the remembered moonlight of the world outside a loveliness it had never before possessed for him,* nay, gave the earth, life itself, for him, another possible beauty, a new reality somehow undreamed-of heretofore. (OFG 16; emphasis added)

In this excerpt, the impact of fiction on reality is described in positive, almost euphoric terms. What matters most, however, is the kind of cinematic awareness that Ethan acquires and applies to reality. A pattern develops within Ethan, turning him into a kind of Expressionist film director.[8]

Deducing the real from the unreal, but just as frequently *reading the unreal into the real,* seems to be Ethan's line of conduct. In the following passage, where he has just returned to the men's section of the Niagara pub, after having chanced upon an advertisement in the washroom for a soup product manufactured by the family of Peter Cordwainer, the friend who committed suicide at university, he hysterically ascribes his dreadful discovery to himself, the demiurge of his fate.

> But now it seemed that by the very act of starting to think about Peter, wanting to tell Jacqueline about him, *he had conjured the family firm back to life again, given it such life as it had never possessed before, at least in Canada, caused it to start expanding, start moving west to Toronto, over the whole country, the whole world,* so that in the end perhaps there would be no place on earth he could hide his head without being reminded every day, every hour, through the fatuous medium of Mother Gettle's Soups, of Peter Cordwainer himself and what he, Ethan, had done. (OFG 47; emphasis added)

Ethan looks upon the reappearance of Peter, in the guise of an advertisement for Mother Gettle's Soups, as the obvious sign of his—Ethan's—own psychic powers. He believes that he has willed this advertisement into existence, and that he has even caused or willed the development of this British product across Canada to plague himself with it and be reminded of his guilt in supposedly encouraging

Peter to commit suicide. Self-persecution seems more enjoyable—yields more jouissance—than persecution alone: thus, paranoia evolves into megalomaniac visions of self-aggrandizement as Ethan's inscape is seen as originating the actual Canadian landscape.

A similar explanation is given by Ethan when, having returned from Europe to his wife and son in Niagara-on-the-Lake, he prays to God, in his own idiosyncratic way, to ask Him for help in order to get over the horrible destruction of his house by fire:

> For "Our Father which art in Heaven," he would find himself saying something like "our fire which art in fear." And out of the word "fear" instantly would *grow* fears; fears of the next day, fear of seeing advertisements, which he now seemed to in almost every newspaper, for Mother Gettle, at almost every street corner—. (OFG 124)

In this case, Ethan establishes a link between the words he uses or, more aptly, misuses, and the mental plague that afflicts him: fears originate in fearful words, in words going berserk, and Logos hits back at him in this uncanny way. Ethan's mental anguish is actually the result of a stubborn belief in his magical powers, of which linguistic distortions are but one variant: he *wills* words of his own into new existence—that is, with a singular dialogic input, or evincing a private network of significations—in much the same way as he wills fire into existence. Likewise, just as he misreads, and confers new meaning on, existing printed words, he sees ominous portents or signs of his damnation in fires erupting around him, as if "the subjective world within, in order to combat that threat, had somehow turned itself inside out: as if the objective world had itself caught a kind of hysteria" (OFG 115–16).

In his willingness to endorse the belief in psychic powers and their involvement in not-so-natural phenomena, Ethan is only too glad to find confirmation of his ideas in *Wild Talents*, a book written by Charles Fort, a recent literary discovery for Lowry, too:

> In no time at all one had been convinced that certain unexplained fires (apart from those that seemed the undoubted work of poltergeists, whatever *they*, finally, were) had actually been feared into existence: that on occasion, feelings of sheer hatred or revenge toward other human beings had been sufficient to cause, without admixture of purposive "magic," disaster, otherwise inexplicable, to others. (So why not to oneself, Ethan thought, as psychiatry implied, by hatred of oneself?) (OFG 139)

Ethan believes that he is "under a curse" and thus becomes afraid of himself. The only solution he can envisage is what he calls a "deconversion from his own secret or semisecret beliefs and obsessions, a deconversion even from any belief in God—either that, or, one day, its staggering and complete reverse!" (OFG 94–95)

While the "staggering and complete reverse," that is, a newly found belief in God, or a *benevolent* form of supernatural power watching over him, seems to fore-shadow the end of the novel, it is too soon for Ethan to abjure belief in the super-natural. Grieving over the loss of two houses (his first house, in Oakville, had to be vacated when Mother Gettle factories started encroaching upon his living space), Ethan decides to "move west," endorsing the philosophy of his father-in-law, The McCandless, who, in a telegram sent to him and Jacqueline after the burning down of their second house, in Niagara-on-the-Lake, had written:

GREATEST COMMISERATION ON YOUR LOSS BUT CONSIDER SOCALLED DISASTER CAN BE BEST POSSIBLE THING FOR YOU BOTH STOP I TOLD YOU LONG AGO WHAT PERILS CAN LURK AT THAT GATE OF UNCHANGE UNQUOTE STOP RELIEVED YOURSELVES TOMMY ALL SAFE BUT SOMETIMES SOUL NEEDS ATOMIC EXPLOSIONS. (OFG 95)

The last subsection of the first part of the novel deals with the idyllic cabin and their enjoyment of life on the beach at Eridanus. In accordance with the coun-sel of The McCandless, Ethan and Jacqueline refrain from looking upon their cabin as something they own permanently. Ethan even compares his new liv-ing experience to a form of divestment of oneself, toward restoring balance, a kind of philosophy he associates with the cabbala (OFG 169). Nevertheless, for all his newly acquired serenity and fortitude, Ethan somehow equates the "bloody awful threat of eviction" (OFG 170) with a new *punishment* from God: eviction from Paradise, as the very title of chapter 23—"Adam, Where Art Thou?"—vividly sug-gests. He thus reverts once more to a well-known subjective pattern of reading the unreal into the real, even if the divine curse is still balanced for a while against the equally powerful idea that "they had not been driven out, they'd left of their own accord" (OFG 172).

At the end of the first part of the novel, as the bus trip nears conclusion and the bus has reached the level crossing, the reader is left with the impression that the scenes from Ethan's past have been relived with such acuity that their "pastness" has been lost sight of. The "presentness of the past" (Grace, *Malcolm* 75) has eclipsed the present and saturated the protagonist's inscape, as well as the read-er's pages. An "atomic explosion" in Ethan's soul is now to be expected.

A MURDERER IS BORN: CO-PRODUCED BY MOTHER GETTLE'S
SOUPS AND B.C.'S LEGAL THEATRICALS

Lowry was aware that his novel would perhaps meet hostile comments from Random House due to the sheer madness of the protagonist (and possibly his own). In his December 1953 letter to Erskine he therefore added, in a post-post script, that "on [the psychological] plane the whole thing can be read slightly differently and in a sense more hopefully, as a kind of abreaction of the past: I like the word cathexis, too" (Sursum 2:700). Since "cathexis" signifies an "investment of mental or emotional energy in a person, object or idea," and since its German equivalent, Besetzung, literally means "occupation," it is easy to see that Lowry was referring to the way in which Ethan concentrates all his energy on people and events belonging to his tormenting past; "abreaction" can also be employed, as Lowry suggests, to describe the main psychological action of the whole novel, since the word means "the release of psychic tension through verbalizing repressed traumatic experience" (Grace, Malcolm 95). More specifically, the end of the bus trip, with the dramatic stop at the level crossing, can be seen as the first active stage of Ethan's abreaction, with the fantasized trial scene in the Ocean Spray bar at Nanaimo (chapter 31) constituting its paroxysm.

First, Ethan, who has been feeling guilty throughout the trip, is confronted with a huge billboard featuring Peter Cordwainer, in full face, advertising Mother Gettle's Soup. Now, with the help of a hangover, his prosecutorial Other takes centre stage in his consciousness. Upon seeing the grinning young man on the billboard, Ethan becomes aware of "this other consciousness, familiar and feared, [which] had now taken command" (OFG 209):

> It was as if the mind of another person, coexisting with the first but utterly independent of it, had begun to work over much of the same material, but with what a different viewpoint! . . . If the first consciousness was the counsel for the defense, this second was the counsel for the prosecution. (OFG 209–10)

This vocal split of his conscience is reminiscent of the Consul's good and evil familiars in Under the Volcano, except that in October Ferry they are glossed over by the narrative voice, not fully dramatized. Ethan will now arrive at a one-word phrasing of his self-incrimination through a specular process, that is, through the agency of a mirror:

> Ethan had often been told he looked rather like Edgar Allan Poe . . . And
> his reflection in the rearview mirror, now opposite him, leaned forward,
> out of the past, as if to corroborate this. . . . Suddenly he saw his whole
> life had been like one long malignant disease since Peter's death. . . . The
> face in the mirror, a half face, a mask, looked at him approvingly, smiling,
> but with a kind of half terror. Its lips silently formed one word: Murderer!
> (OFG 215–16)

His prosecutorial voice actually takes shape in the face or mask looking back
at him. The vocal split goes together with a visual type of schizophrenia: the
face reflected in the mirror is perceived by Ethan as the Other in him, a Poe-like
double. In spatial terms, the visual emergence of a self-incriminating double, no
matter how self-deceptive and warped, precludes a harmonious coexistence of
Ethan's self with life "out there," while reasserting the power of his guilt-laden
inscape.

The second climax occurs in the men's section of the Spray Inn Bar, a suitably
claustrophobic space, where Ethan, in the course of a fantasized trial, morphs
from defence lawyer to defendant. The trial brings us back to the Chapman
boy, an adolescent who allegedly caused the death of a girl by suffocation when
attempting to rape her (OFG 266–68). Ethan Llewelyn failed to defend him, so
the boy is due to die by hanging. Ethan's claustrophobic surroundings are an
"objective correlative" of his gloomy inscape and constitute a perfect venue for
his fantasized professional acting out. His defence comprises several stages: he
first criticises British Columbians and the province's lawyers for not sublimating
their murderous instincts through the production of quality literature, in particular, a theatrical production that could advantageously replace the real-life Grand
Guignol–type executions on the scaffold (OFG 264–65).

Ethan acknowledges that it is difficult to defend a rapist and a murderer such
as the Chapman boy: it might have negative consequences, so he claims, not only
for the defence lawyer, but also for the community in which he lives. Needless
to say, Ethan is already thinking of Eridanus, but his concern for his lost paradise becomes even clearer when he resorts to quoting a passage from Hermann
Hesse's *Demian* in defence of adolescents:

> In the average person [puberty] is the only time in their lives that they
> experience the sequence of death and rebirth that is our fate, when
> they become conscious of the slow process of the decay and breaking
> up of the world of their childhood, when everything beloved of us leaves
> us, and we suddenly feel the loneliness and deathly cold of the universe

about us. And for very many this pitfall is fatal. They cling their whole life long painfully to the irrevocable past, to the dreams of a lost paradise, the worst and most deadly of all dreams. (OFG 268)

In this passage, Hesse's voice is dialogized by Ethan's own intentions.[9] In defending Chapman through this depiction of adolescence, he is really defending himself. Indeed, in Hesse's prose are to be found the very words that Ethan needs to achieve his twofold defence: that of Chapman's adolescent vulnerability and that of his own nostalgia, which, from Lowry's perspective, is also a form of prolonged adolescence in his character. However, in the double entendre of this fantasized trial lies also the germ of Ethan's own prosecution. A voice doing the prosecutorial bit (ascribable to Ethan's prosecuting self, or to an externalized variant of that familiar in the fantasized audience) turns against the defence lawyer and exposes his real motivations:

> "Yes, we like that, Mr Llewelyn. Especially the bit about the irrevocable past, and the dream of a lost paradise. Is it not because you are still clinging to such a dream, to such an irrevocable past, that you, who of all people might have done some good, who would in fact quite possibly have been retained to defend the boy, did not raise a finger to help?"
> "I?"
> "Yes. You. Did you not say, 'For to speak out in this instance not only might involve an individual risk to the speaker, but to the whole community in which he lives?' And . . . what community could that be, other than that of your own—you squatters on those float houses in Eridanus?"
> (OFG 269)

Within the logic of Ethan's scenario, his prosecuting double is denouncing his hypocrisy. Evading his professional duties as a lawyer on account of his own personal immaturity is the crime Ethan thinks he is guilty of. Interestingly, the dramatization of his guilt brings us back to the very nature of his inscape. Ethan's mind, much like that of his real-life creator, dwells overwhelmingly on paradigmatic correspondences. Clinging to the past is indeed the link between Ethan and the Chapman boy in the paradigmatic class of prolonged adolescence opened up by Ethan via Hesse's *Demian*. Such correspondences haunt him, as is suggested by the hypertrophied textual space devoted to Ethan's guilt-laden inscape. At this stage, the claustrophobic bar in which Ethan is seated fittingly enhances the predominantly static dimension of this unorthodox road narrative, giving pride of place to his engulfment in self-flagellation and paranoia.

The piece of legal madness continues with a *Volcano*-like, multi-layered series of utterances, as Ethan's sentencing climax finally takes place:

"Save him!"
"Oh, shut up!"
"It's no good, this kind of life."
"But you, Ethan Llewelyn, what did you say? What did your able pen do, your pen more able than mine, or your still small voice, the one voice, the one pen still able to save him?"
"Hang him!"
"Hang him!"
"The appeal for clemency of Richard Chapman, the fifteen year-old rapist has been refused by the Cabinet today. Richard must keep his date with the hangman next December thirteenth."
"Hang him!"
"Hang Ethan Llewelyn!" (OFG 271)

If this passage does not read exactly like the psychotic polyphony obtained in the "Cave of Winds" episode from chapter 10 in *Under the Volcano*, the temporal disjunction of the various speeches once again emphasises the static/paradigmatic dimension of the narrative sequence. Indeed, some utterances come from the men's section of the Spray Inn Bar, where Ethan is seated, while others seem to be generated by Ethan's inscape. The italicized statement reads like a sample of journalese, a written reminder of Chapman's scheduled execution, remembered or read by Ethan. The final sentence of chapter 31 spells out the ultimate punishment for Ethan's "crime": death by hanging. The juxtaposition of his two forms of abreaction makes the sentence inevitable: Ethan Llewelyn is guilty of two counts of murder at one-remove: by encouraging suicide and through professional inertia. He is also guilty of criminal nostalgia—he is a romantic "psychopath"—and of deceit as well as self-deceit. In Ethan's death-wish fulfilment, death by hanging reads then like poetic justice.

Thus, at the end of the second part of the novel, Ethan has woven together the two strands of his existential malaise. Now that the release of tension has been achieved, it remains to be seen whether Ethan's redemption can take place: will he outgrow his alienating inscape and how shall we, as readers, assess his progress in spatial terms?

A RECOVERY OF SORTS:
IS THERE ANY NEW VIABLE SPACE IN THIS TEXT?

Ethan has gone through a hallucinatory process of self-revelation in a narrative in which he is said to be directionless. This overall impression of disorientation is perhaps strengthened by the antithetical forces of nostalgia and forbearance presiding over Ethan's psychomachia. Throughout the road narrative, he has been emphasizing that he and his wife are very much alive to the impermanence of things, including that of their most treasured place:

> Moreover they'd never looked upon their little beach cabin, however beloved, as a permanent thing. That impermanence, indeed, the ramshackle tenuity of the life, were part of its beauty. (OFG 171)

It is essential to realize how this belief in impermanence is constantly seen as a counterweight to the power of *nostos*, the deeply rooted nostalgia that besets Ethan and, to a lesser extent, Jacqueline. However, nostalgia dies hard and Ethan's abreaction of the past, while a necessary acting out of his anguished fantasies, does not amount to a permanent cure from his longing for Eridanus. If the couple has left their little paradise of their own accord in order to escape eviction, the vivid memory of the place continues to haunt Ethan so much that, once aboard the ferry leaving for Gabriola, he briefly contemplates suicide to escape his "fear of the future, fear of himself" (OFG 300), and subsequently looks upon this moment as "a genuine impulse, of which he still even could feel the sickening and desperate volition" (OFG 301). Right through to the end of the chapter, ironically titled "Outward Bound," the past and the future fight it out in Ethan's mind, and this is expressed most forcefully and poignantly in the closing paragraph:

> And still Gabriola drew nearer, though not much nearer. Baffling heavy seas, and a head wind, the ferry had not traversed a quarter of the distance yet. And still Eridanus and the little cabin drew nearer, though ever farther away. (OFG 302)

The poignancy of the passage lies in the chronotopic paradox spelling out Ethan's emotional proximity to Eridanus and his unstated desire to maintain Gabriola beyond the offing. In terms of geographical reality, there is no paradox: it is true that Ethan gets closer to the mainland again (and, thus, to Eridanus) when he takes the ferry from Nanaimo to Gabriola than he had been when starting out from Victoria. However, the slow advance toward Gabriola, as perceived by the protagonist, stresses the mere tentativeness of his future, while Eridanus' relative geographical proximity is both real and delusional since the temporal separation from it is inexorably increasing.

In the penultimate chapter, titled "Not the Point of No Return," reality even seems to outmatch Ethan's delusions when the ship is forced to return to Nanaimo because of a black-attired passenger who needs to be disembarked due to her profuse bleeding. The lady in black is perceived as one more example of God's momentous tricks, but both Ethan and Jacqueline take this incident in stride and surrender to fate. Following a discussion with a Catholic priest, Ethan has learnt to view such expressions of fate as those of a "divine supernatural order" (OFG 320). In the to-and-fro movement that the narrative has now adopted, the final twist is the ironical news of a reprieve for the squatters in Eridanus, as the ferry is about to leave for Gabriola again. This piece of news is conveyed to Ethan by the *Vancouver Messenger*, tossed on board by a newsboy. Yet the ferry, no longer seen as "Charon's boat" (OFG 287), a reference to the ferryman of Hades, is once more outward bound and, unlike Jacqueline, who momentarily clings to the dream of regained paradise, Ethan decides to go along with the "current" of things and dismisses this reprieve as a false return, alive as he now is to the transience of things.

In the ultimate chapter, where faith in the future seems to abound ("Uberimae Fides"), the last page of the novel is of paramount importance in determining what possibilities the longed-for island of Gabriola contains, both diegetically and narratively speaking. Looking at the novel in its entirety, and bearing in mind the textual portion devoted to nostalgic reminiscences and guilt-laden associations, it is hard for the reader to suspend disbelief and view the ending as redemptive by lending credence to Ethan's so-called rebirth in Gabriola. Furthermore, the final page, in its ambiguity and tentativeness, seems to suggest a dubious new beginning:

> The island lay before them in the last of the sunset light, *a long dark shape, spiked* with pines against the fading sky. There was *no splendor of gold and scarlet maples, it was a splendor of blackness and darkness.* And as they approached, there seemed *no beach,* just the high, foolhardy cliffs dropping straight into the sea. Behind Nanaimo *the sky turned a sullen smouldering red:* the mountains on the mainland melted into the twilight. Then *the light was gone* and Gabriola too lay in *the immense shadow.* The wind blew sharp and salt and cold.
>
> Gabriola . . . Ah, how wild and lonely and primeval and *forbidding* it looked! *Not a light glimmered, not a house shone through the trees,* there was

nothing but the cliffs, so high the trees on the top seemed dwarfed, mere broken bottles guarding the rim, the cliffs, and the uproar of *the black sea* at their base. (*OFG* 332; emphasis added)

It is a forbidding, cold, and dark landscape that opens up before Ethan. The absence of light and colour could not be more strongly emphasized than it is here through the repetitive use of negative constructions and the deployment of the paradigm of void and darkness. Nanaimo's backcloth is now a sky "turned a sullen smouldering red," as if the past hell is now left behind only to make room for a cold, colourless, and somewhat frightening darkness. At any rate, this is hardly a vision of paradise, with its expected promise of light.

The very last lines steer the text even more toward something that looks like an unreal landscape:

Deep in the dark forest behind was the glow of a fire with red sparks ascending like a fiery fountain; yes, someone *was* burning the stumps to clear his land. The sound of lowing cattle was borne to them and they could see a lantern swinging along close to the ground. A voice called out, clear, across the water. And now they saw the dock, with silhouetted figures moving against a few lights that gleamed in the dusk. (*OFG* 332–33)

The colour red has now endowed the landscape with some life. Noise and movement—a clear voice (perhaps the only positive sign)—have also endowed the immense dark void with minimal human presence (underlined by the indefinite article as in "a lantern swinging," "a voice called out"). And when plurality is finally granted to the description of the place ("silhouetted figures moving against a few lights that gleamed in the dusk"), it is only the better to emphasise the illusoriness or sketchiness of human life, the "silhouetted figures," not individuals, being somewhat reminiscent of Plato's cave. Most importantly, the passengers on board the ferry are never seen disembarking and setting foot on Gabriola.[10] The reader experiences a kind of suspended animation, which the final typographical sign of the text—suspension points—forcefully underlines. Thus, there is something ideational about the final vision: it is akin to a dreamlike, wished-for place that can only yield darkness, silhouettes, and tentative life. The Llewelyns have approached the new land they have been yearning for, but in this very yearning, the tentative, and possibly the delusional, are inscribed, as the de-realization of the ultimate vision suggests. *October Ferry to Gabriola* plays out the tension between past and present/future. Thus, the textual open-endedness is best suited to this ambivalent narrative of withdrawal and return: being on the threshold of things is indeed the most poetic anti-closural strategy.

Finally, "outgrowing the alienating inscape" also has narrative implications. To outgrow one's inner obsessions, to take the voyage out, implies a form of narrativity which, ultimately, is uncongenial to Lowry's writing ethos or *modus scribendi*. Likewise, the idyllic mode seems hardly compatible with the novelistic genre in Lowry's case. "The Forest Path to the Spring," because of its self-contained novella format, could harbour healing visions, but when Lowry gradually turns his novella into a novel, as was the case for *October Ferry*, hell breaks loose, narratively speaking for him: the Otherness of language invests textual space in the guise of excruciating signs and reminiscences. Lowry's own circuitous interpretation of the novel's ending is quite revealing—it is no longer paradise regained, but purgatory:

> The storm has now dropped and the ferry once more proceeds to Gabriola but the whole book, and with it the ferry . . . now rises to another level: whereas before the ferry was a Charon's boat proceeding to a kind of hell, now it is another sort of ferry proceeding, as it were, toward the Mount of Purgatory (Mount Baker). With this too, Gabriola loses its ambivalence on the lower plane: assumes it on a higher. Centrally and realistically it becomes now the accepted future. (Lowry, *Sursum* 2:698)

Lowry eventually offers a religious interpretation of the novel. Several critics have followed suit by proposing a salvational reading of the ending.[11] Given that this text engages us by offering no conclusion, this essay begs to differ, underscoring the overall ambiguity of the passage in the published version, mulling over the beauty of an idea—Paradise—while the incompletion of the quest, mirrored in the suspended narration, opens up all sorts of vistas and endless textual voyages for the gratification of the reader.

NOTES

1. The novel was published for the first time in 1970. Further textual references will be made to that edition using the parenthetical abbreviation OFG.

2. In a letter to his literary agent, Harold Matson, dated October 2, 1951, Lowry had presented a new book in the making, containing six stories: "Through the Panama," "October Ferry to Gabriola," "In the Black Hills," "Strange Comfort Afforded by the Profession," "Elephant and Colosseum" and "The Forest Path to Spring" (Lowry, *Sursum* 2:436–37). *Hear Us O Lord*, published posthumously in 1961, does not contain "October Ferry" or "In the Black Hills" (the latter published in 1975, in *Psalms*

and Songs), but includes three other stories: "The Bravest Boat," "Present Estate of Pompeii," and "Gin and Goldenrod."

3. Ethan Llewelyn had failed to empathize with his friend Peter Cordwainer and actually mocked his threats to commit suicide: "If only he [Ethan] had not gone out that night for the last bottle of gin. 'Let the bugger die!' they had shouted that night in the Headless Woman just before closing time [. . .]" (OFG 47). Significantly, Lowry himself felt guilty for the death in 1929 of his Cambridge friend Paul Fitte for similar reasons.

4. Lowry himself was aware of the paradigmatic density of his novel and claimed in a letter to Matson dated January 25, 1954 that "if the narrative doesn't move horizontally, it certainly can move, if in a bizarre fashion, vertically" (*Sursum* 2:709).

5. This portmanteau word, as Douglas Porteous explains, "is derived from the poet Gerard Manley Hopkins, who originally meant it to refer to the inner beauty of natural forms as they reveal themselves to the observer. . . . The concept was later extended to embrace the notion of the observer's mental landscape, the landscape of the mind" (123).

6. In "The Forest Path," Lowry's closing novella in *Hear Us O Lord*, "Wywurk" and "Four Bells" (not "Eight Bells") are the humorous names of two shacks (216–19).

7. The last sentence from Scott Fitzgerald's novel reads: "So we beat on, boats against the current, borne back ceaselessly into the past" (188).

8. For an insightful examination of Lowry's brand of expressionism, see Grace, *Regression* 163–84.

9. For a clear explanation of the double-voiced effect referred to as dialogic by Bakhtin, and resulting here in the internal dialogization of Hesse's prose by Lowry's/Lewelyn's discourse and intentions, see Bakhtin 324–25.

10. This, as Victor Doyen kindly explained to me, seems to have been Margerie Bonner Lowry's editorial choice, for Lowry actually had the Llewelyns set foot on the island in his last draft of the novel. Margerie may have abused her editorial powers, thus evincing her own authorial self interacting with Lowry's voice in the writing process of *October Ferry*.

11. Grace offers a reasonable version of this redemptive reading by emphasizing the quest rather than the reaching of the goal: "for Lowry it is not the finding but the *searching* that is important, and *October Ferry* ends with a sense of movement and expectation. . . . With *October Ferry to Gabriola* the Lowry voyager escapes (for the moment) the negative circle of self and distorted perception, and the trap of the past." (Grace, *Malcolm* 98)

WORKS CITED

Bakhtin, M. M. *The Dialogic Imagination: Four Essays*. Edited by Michael Holquist, translated by Caryl Emerson and Michael Holquist, Austin: U of Texas P, 1981.

Fitzgerald, F. Scott. *The Great Gatsby*. 1926. Harmondsworth, UK: Penguin Books, 1982.

Grace, Sherrill E. *Malcolm Lowry and the Voyage That Never Ends*. Vancouver: U of British Columbia P, 1982.

——. *Regression and Apocalypse: Studies in North American Expressionism*. Toronto: U of Toronto P, 1989.

Lowry, Malcolm. *Hear Us O Lord from Heaven Thy Dwelling Place*. 1961. London: Jonathan Cape, 1962.

——. *October Ferry to Gabriola*. Edited by Margerie Lowry, New York and Cleveland: World Publishing, 1970.

——. *Psalms and Songs*. Edited by Margerie Bonner Lowry, New York: New American Library, 1975.

——. *Sursum Corda!: The Collected Letters of Malcolm Lowry*. Edited by Sherrill E. Grace, vol. 2, 1946–1957, Toronto: U of Toronto P, 1996.

——. *Under The Volcano*. 1947. New York: New American Library, 1971.

Porteous, Douglas. "Inscape: The Landscape of the Mind in the Canadian and Mexican Novels of Malcolm Lowry," *The Canadian Geographer*, vol. 30, no. 2, 1986, pp. 123–131.

13

The Path to Translation:
Ex-isting and Becoming in the Divinely
Grotesque Comedy of "Elephant and Colosseum"

PASCALE TOLLANCE

Malcolm Lowry's short story "Elephant and Colosseum" follows a writer abroad, a European back in Europe, but yet a writer still in exile, both from his native land and from the other continent to which he has exiled himself. In this case, the sense of displacement experienced by the character is reinforced by the fact that Cosnahan, the protagonist, is thwarted in his expectation to "find himself translated in Italian" (the same phrase is used several times). What Cosnahan actually "finds" half way through the story is that neither he nor his book, Ark From Singapore, has any existence for the Italian publisher who has supposedly taken on the translation. If it all boils down to a mistake in the end, and if, as much else in the story, things and people simply fail to appear at the right place at the right time, the incident takes on huge significance for a writer who has found himself unable to write since he has become successful. Failing to recognize himself in the multiple images offered by the rest of the world, failing, equally, to find due recognition in his publisher, Cosnahan "seeks comfort" (Lowry, "Elephant" 160) in the nearby zoo (and not, in contrast to the previous story, "Strange Comfort Afforded by the Profession," in a museum containing the relics and letters of a dead fellow writer). In fact, Cosnahan finds more than comfort in the zoo, because he is "recognized" by one of the elephants, named Rosemary, whom, it turns out, he looked after years ago on her long sea voyage to Rome, and who provided the inspiration for the novel whose translation he is presently trying to track down. Rosemary, the "heroine" of Ark From Singapore, formerly having been saved by Cosnahan from a storm during their shared voyage, finally has the privilege of saving Cosnahan in her turn, as it were, as her encounter turns into an intense epiphanic moment that restores to the writer his powers and desire to write.

Incongruous as it may seem, the story offers sharp insight into the process and space of creation, the overwhelming concern of all Lowry's later texts. The narrative can be described as a journey that loosely follows the Dantean pattern so very dear to Lowry. Eventually, what helps the writer overcome a paralyzing sense of isolation and alienation is a form of love—albeit love for an elephant. To an already extensive bestiary, "Elephant and Colosseum" thus makes a major and original contribution. Rosemary is perhaps the only animal in Lowry's fiction that offers a purely comedic function, making possible the remarkable assertion "that life, all life must have a happy ending," and "that it [is] our tragic sense that [is] the more frivolous" (172). The story is "a serious story," as Lowry repeatedly maintained in his correspondence, although it is also, in the words of its author, "a Moby Jumbo" and "a comic strip for the infant Panurge."[1] To the Consul's affirmation that "the gods exist, they are the devil" (Lowry, *Volcano* 252), "Elephant and Colosseum" opposes an equally momentous claim: "If there was a creation that testified to the existence of almighty God, and His wide wild humour, it was the elephant, that marvellous juxtaposition of the grotesque and the sublime" ("Elephant" 162). And contrary to the Consul, who ends up, dead, at the bottom of the ravine with a dead dog, Cosnahan feels in the last lines of the story that he has been "translated . . . into a conscious member of the human race" (174). The puzzling question is how a detour through the zoo is what makes this translation into humanity possible.

"AN ETERNAL WRITER ETERNALLY SITTING IN THE ETERNAL CITY"

The relatively lengthy text of "Elephant and Colosseum," in its density and intricacy, weaves together many threads. The multidirectional nature of the narrative finds its geographical equivalent in the labyrinth of narrow streets and alleys through which Cosnahan "drifts," "steering as by dead reckoning" (143). But the seemingly random progression is nevertheless counterbalanced by a very strict pattern. The story clearly falls into three parts: a first part, where Cosnahan seems glued to his chair on the terrace of the restaurant Rupe Tarpea, and only allows his mind to stray; a second part, where he decides to go in search of his translated book and its publisher, and in so doing repeatedly loses his way amid the busy streets and dangerous traffic of Rome; and a last part, where the writer suddenly realizes he is near the Borghese Gardens and finds himself drawn to the zoo, where he stumbles upon Rosemary. The shadow of Dante is present from the very first page, introduced with a humorous angle: as Cosnahan tries to order a drink in a language he cannot speak, his linguistic predicament expresses itself in his murmuring to the waiter "something like 'Nel mezzo del cammin di nostra vita mi ritrovai in—'" (114). In a letter he writes to his wife while sitting in a restaurant terrace, Cosnahan describes the Piazza Venezia as an "inferno" (129), and as he later approaches the wooded area of the Borghese gardens, he repeats "Nel mezzo del camin di nostra vita mi ritrovai in," and continues "And here was the bosca oscura, the obscure boskage" (159).[2] Yet, in this case, the dark wood is next to the garden where Cosnahan is about to be "saved" by Rosemary. Cosnahan ends up, by a roundabout path, where he began. Through his particular use of the figure of the circle, Lowry summons up and reworks the Dantean geography. The three parts, each of which takes us back to the point where they started, can be described as forming three circles that are enclosed within the wider circle formed by the whole story. Each can be seen as an attempt to break the previous circle, an attempt which only succeeds in the last part, although we are given the impression that we have not moved at all, with Cosnahan sitting "once more under the awning of the Restaurant Rupe Tarpea" (170) feeling "that he'd woken up" (170). In other words, the journey or the "voyage" of the writer through Rome leads to the revelation of something that is new and yet which has always been there. The progression that breaks the circle is also what allows matters to come full circle.

What dominates most of the story, particularly before the encounter with Rosemary, is a paradoxical feeling with which the Lowry reader is familiar: a feeling of intense and immediate participation inextricably combined with a sense of remoteness and alienation; the impression of being an outsider nevertheless trapped, in this case, in a beautiful garden, or city, from which one has been expelled, or to which one has never belonged in the first place. What characterizes "Elephant and Colosseum" is that this feeling of exclusion is subdued, as if the magic of Rome had almost the power to dispel it. One is nearly allowed to forget Cosnahan's uncomfortable situation—and yet not quite, as the character is introduced sitting in the Rupe Tarpea, a place named after the famous cliff of the Capitoline Hill, an execution site during the Roman Republic. Being thrown off the cliff did not only mean death, it was a potent symbol of the city's will to discard those who threatened its law and order. Later, the reader is told that Cosnahan, the Manxman who says he still thinks in Manx but can no longer speak it, has found that Manx Gaelic is about the only language which does not feature on the confession boxes in St Peter's. Throughout, Cosnahan experiences the sense of being set apart from the vast crowds that fill the streets, from which he cannot detach his gaze but with which he cannot mix, if only because he is stuck in his seat for a large part of the text. For despite the impression Cosnahan might give of musing in a free and leisurely manner, the text makes it clear that the character is stuck in the Rupe Tarpea, being unable to ask for the bill in Italian. Cosnahan is miraculously freed only when a new waiter, who approaches him with a smile, puts an end to his "ordeal" with a few words of English.

From the first sentence, the writer's predicament is approached with delib-erate humour: "under the awning of the Restaurant Rupe Tarpea, crowded by men and women talking, a lone man named Kennish Drumgold Cosnahan sat drinking a glass of milk with an expression of somber panic" (114). The dialogue which follows between "Drumgold" and "Cosnahan" appears as an illustration of Freud's analysis of humour: a paradoxical defensive strategy used by the ego, which manages to assert its invulnerability by dividing itself and siding with the superego. A thin barrier against panic and terror, the victorious displacement of affect that humour achieves does not conceal that Cosnahan is struggling at that moment to find an image of himself he can present to the rest of the world. As a writer who has achieved success, he has become "someone." And yet, far from strengthening his sense of identity, success seems to have made this identity more elusive. Asked to provide his Italian publisher with a detailed biographi-cal portrait, the writer puts himself in the position of the reader, compiling and editing the various reviews and blurbs about himself that he happens to possess. There is no mirror on the terrace of the restaurant, but Conashan can see his face simultaneously in the window and in the photo on the back cover of his book: the face is described as the same, yet not quite the same, just as the critics' reviews echo each other without being identical. Cosnahan is always almost someone, and yet, not quite: "a mixture of Conrad and Algernon Blackwood at his best," "a mixture of early Conrad and Wodehouse at his funniest," "a combination of Jack London, James Stephens and James Oliver Curwood" (118). Unsurprisingly, "reading these later eulogies produced in Cosnahan a bizarre mental commotion as of some endless mirrored reduplication" (118).

The multiplication of images in the virtual mirror only increases a sense of strangeness, which expresses itself in temporal terms: "for a moment he felt like an eternal writer eternally sitting in the eternal city, eternally reading precisely the same sort of notices . . . though in another way, of course, it was always as if he were reading them for the first time" (118). The cliché of Rome as the eternal city is displaced to convey the impression of being in a strange time warp. At this point, it might be of interest to remember the title of the first, seven-page version of the story: "Sooner or Later or So They Say," which, as Gordon Bowker reminds us, derives from the saying "If you sit here long enough, sooner or later, so they say, you were certain to meet someone you knew" (Bowker 474), and which is actually explicitly referred to in the text: "Cosnahan wondered if this was the very place where, if you sat long enough, so they say, you were certain to meet some-one you knew" ("Elephant" 133). The eternal writer eternally sitting and reading (but not writing) endless articles is also eternally waiting, waiting for someone to appear, his brother or his publisher, "either of whom might turn up there" (129).

Eternity becomes associated with vacancy and indeterminacy, as suggested by the "sooner or later" (or the "either of whom"), which, for the Lowry reader, echoes the "anyhow, somehow" by which everything seems to be, or to happen, in *Under The Volcano*. Clément Rosset dwells on this "anyhow, somehow" in *L'Idiotie du Réel*, and analyzes it as a perfect expression of the "insignificance of the Real,"[3] of which the Consul allows us to share the most profound experience. Unlike the Consul in his "stone retreat" (Cervantes's toilets), who "would have been glad of a mirror to ask himself the question, 'Why was he here? Why was he always more or less here?'" (*Volcano* 336), Cosnahan is surrounded by the multiplication of reflections.[4] But he seems to experience the same feeling of dissociation, a dissociation so acute that it almost cancels itself into neutrality. Exile in the eternal city becomes the translation of a form of disjunction that goes beyond a simple feeling of isolation and inadequacy. It is like being caught in a void, in a here and now that is at the same time nowhere.

EX-ISTING

The English words uttered by the Italian waiter at the end of the first part seem to break a spell as Cosnahan very suddenly stands up laughing and launches through the streets of Rome, remembering that he had an appointment, that his "presence in Rome was not altogether without purpose" ("Elephant" 135). Initially, this second part could be taken to announce a return to practical reality, a reality with which Cosnahan appears firmly decided to deal as he actively goes in search of his Italian publisher. Very quickly, however, this impression is dispelled and we find ourselves in a world that can be described as both dreamlike and nightmarish, the writer being put through another complicated ordeal. The reader is constantly reminded of the risk of losing one's way in the complex network of narrow streets and in "the titanic thunder and confusion of the traffic" (147). Besides, we are told that Cosnahan's present journey is in fact the resumption of a journey attempted a few days earlier, which failed so badly that Cosnahan has "allowed three days to elapse before trying again" (138). Tracking down his translated book transforms itself for the writer into a monumental task, all the more so as his whole life seems to depend on it: for the character, "to find himself translated" means finding proof of his existence vis-à-vis the existence of his translated book. As the latter turns into a will-'o-the-wisp, Cosnahan himself is reduced to an insubstantial shadow. Interestingly, the writer comes across various processions and groups, which he observes with meticulous attention, but which do not seem to see him, or which "recognize him for what he is not" (148): when truckloads of waving Italian soldiers throw green leaves to the writer, who waves back to them, the scene of "triumphant recognition" that Cosnahan calls "deliciously ironic" is said to have "caused him to feel his loneliness most of all" (148). As he tries to mix and merge with the crowds, the writer momentarily disappears, carried by one of the numerous processions: "After a while Cosnahan, like a snag of driftwood caught in a current following some colourful boats downstream, found himself joining in the procession" (151): the consonantic effects and the main alliteration (Cosnahan / caught / current / colourful) strengthen the impression that Cosnahan is one with the crowd, an impression confirmed when the writer becomes totally absorbed by the sight of those around him. Thus, the two long descriptions of the Roman priests turn into a brilliant verbal exercise strongly reminiscent of the description of the Babel of names of liquor bottles in Under the Volcano: "priests with bowler hats, with flat-topped hats, with briefcases, with no hats at all, bearded priests carrying brown paper parcels, black-velvet-hatted priests carrying small briefcases, more tall solemn ones carrying their hats behind their backs" (153). But as Cosnahan "bows and smiles" to two of the priests whom he has encountered previously, he notices yet again that they don't "recognize him" (153). Colourful, funny, or beautiful, the Roman crowd seems nevertheless out of reach even as Cosnahan mingles with them and tries to capture them through his endlessly detailed lists. Conversely, Cosnahan seems to have become simply invisible to them, as if he were not among the living. Amid such uncertainty, it is not entirely surprising, then, that Cosnahan should "see" his 'fellow writer,' Gogol, who wrote Dead Souls in Rome one hundred years prior, three times throughout the story (the sightings are referred to as a "half-hallucination," [170]). Worse than being mistaken for someone else, or caught between alienating reflections, there is this plight which Cosnahan shares for a moment with the Consul: that of being out there, in the midst of it, and yet exiled or banished, "unseen, cut off from God" (Volcano 177).

Once again, one might ask whether Cosnahan is truly present, among the crowd, or the eternal writer caught in a time warp. It is the very question the character asks himself, in fact, as, having sat down in a café to make a few notes, he suddenly finds himself in the very place which he has been trying to reach for several days: "And now, the next moment, [he] found himself waiting in the enormous silent coolness of his Italian publisher's office. Well, he was here, wasn't he? Or was he?" ("Elephant" 155). Slightly disturbed by the sudden ellipsis which brings him without transition to the long-awaited moment of truth, the reader might be even more put out by the disengagement of the narrator when introducing the crucial confrontation between Cosnahan and his publisher, and the final verdict:

Cosnahan . . . had just seen another cover that might be his, unfortunately it was André Obey's *Noah*, when the young Italian returned.

Afterward it seemed their conversation went something like this . . . (156)

The dialogue, framed as such, thus becomes an approximate reconstitution of something one cannot be sure has happened, a piece of fictional dialogue flaunting its fictional nature. Although the narrator is relaying the sense of unreality felt by the character through internal focalization ("it seemed "), he also gives the impression that all he can do is supply inadequately for the failure of his character ("something like this"). And what is about to be announced to Cosnahan is that, as far as his Italian publisher is concerned, neither he nor his book exist. Although present in the flesh, with his original copy of the book and its cover photograph in hand, Cosnahan is told: "Yes, but we don't have you *here*, Signor" (156).

THE SMILE OF THE ELEPHANT

At the end of the second part, Cosnahan finds himself truly in the "bosca oscura," an eternal writer in an existential void where humour is no longer available: "For once in his life, Cosnahan had not only lost his sense of humour but felt really desperate" (158). The epiphanic revelation that is about to take place, thanks to the elephants "feeding fodder into their kindly, sardonic mouths" (162), is brought in step by step, yet the whole episode may be described as incongruous for many reasons. Some may remain perplexed by what seems like a miraculous intervention that propels the story to its comic ending. The "recognition scene" (Rosemary "regard[s] Cosnahan with shrewd small intelligent eyes" and suddenly trumpets) is, in fact, described by Cosnahan himself as the most "preposterous" in literature.[5] The ending only makes sense, of course, in light of the beginning. The writer who has so far obsessively been trying to find proof of his existence in the eyes of Rome declares, at the end of the story, that meeting Rosemary has been "a little like meeting himself." On the one hand, the apparition of the elephant can be looked at as a sort of magical intervention (at one point Cosnahan sees it as a sign from his mother, who is a bit of a witch); on the other hand, it is made to appear as a perfectly logical occurrence. Rosemary was there from the start and, moreover, found her way to Rome thanks to Cosnahan, as the narrator repeatedly reminds us: "How could he have forgotten?" (165); "he never really could have forgotten" (165); "it had not been easy to forget" (167). Being able to see Rosemary (who, unsurprisingly, has not forgotten him) is, then, just a question of looking toward the Borghese Gardens and detaching his eyes from the blurbs and reviews, and from the effect of the "endless mirrored reduplication" they produce. As it appears, little by little, the "self" that Cosnahan declares he has met thanks to Rosemary is not a fully constituted image; it is not the author of the photograph on the back cover of the book, the much desired, but also perhaps much dreaded, translation of oneself. It is instead the writer who once wrote the book he is holding, the writer who writes and will write, the writer Cosnahan still needs to become, or rather, what he must keep becoming, "somehow, anyhow."

Unlike many other animals in the Lowryan bestiary, Rosemary does not function as a double, even if we might initially think we are witnessing an odd form of identification made possible by the personification of the animal. Very quickly, Cosnahan dismisses that idea when he says, "It was usual to sentimentalize about elephants, and much has been written about their memory, longevity, fidelity, their patience and sapience" (162). Claiming that it is for its own "elephantine virtues" (163) that he feels drawn to the elephant, he nevertheless indulges in what appears as a fantasmatic projection: the elephant is presented as a "profoundly meditative animal" (164): "Like the sacred ibis who has the habit of standing on one leg for hours at a time by the Nile, in a manner which can strike most human beings as idiotic, so, in its state of deep abstraction, with the elephant" (164). It is the vacant gaze, the gaze turned toward something that remains out of sight, which exerts its imaginary power here; not something that fills the field of vision or stares back, but something that directs the eye toward an indefinable object. The "idiotic" attitude becomes an expression not of sheer vacancy, but a positive absence, an inspiring silence that is also emblematized by the Cosnahans' family cat, Citron-le-Taciturne. And like the grin of another, more famous, cat, it is the gaping mouths of the elephants, "smiling softly to themselves, enjoying at the same time some transcendental joke," that catch the observer's imagination. The joke cannot be shared: by their inscrutability, the elephants leave the observer out. But like the Cheshire cat, they also leave something for him: the soft contour of a smile, which, in the case of Cosnahan, suddenly seems to hold things—something, anything—together.

In this case, a vital, magical ingredient is nevertheless necessary for this vision to be sustained: "But in order to understand these things it was perhaps necessary to have loved an elephant" (164). The strange kind of love Cosnahan feels for Rosemary (he jokes about Androcles and the lion and *Tarzan of the Apes*) leads him for the first time to make light of his narcissistic search for himself. The question of whether he exists in the eyes of the world ceases for a moment to be relevant to the writer. Between endless alienating reflections and an existential void, Cosnahan discovers what he knew all along: that there is his work, which is perhaps as much a labour of love as looking after Rosemary ("his first great unselfish love" [171]) through the storms of the oriental seas. In any case, it is toward his book that Rosemary finally causes Cosnahan to direct his glance as he decides he has to "abandon . . . his futile search":

> And abandon for what? What but his work! Yes, his precious, ridiculous, second-rate, and yet to him, and to his wife too if they must live, all-important work: it was this he had been missing all along, seeking some stimulus, somewhere, anywhere, to begin again, and in the act of seeking, the excuse to postpone that beginning; and now at one of those rare points where life and poetry meet, Rosemary had appeared; for Rosemary, so to say, *was* his work—Cosnahan glanced down at the cover of his book again. (173)

Rosemary reminds Cosnahan of the material presence of his book in which the elephant undergoes all sorts of transformations (as it does in the story), while remaining somehow untouched as the force that holds the book together. From her various associations with the figure of the mother, one could be tempted to see Rosemary as just a large protective maternal body. But it is not a fantasy of primitive fusion that Rosemary inspires but, rather, the feeling that some continuity, coherence, or cohesion can be maintained *despite* all the separations, losses, and transformations imposed by the hazards of life, but also by the process of writing. It is this acceptance of separation that is not sheer loss but entails infinite possible transformations that is finally underlined when Cosnahan realizes that meeting Rosemary has also allowed him both to see, in a vision, his mother, whom he had failed to see before she died, and to let go of her: "by accepting his mother's death, and now he had for the first time fully accepted it, he had released her, and he seemed to see her now flying up through the blue Roman clouds" (172). Having witnessed the metamorphoses of Rosemary that actually seem to take place "before his eyes" (169), Cosnahan then finds himself, by another ellipsis, in the very spot where the story started, with the same waiter in front of him. Everything is the same and yet not quite the same. What may be thought disturbing and perhaps slightly "preposterous" is the uncertainty maintained by the text as to the nature of what has actually taken place since the transformations that occur are made to appear as literal as possible. The text associates and blurs the magical and the religious to emphasize a process which is of the body while resisting any simple materialistic interpretation—just as writing may be described as the very material act of composing letters, an act which nevertheless cannot be reduced to the mere physical inscription of marks on a page. It is the image of resurrection that triumphs in the final pages, with the vision of Mother Drumgold floating upward on her celestial journey among the "irreverent angels" of his thoughts, and, finally, at the close of the text, the renewed allusion to the incredible story of "Illiam Dhone, who was hanged. And yet lived." Rosemary has resurrected the past for Cosnahan, but she has also, crucially, resurrected the future. The "knowledge that he would work again" frees Cosnahan from the eternity to which he seems to be confined at the beginning—or at least changes the face of eternity for him. In the third occurrence of the puzzling vision or "half-hallucination" of Gogol going up the Via Veneto in a horsecab, the description undergoes a significant change: the Russian writer is no longer "eternally plodding" (128) or "clopping up eternally up the street" (133), but simply "still plodding up the hill" (170); at the same time, his face disappears completely, together with "the tragic beaming nose" (128) or "his eternally beaming nose" (133). In fact, the writer is "visible now only *as a cigar coal*" (170; emphasis added). Gogol's face and Gogol himself have receded to the single light of a cigar butt. This small but nonetheless striking detail underlines perhaps that the resurrection that finally takes place does not involve the restoration of identity, but rather its dissolution or dismissal. The sense of existing as a self which is never itself, the question of being someone and the fear of being no one, have gone to make room for the desire to be one of many—hence the final litany of Manx names that closes the story and follows Cosnahan's assertion that he has been "translated . . . into a conscious member of the human race":

> And who might that be? Who was he? Who was anybody?
> For the papers said that man was Smithers, they might even say that he was Drumgold. Cosnahan, they might say that man was. And somewhere they had got the notion that he was as common as the century . . .
> But man was Quayne, and man was Quaggan, man was Quillish, man was Qualtrough, man was Quirk and Quayle and Looney, and Illiam Dhone, who had been hanged and yet lived—because he was innocent? (174)

The path to salvation does seem to involve a "translation" in the end. But this translation is not dependent on the recognition and interference of someone who would have the power of bringing the writer out of the darkness and into the light, of making the invisible visible or the insignificant meaningful. It transforms Cosnahan into what he already is, while requiring his own power of recognition, an active transfer of the gaze and the imagination that will make him desire to continue to do his "precious, ridiculous" work, just as one (anyone) among the crowd. Rosemary is a key agent in this translation, precisely as she takes Cosnahan's eyes away from, or through, the mirror, where the absence of reflection can exert its positive effect. As a creature, one cannot be *like* but one can be *with*, or as a creature that cannot be known and can only be loved, she enables Cosnahan, within the space of the zoo, to undergo his translation into a simple writer and, simultaneously, into a simple "member of the human race." And because she can only point the way to what Cosnahan must keep becoming, she too must be released: just like in Dante's *Divine Comedy*, Rosemary, the guide, finally leaves the writer to his own devices.

In reading "Elephant and Colosseum," one cannot help thinking of Gilles Deleuze's "Devenir-intense, devenir-animal, devenir-imperceptible," where the philosopher approaches the notion of "becoming" in the perspective of a meta-morphosis that bypasses identification and implies the cancellation of identities and individualities. Deleuze gives some examples of this process in some writers such as D. H. Lawrence and Virginia Woolf, and talks about "the becoming whale" of Ahab in *Moby Dick* ("Achab a un devenir-baleine irrésistible" [298]). Deleuze's radical perspective cannot be made to fit entirely Lowry's text where too many different associations are conjured up to make sense of the encounter with Rosemary, but the story does seem to draw on the creative power of what Deleuze calls an "alliance" with the non-human (after all, Cosnahan's "first unselfish love" features in a novel called *Ark from Singapore*). What seems particu-larly interesting in the case of "Elephant and Colosseum" is Deleuze's idea of an intimacy between what he calls "becoming animal" and "becoming writer" through a process which departs altogether from filiation: "Si l'écrivain est un sorcier, c'est parce qu'écrire est un devenir, écrire est traversé d'étranges devenirs qui ne sont pas des devenirs écrivain, mais des devenirs-rat, des devenirs-insecte, des devenirs-loup" (293–94; The writer is a sorcerer because writing means becoming, writing involves strange forms of becoming which are not becoming a writer, but becoming a rat, an insect or a wolf). Rosemary makes the question of whether Cosnahan is a new Conrad irrelevant; she makes him forget who he might be or whom he might be like. She simply restores his powers, making him feel "as happy as some old magician who had just recovered his powers and brought off a masterstroke" (Lowry, "Elephant" 174). As Deleuze points out, it is not so much what you become that matters, but the becoming itself. At the same time, in this case, the particular qualities of the elephant, and "the strange primal peace an elephant inhabit[s]" (164), continue to feed the imagination, if only to offer the image of an infinite space where one can precisely forever "become." The successive metamorphoses that we are allowed to witness after the encounter with Rosemary and the impression that the text starts undergoing an uncontrolled proliferation suggest that the renewal of the creative process is already at work and, again, bring to mind Deleuze's words: "Chanter ou composer, peindre, écrire n'ont peut-être pas d'autre but: déchaîner ces devenirs" (333; To sing or to compose, to paint or to write might have no other purpose but to unleash these becomings).

Eventually, the smile of the elephant transfers/translates itself to Cosnahan and turns into a "gigantic attack of laughter," as if the writer had truly become one with the huge body of the elephant. The fascination with gigantism is particularly striking in the way Lowry describes his story in his correspondence: "a short story for Titans," "a Pantagruellian fancy or multum in colosseo," "a comic strip for the infant Panurge," "a monster" (Sursum 2:435). The sustained reference to Rabelais underlines the presence of a grotesque synonymous with an enormous vitality that is itself intimately connected with the infinite powers of language. Humour can then appear less as a defensive weapon than as a way of fully trusting words and relinquishing one's power to them. Let us not forget that after all, the whole story is a play on words, as Lowry's Roman "Elephant and Colosseum" is made to sound like a geographical translation and linguistic equivalent of London's fanciful and incongruous "Elephant and Castle." The fear of totally losing control and being "written by one's text," a major concern for Lowry's protagonists (and for Lowry himself), might best be overcome by allowing words to do their tricks. This surrender to language is perhaps, as Deleuze might put it, what prevents the fundamental crack that every Lowryan character bears from reaching irreversibly into the depth of the body and destroying it.[6] Then indeed it becomes possible, for a moment at least, to assert that "it is our tragic sense that is the most frivolous."

NOTES

1. Letter to Harold Matson, October 2, 1951 (Lowry, Sursum 2:435).

2. In his use of the phrase "bosca oscura" for Dante's "selva oscura," Lowry here repeats an error from chapter 7 of Under the Volcano.

3. "Nous appellerons insignifiance du réel cette propriété inhérente à toute réalité d'être toujours indistinctement fortuite et déterminée, d'être toujours à la fois anyhow et somehow: d'une certaine façon, de toute façon" (Rosset 13).

4. Rosset defines "idiocy," which etymologically means simple or unique, through the inability to be reflected, to appear as a double in the mirror: "Toute chose, toute personne sont ainsi idiotes dès lors qu'elles n'existent qu'en elles-mêmes, c'est-à-dire sont incapables d'apparaître autrement que là où elles sont et telles qu'elles sont: incapables donc, et en premier lieu, de se refléter, d'apparaître dans le double du miroir" (42).

5. Let us note, among other things, that the reference to Aristotle's *anagnorisis* is displaced from tragedy to comedy.

6. I am referring to Deleuze's parallel meditation on Fitzgerald and Lowry in "Porcelaine et volcan," and to his question: "Est-il possible de maintenir l'insistance de la fêlure incorporelle tout en se gardant de la faire exister, de l'incarner dans la profondeur du corps?" ("Porcelaine" 183). In this respect, we can think of the particular role devoted to humour, to which Deleuze repeatedly refers in *Logique du Sens* as "the art of surfaces"—without losing sight of the paradox illustrated by his quote of Paul Valéry's "deep words'": "there is nothing deeper than skin" ("le plus profond c'est le peau" [20]).

WORKS CITED

Bowker, Gordon. *Pursued by Furies: A Life of Malcolm Lowry*. London: HarperCollins, 1993.

Deleuze, Gilles. "Devenir-intense, devenir-animal, devenir-imperceptible," *Mille Plateaux*. Paris: Éditions de Minuit, 1980, pp. 284–380.

——. "Porcelaine et volcan." *Logique du Sens*. Paris: Éditions de Minuit, 1980, pp. 180–189.

Lowry, Malcolm. "Elephant and Colosseum." *Hear Us O Lord From Thy Dwelling Place & Lunar Caustic*. 1961. London: Picador Classics, 1991.

——. *Sursum Corda!: The Collected Letters of Malcolm Lowry*, edited by Sherril E. Grace, vol. 2, 1947–1957, London: Jonathan Cape, 1996.

——. *Under The Volcano*. 1947. London: Penguin Books, 1985.

Rosset, Clément. *Le Réel. Traité de l'idiotie*. Paris: Éditions de Minuit, 1977.

14

Placing Agency in the
Cultural Landscapes of La Mordida

RYAN RASHOTTE

Inspired by Malcolm Lowry's final trip to Mexico, in 1945/46, the posthumous *La Mordida*, a novel in progress at the time of his death, finds protagonist Sigbjørn Wilderness on a bitter honeymoon in an "Americanized" Mexico. This incipient but widespread Americanization that he associates with mass tourism in Acapulco is disappointing, not least for supplanting the outpost cosmopolitanism he remembers fondly of expatriate life there in the 1930s; Wilderness elegizes that Mexico has become susceptible to a contagious American modernity, and that the country's mythic cultural landscape, once such a profound stimulus for his literary endeavours, is now endangered by beachfront resorts and an invasive species of American pleasure seeker.

The crux of the story that follows—Wilderness's refusal to pay a fifty-peso *mordida*, or bribe, to local police, ostensibly to cover the penalty for an overstayed visa (Wilderness refutes the charge, as Lowry did during his own trip to Mexico)—stems partially from Wilderness's desire to distinguish himself from the new, profligate mass tourist, who he suspiciously believes is complicit with the Mexican government, and a burgeoning business culture of contemporizing "timeless" Mexico that is, if not altogether in the United States' infrastructural image, then in its commercial service (though the two fates are largely indistinguishable here). By not paying the *mordida*, Wilderness summarily denies a pecuniary basis to the host–guest relationship, and declares his intimacy with "mythopoeic" Mexico, while spurning that nation's modernizing agents (and doing so, not insignificantly, in a year when British imperialism—and the sort of expat cosmopolitanism it enriched along modernity's frontiers—was well entering a decline).

Wilderness's refusal is more than conscientious objection, however. And on a deeper level, it has nothing to do with moral logic, nor is it an act of will (on his part, at least). Its function is, above all, fatalistic, which is to say literary, as it sets in motion the events of this triumphant novel about writing a tragic novel predestined by yet another tragic novel. Each refusal to pay his *mordida* increases the severity of his punishments (real and imagined) from the Mexican authorities, and, accordingly, makes the trauma of revisiting his sordid past all the more pronounced. And the more he suffers, the more metonymy he is able to pull from the storm clouds lingering over the charmless beaches of Acapulco in 1946 and read it according to the cultic, timeless mysteries of "Wilderness in Mexico."

In this regard, "refusal" and "allow" are the wrong words; it was never as though he had a choice. When tragedy sets in, Wilderness begins to fantasize that he is a character being composed in real time by a daemonic narrator. His circumstances are placed outside his control, and his one recourse to agency—recording his oppression in the form of a paranoid novel identical to *La Mordida* itself—is no mode of agency at all. All it does is codify his lack of influence on the bureaucratic meta-nightmare of the daemon's plot as it moves torpidly toward one of two unfortunate ends: death or the United States.

This "literary" persecution is both banal (a novel of offices and hotel suites) and fantastic (Joycean in its ur-cartography). Most often it is fantastic in its banality, as when his case transfers from office to office and the Mexican authorities come more and more to resemble the daemon's co-conspirators, their charges against him sinisterly delving deeper into his past; as when he cocoons himself in the existential paralysis of his incomplete novel so thoroughly that every slight or dirty look from its minor characters portends the final stage of disaster. Calvinist diablerie, we might call it: when everything horrid is preordained, what else can one do but write it down and push on toward the catastrophe? (Or drink; there is a lot of drinking to be done here, as well.) Wilderness calls it "the machinery of the mordida," and by surrendering to his daemonic narrator and refusing complicity with Mexican authorities, he is duly pummelled through it to record the uncanny and intertextual synchronicity such pummelling affords (Lowry, *Mordida* 192).

The collapse of the public and private, the past and future, the real and literary, forces Wilderness into a "state of exception": he must cede agency to the parallel antinomies of state and narrative sovereignty to the point where his death seems imminent. When redemption finally arrives, it comes in the form of restored national and narratological agency: Wilderness escapes his daemon by crossing into America, where, as a privileged British citizen, he is incorporated into an unprejudiced juridical order (in the text's terms). The daemon secedes destiny back to Wilderness, his Texan "brothers" offer homecoming, and the story takes a final turn for the triumphant (314).

What makes his redemption a pyrrhic victory, however, is not only Wilderness's loss of a cherished creative stimulus (in mythopoeic Mexico), or his proselytizing and maudlin praise of the United States (a more extreme biopower here, in its frankly dumb carnality); it is also his inability to find a liveable context for *mordida* culture, which is to say Mexican culture, beyond the limits of Euro-American legal epistemology, just as he is unable to find intimacy with Mexico beyond the mythical patterns he has mapped of it and the resort it has led him to. The juridical fallacy of *La Mordida* is its uncritical partitioning of biopolitical borders—rendering certain nations stable and unstable, certain sovereignties arbitrary and reliable, in terms of narrative affect—and at the end of the novel not even Wilderness will be satisfied with his division. Like Lowry, he is left struggling to accept the foreclosure of a literary and personal relationship with Mexico. And though Lowry would head north, soon to discover the celebrity that had eluded him, it would not be hyperbolic to suggest that his banishment from Mexico continued to haunt him for the rest of his life.

AMERICANIZED MEXICO

The threat of the past underlies Wilderness's trauma from the novel's start: a fear that the present is merely the recycle of past events, that juvenile mistakes will require latent retribution; that *The Valley of the Shadow of Death*, the protagonist writer's *Under the Volcano*, has coded his present Mexican excursion with cryptic tragedies he will have to decipher and suffer. Posing just as great a threat, however, is the idea that the past is disappearing: that mythopoeic Mexico is facing extinction in the wake of modern industrial hospitality.

Early into his ordeal, while waiting in an immigration office in Acapulco, Wilderness is impressed by an article called "Vanishing Enchantment" in the journal *Modern Mexico* ("Vanishing Enchantment was right—in Modern Mexico," he quips [177]). He agrees with the argument that "Prosperity and Inflation were changing beautiful Mexico into Ugly Mexico"[1] and applauds its abstruse conclusion that "[the] world of supreme and archaic illusion, which man had built to be the foundation of his consciousness as history in a mythical sense is dispelled, and poetry disappears from the world" (180). For Wilderness and Eduardo Rendon, the real article's author, the commercial and infrastructural modernization of Mexico has endangered its "poetic" and "historical" character by denying the mythology of its cultural landscape. "In the U.S.," Wilderness quotes Rendon, "man is no longer part of the myth;" and Wilderness fears Americanization promises the same fate for Mexico (180).

The argument has played out in a series of ruminations since the honeymooning Wildernesses' arrival in Acapulco by bus, when "Wilderness could see, far beyond, hundreds of new white houses like California on every hill and mostly looking in stupid modern style" (52). In the town, he reflects on how after 8 years [it] seemed so much changed it was as if a gang of bucket cranes had been at work simply plucking up large sections of the town and dumping them down elsewhere . . . Acapulco . . . had always been, to his mind a supremely characterless dull little town, of a quite remarkable ugliness: but not this kind of ugliness. Now its ruination, by virtue of its reconstruction, seemed complete. (52–53)

The passage continues at length to describe this vacuous "reconstruction," suggesting a kind of spiritual impoverishment in its "ruination." Lowry himself declared more than once on his second trip that "[the] abomination of desolation was standing in the holy place of Mexico" (Bowker 360).

Earlier on the bus ride, Wilderness had encountered a prophetic advertisement in the ubiquitous signs for "Alemán" running along the Xopilote Canyon (Lowry, *Mordida* 38). In fact, the 1946 presidential candidate would become known as the "father of Mexican tourism" (Clancy 43). During his tenure as interior minister and as head of the department of tourism, he worked rigorously to market an image of "romantic Mexico," which, by 1946, had helped inaugurate a tourism boom (Berger 76–90). Between 1945 and 1950, the number of tourists entering Mexico more than doubled, in part due to the expedited reconstruction and commercial branding of Acapulco (Clancy 43).

One manifestation of Americanization, as Wilderness sees it, is the multitude of middle-class Americans sunning themselves on the beachfront of his "infernal paradise." Unlike the cosmopolitan set of the 1920s and 1930s, those interested and interesting classes, these new tourists care little for cultural pilgrimage, preferring the novelty of pleasure tourism. And indeed, Wilderness has a point; in his eight-year absence, the Americans had arrived in Acapulco and their *raison de voyager* had evolved. In 1941, Mexico strengthened commercial ties with the United States under the auspices of Franklin D. Roosevelt's Good Neighbor policy. With war limiting travel from Europe and restricting American tourism overseas, Mexico began focusing its tourist marketing on American consumers (Saragoza 102). For this new tourist, as Alex Saragoza explains, interest in post-revolutionary politics and the renaissance of *lo mexicano* had lost cultural currency: "[in] contrast to the heritage-laden publicity of the past, by the 1940s the state's tourist effort modified its picture of Mexico, reducing the focus on culture and lore for greater attention to romantic, sensual settings and leisure . . . [with] modern amenities" (104–108).

Certainly, on one level, Wilderness' desire for exotic stasis aligns him with the American tourist he is pleased to criticize. The difference is that, for Wilderness, the romance of Acapulco is a distasteful simulacrum, and he is quick to see through its commercial ruse. How different is the Wilderness' arrival into Acapulco from Yvonne's disembarkation eight years earlier in *Under The Volcano*, where the Consul's ex-wife encountered "a hurricane of immense and gorgeous butterflies swooping seaward to greet [the ship]" (*Volcano* 88), the Wildernesses are now "besieged, swamped with boys trying to grab their shopping bag . . . and jabbering, and a hundred taxi drivers shouting: 'Hotel!' 'You want Hotel!' 'Mister O.K. what you want'"? (*Mordida* 53)

It is not merely the infrastructural development of Acapulco that troubles Wilderness, but that industrialization has conscripted Mexicans themselves into the commercial project of marketing their culture on the broadest horizon. To the detriment of their holiness enters the desire for modern wealth and ubiquitous US-pop stupidity: "[The] surroundings in Wilderness's eyes were ruined . . . by bad taste and stupidity, and by American bad taste in the bargain" (62). He remembers wistfully the Hotel Paraiso de Caleta, one of his old haunts now permanently shuttered, and acerbically wonders whether the new hotels are being built further from the beach to encourage revenue for taxi drivers. He concludes,

> Acapulco was but another department of the vast dairy farm that Mexico was becoming, for the purpose of milking Americans, as an unconscious revenge for which America was with her money advancing her [sic] bad taste at such a liberal rate of interest that soon Mexico per se was vanishing. Her voice would be deafened by juke boxes, which they would fall upon much as a defeated army would fall upon opium. (62)

Such criticism anticipates the novel's greater theme of the greedy state unconscionably trying to secure foreign capital at the expense of a mythic heritage. But it's also symptomatic of larger international anxiety. Though Wilderness presents himself as a cosmopolitan world traveller, an austere memorialist of expatera Mexico (and sometimes as a Canadian novelty), his fear of Americanization could also stem from Britain's waxing authority in the affairs of the developing world. In her materialist analysis of *Volcano*, Luz Elena Ramirez argues that Lowry's best-known novel is partially a response to Mexico's post-revolutionary pull for economic independence—the country's nationalization of key mining, locomotive, and oil industries—which came at the expense of Euro-American corporate control and diplomatic influence (Ramirez 135). The novel's "theme of deracination," she argues, "typifies not just the identity crisis of the modern self, but that of the British Empire in the twentieth century," an empire now beleaguered by post-war expenses and soon to be challenged from within by colonial independence movements (126).

The theme extends into *La Mordida* as well, and not only because the events of Wilderness' *Volcano*-esque novel threaten at all times to influence the present. Because of strengthened Mexican-US relations, Britain soon found itself alone in protesting Mexico's oil expropriation. Even though diplomacy between Britain and Mexico resumed in 1941 (a year before Mexico joined the Allies), the terms and figures of Britain's remuneration remained in limbo until 1947, when Mexico had succeeded at lowering its $257 million debt to $81 million (Meyer 163, 167). Britain's urgency to settle had critically weakened its bargaining agency—a fact obvious to Mexico; by the time Lowry returned, the country no longer viewed Britain as a threat to nationalization (165). And since the United States, the emergent superpower of the post-war period, had proven itself reluctant to side with Britain on the terms of a settlement (165–66), Wilderness's smug condemnation of Americanization may very well reflect his anxiety about the incipience of post-colonial agency and post-war American hegemony.

But things are not all that bleak. As much as Wilderness laments tourism, it needs be mentioned that the couple, at least in the early stages of the trip, frequent the new tourist zones and take some pleasure in Acapulco's recreations. Even if the vacation is sometimes endowed with higher (meta)physical potential—Acapulco, "the centre of every kind of vice" (Lowry, *Mordida* 32), paradoxically offers the dissipating Sigbjørn "moral rescue" (38), and its sea presents "an image of health and escape" (77)—this is still a belated honeymoon, after all. With touristic bathos, Wilderness recalls how the hotel "fulfilled the most roseate view of the advertisements. . . . There was a glorious view and, reasonably cheap. . . . [The hotel] had all the advantages of great hotels and few of the disadvantages" (85). Passages like this one scan with minimal sarcasm (in *La Mordida*, we know when irony enters the page). Despite the mosquitoes that interrupt their lovemaking (to foreshadow the greater "bite" [the *mordida*] that will soon poison their enthusiasm), the Wildernesses seem sincerely happy for a time playing tourists (70). Even if part of their joy comes from criticizing "loud-mouthed" Americans (a perennial pastime of Canadians abroad) and boasting of their adventures off the beaten path (102).

STATE OF EXCEPTION AND THE MACHINERY OF *LA MORDIDA*

Lowry envisioned *La Mordida* as the companion novel to *Dark as the Grave Wherein My Friend is Laid*. Both books, published posthumously, draw heavily on the events of the Lowrys' Mexican "honeymoon," a trip haunted by the imaginary of *Under the Volcano* (a new draft of which Lowry had just submitted to publisher Jonathan Cape; his famous defense of the manuscript was composed on this trip) and by

Lowry's dipsomaniac past (however lurid his current debauches, they tended to begin in nostalgia). On the last leg of their trip, Malcolm and Marjorie Lowry were solicited by police to pay a fine for an overstayed visa. Believing the fine to have had been settled eight years ago and refusing to pay it again, Lowry soon found himself caught in the sluggish and paranoid ordeal with Mexican immigration that would inspire this fictional account.

Whereas *Dark as the Grave* concludes by celebrating the beneficence of the Mexican state (as a symbol of transcultural friendship), the state returns in *La Mordida* as an impersonal, vindictive, and altogether terrorizing institution; it prolongs Wilderness's abjection as a foreign undesirable, delving into his past for evidence of criminal behaviour, and manufacturing a pretext to deport him and his wife. The early tensions between Americanized Mexico and "mythic" Mexico now reach a sort of synthesis in the "machinery of the mordida": a system both modern in its bureaucracy and pre-modern (read: savage) in its improvised policy; impersonal in its dealings with the couple, but almost divine (or daemonic) in its awareness of Sigbjørn's past and its ability to punish him for it.

Never formally charged with a crime, Sigbjørn and Primrose are instructed to remain in Acapulco, "imprisoned in paradise," until Sigbjørn's case is transferred to authorities in Mexico City (168). At the national immigration office, his case is taken up by Señor Corruna, "an absolute devil . . . perhaps indeed . . . the Devil himself," who charges the couple for failing to secure work visas (they have confessed to being writers, an executable crime in *Volcano*) (266). After weathering long bouts of alcohol-fuelled paranoia, and longer hung-over paranoia, while their case shuffles between branches of juridical limbo, the Wildernesses are finally incarcerated, robbed in prison, and taken to the border under custody where they are threatened into signing deportation papers (and forbidden from re-entering Mexico).[2]

From the moment he refuses to pay, Wilderness' *mordida* places him in a state of exception: more than just denied civil right, his very presence in Mexico is arbitrarily and meaninglessly criminalized. Because he has not broken an official law, his persecution is unappealable even as it more intently impeaches his privacy. And just as his "crime" is perpetually redefined by various state authorities, it becomes overdetermined by a host of Wilderness's fears, spanning the banal to the cosmic, in his struggle to align their significance with his circumstance. "Sigbjørn and Primrose are caught in an antimony," Lowry writes, "because there is the law itself that is changing" with regard to "civil rights." "They are both in the right and the wrong" (185). An Agambenian reading would suggest that the aporia inherent to the Wildernesses' antinomy betrays the origin of *nomos* itself: "the principle that, joining law and violence, threatens them with indistinction"

(Agamben 30–31). In persecuting Wilderness without due cause, the law of the state reveals its foundational violence through the force and arbitrariness of its application, exposing national sovereignty to be mercilessly unstable.

In an analysis of *Under the Volcano*, Andrew John Miller claims that Lowry's protagonists resist national sovereignty on principle and "[embrace] . . . fantasies of free-floating authenticity and autonomy," because they find "growing irrelevance [with] national citizenship as a source of identity and solidarity" (Miller 1–2). "Lowry," he asserts, "is a postnational writer for whom the nation-state no longer seems a stable principle of order" (5). On one level, this seems perfectly congenial with Wilderness' perspective. National sovereignty in *La Mordida* breeds anxiety and alienation in the cosmopolitan mindset: "The feeling that you are in a country where you have no right to be . . . persisted in these days in almost any country, including your own . . . [and] feeling that you have legally no right to be where you are is awful in the extreme" (*Mordida* 115). In Mexico, however, this alienation is more fundamental, culturally rooted: "[it] is there anyway, to some extent, from the start . . . because of the churches, the faith, particularly poignant" (115). If Wilderness is suggesting that sovereignty in a post-national world is more tolerable in countries with a familiar Anglo–Protestant heritage (the end of the novel hastily suggests the same), the central proposition of *La Mordida* counters that, more than any shared religious sensibility, it is the stability of modern juridical framework that makes certain nation states more desirable than others.

Reading the novel according to Agamben, Wilderness's victimization would demonstrate the very logic of (trans)national sovereignty because it exposes the primary violence of *nomos* itself. But, in *La Mordida*, only in Mexico is that violence provoked. When the couple enters America at the end of the novel, and is received with warm familiarity by American citizens and immigration officials, the novel partitions the two states in terms of the sovereignty they allow non-nationals: violence and law remain distinct north of the border (at least for the privileged Wildernesses), and the state of exception becomes ideologically territorialized in the Mexican state, transferred or displaced onto a juridical framework deemed democratic in form but totalitarian in procedure. What validates this juridical fallacy is not the novel's polemic (the best example of which is in the introduction, a letter Lowry actually sent to his American lawyer describing the couple's ordeal) but the narrative's affective investment in Mexican antagonism and the catharsis of American sovereignty.

Again, there may be post-imperial subtext to Wilderness's dilemma. As I suggested earlier, his loss of agency echoes the waning authority of the empire in contemporary British-Mexican economic negotiation (particularly when it comes to the matter of unpaid debts). When the Wildernesses do appeal to British and American consulates for legal advice, they receive little help and so continue to adopt other forms of strategic nationalism to establish their difference in a country where "the amount of money a gringo has is perhaps the sole criterion of his merit" (102). Their constant refrain, "Nosotros no somos americanos ricos—pobres—Canadianos [sic]," is at once a playful request for discounts on hotel rooms and an implicit rejection of the commodification of Mexico for American pleasure seekers (53). It also declares a kind of sovereign liminality in the suggestion of mutual frontiers ("Canada" in the novel means an isolated cabin in Dollarton, British Columbia), in its appeal to circuit official rules in the spirit of friendship (however cloying such an appeal would probably sound to struggling Mexican entrepreneurs).

But if personalization fails in *La Mordida*, it does so most significantly in Wilderness's refusal to pay the bribe: for all his self-declared cosmopolitanism, ignoring this bit of juridical protocol truly demonstrates the limits of his transculturation. In an essay on corruption in Mexico, Gabriela Coronado argues that the rhetoric used by members of developed nations to criticize Mexico's *mordida* system is often selfish and hypocritical: "the Anglo/Protestant/Western behaviour, 'our way,' is naturalized as the 'right' behaviour, while alternative practices from other nations, 'the other's way,' are implicitly assumed to be wrong: inefficient and immoral" (Coronado 7). She suggests that reducing the *mordida* to a simple act of corruption is insensitive when *mordidas* can in fact "demonstrate creativity, innovation, or merely a struggle to survive" (2). Post-colonial scholar Boaventura de Sousa Santos suggests deeper epistemological roots to the politics of such misunderstanding in arguing that modern juridical theory delegitimizes notions of legality that exist beyond the rigid binaries of the Euro-American context: "This central dichotomy [i.e. between the legal and illegal] . . . leaves out a whole social territory where the dichotomy would be unthinkable as an organizing principle, that is, the territory of the lawless, the a-legal, the non-legal, and even the legal or illegal according to non-officially recognized law" (2).

Mordidas were standard practice during the Lowrys' trip; Mexicans and tourists were equally solicited. In fact, 1946 marked the beginning of unprecedented bureaucratic corruption with the presidential inauguration of Miguel Alemán ("the father of Mexican tourism" grafted voluptuously from that industry) (Krauze 556–57). And it does not seem to bother Wilderness in *Dark as the Grave* when the "swarming" American tourists in Cuernavaca get the pinch (Lowry, *Dark* 105). Police chief and former acquaintance Eduardo Kent explains the ubiquity of "'put-up jobs" to exact money from "Americans [who] come here [and] . . . lose their heads": "There's no mystery about that part of my job—it comes straight from the Governor. They want the tourist trade and they don't want Americans to get in trouble. If it comes to that [i.e., bailing an American out of jail] it's all a matter of dollars" (Lowry, *Dark* 148–49).

The mystery arrives only when Wilderness himself is solicited, and it is precisely the personalization of the *mordida* that so terrifies him because he believes he is being targeted for some sort of cosmic retribution. Thus, if *La Mordida* is a machine (in the novel's metaphor), it functions more than just an extra-juridical culture of bribery but as a wider narrative structure, fusing state, personal, and textual antagonism in its abjective production.

The state, as we have seen, operates on multiple zones of indistinction. Its bureaucracy refuses to distinguish juridical and extra-juridical procedure. The levels of state power—regional and national, official and civilian—collapse in its surveillance and arbitrary policing. And when Wilderness's alcoholic excess and literary efforts become quasi-criminal activities under the scrutiny of Mexican authorities—it is no longer simply that he failed to pay for a visa extension; officials now have proof that he is "borracho . . . siempre ebriedad" (Lowry, *Mordida*, 178); they warn him, "You say bad things about Mexico and wrote—we know—we have it all" (287)—his own self-persecutory impulses become externalized in (un)official punishment (McCarthy 147). Thus, as Agamben says of Kafka's *The Trial*, "[the] existence and the very body of Joseph K. ultimately coincide with the Trial; they *become* the Trial," Wilderness becomes his *mordida* (Agamben 53).

His subjectivity undergoes a kind of schism, dividing Sigbjørn Wilderness, acting and more often failing to act in the economy of the text (and of the country); and the daemonic narrator who reduces Wilderness to his bare life, a mere character "in an unimaginable novel, not of this world, that did not, indeed, exist" (Lowry, *Mordida* 49). Externally, the daemon denies Wilderness's agency and propels him moribundly through the *mordida* machine; internally, he effects Wilderness's suspicion that Wilderness's past is somehow unconsciously creating his trouble (McCarthy 147). His uncanny terror is the crisis of narcissism exceeding subjectivity and bending the world into tragic self-importance.

The text then is the very code of this *mordida* machine. It is *The Valley of the Shadow of Death*, the revised and revised *Volcano*-esque novel that haunts the present; the "forest of symbols" around him, revealing the gap between life and fiction, the personal and universal. It is also the real-time novel of his daemon with its ruthless logo-masochism and tragic foreshadow on every page (McCarthy 146–47). Refraining from drinking or writing, choosing to see synchronicity as coincidence—taking any rational measure to resolve his problems would be as impossible as paying the *mordida* because the choices he makes have been preordained by crueller forces (Lowry, *Mordida* 297). Like the constant shakes he suffers every time he has to sign his name, his decisions are beyond self-control, "as something within him seemed inextricably bound, impossible of disengagement from, the machine" (60). Patrick McCarthy diagnoses this paralysis as Prufrockian fear: "whatever action he takes could upset the balance of the universe and make him responsible for the result" (160). And thus, writing and drinking fuel the self-fulfilling prophecy of a narrative in which Wilderness can be only an inactive observer, a character addicted to fate and dutifully bound to record its realization.

The novel concludes by giving back Wilderness a lost or repressed self-control, a narratological agency, which, in the manner of its return, is inseparable from national agency. In the final chapter, the Wildernesses arrive at the Nuevo Laredo border under the custody of an immigration officer who implies that he plans to murder Sigbjørn rather than deport him (Lowry, *Mordida* 297). Seizing an opportunity to escape, the couple crosses the border and meets "bronzed tall Texans," "the courteous Texan," "another polite Texan" (313–15). "'They are my brothers,' Sigbjørn almost purred, for the situation was causing him the most benign joy he had ever experienced" (314). Unlike their Mexican counterparts, the American border officials escort the Wildernesses into their country with sensitivity and civility. Any fear that Sigbjørn will be denied entry into the United States and separated from Primrose (an American citizen) immediately dissolves. "If the Texans like to think they are the best people in the world . . . so far as I'm concerned they are," Sigbjørn confirms (316). And though the couple repeats their thrifty refrain, "Nosotros no somos ricos Americanos" to a Mexican hotel owner on the northern side of the border, "[the Wildernesses] don't really care" (316). They are no longer worried about saving money and what earlier may have been the desire to distance themselves from Americans has been replaced with the joy of homecoming.

It is precisely at this moment, finally alone in a Laredo hotel room, that the daemon relinquishes his power over Wilderness and the catharsis is complete. Across the border, Wilderness has found liberation from the "machinery of the mordida": the daemon's control, the Mexican authorities, and from the text itself, as the novel will conclude two pages later.

AGENCY BEYOND *LA MORDIDA*?

But if this is supposed to be a triumphant ending,[3] why does the American homecoming somehow feel more illusory than the daemon's fiction? Is the welcome his Texan "brothers" extend not just artificial pleasantry, more of that cultural "stupidity" that was devouring mythopoeic Mexico? Moreover, if Wilderness's entry into the United States indicates a revitalized agency, how do we excuse that he had been pushed through the border as passively as through "the machinery of the mordida?" How secure really are the guarantees of American sovereignty when once more he has been automatically selected by immigration authorities because of his race and British heritage for "exceptional" treatment? How stable is sovereignty if it is granted by a state that can just as easily take it away?

Mary Pat Brady argues that the border renders its crosser "[transmogrified] . . . into someone either more or less advanced, more or less modern, more or less sophisticated" (Brady 50, 59). The border is an "abjection machine," "producing subjectivities, differences and cultures in terms of itself": making some subjects "intelligible," "human," and "legal," and others "alien" and "ontologically impossible," while "[erasing] the signs of its labor" (50, 60). Being selected for American sovereignty forces a different kind of self-schism in Wilderness: it corroborates the notion that his experiences in Mexico were "unintelligible," impenetrable, and, now, forever beyond understanding. "In America man is no longer part of the myth" (Lowry, *Mordida* 180), he had said weeks earlier in Acapulco; in America is now where he stands. And if he has not exactly chosen America, America has chosen him, which means that he has accomplished nothing more than exchanging one form of invasive, surveying biopolitical order for another that seems just as automatic and perhaps even more totalizing if the "bronzed tall Texans" embody the state itself in his reception.

In the novel's conclusion, it becomes clear that, more than just a mythopoeic cultural landscape, Mexico meant for Wilderness the possibility of a kind of intimacy the Texans could never offer. It meant the friendship he had gone to rekindle in *Dark as the Grave*. The spirit of that friendship surfaces quietly in *La Mordida*: we glimpse it in "the good Mexican" who had been terrorized by US immigration officials and who offers to cover Wilderness's *mordida* to spare him a similar fate (194–95). We see it again in the junior immigration officer who risks his position by assisting the couple across the border before his superior can inflict further humiliation and violence (312). Both gestures of friendship demonstrate a sympathy that is overtly hostile to state sovereignty (unlike the friendship of the Texans who, again, are practically state ambassadors). And one wonders if the loss of the possibility of friendship was partly what Wilderness had in mind on the last pages of the novel when he opens the curtains in his Laredo hotel room and takes one last look across the border: "And there, separated from them by the Río Grande, by centuries, by eternity, was ancient Mexico, great dark Catholic mysterious Mexico, to which perhaps [the Wildernesses] could never return.

What was Mexico? What did Mexico mean? Why was the thought that one could not return so terrible?" (317–18)

In *The Logic of Sense*, Gilles Deleuze suggests that Lowry's alcoholism warps his characters' perception of time so that "every future is experienced as a *future perfect* ("futur antérieur"), with an extraordinary precipitation of this compound future (an effect of the effect which goes on until death)" (Deleuze 159, 349). This may explain why the promised triumph of *La Mordida* cannot remain territorialized in America (nor, for that matter, in any present surroundings) and is instead differed to "Eridanus": to "[the] glory of a blue morning in Canada at home" where the Wildernesses may be finally domesticated (Lowry, *Mordida* 297). (This reads triumphant after all that has happened, though the victory it suggests is a lonely one.)

But if we take Deleuze literally, by which I mean grammatically, the future perfect reveals something else just as telling of Wilderness's—and Lowry's—failure: the tense demands the settlement of the past as the condition for a syntactically possible future ("I will have done"). It is an affirmation to improve the present for the stability of the future even if it betrays the solipsism of predestination ("thy will be done"). It is this antinomy, of hope and hopelessness, that will prove the final post-textual struggle for Wilderness, and the one he won't be able to resolve. Fate will continue cycling, the debts of his past will never be settled, exile will endure.

Sherrill Grace argues that when the Consul in *Volcano* is shot by the fascist *sinarquista* police, his death is authorized because he has been placed in a state of exception (reduced to bare life, the *homo sacer* who may be killed without reprisal), just as the Consul once authorized a state of exception for German prisoners of war. His death, the repetition of his own crime, according to Grace's reading, is the result of tragedy gone un-mourned, of trauma denied abreaction (Grace 207–209). *Dark as the Grave* is essentially a novel about mourning a lost friend that begins by mourning a lost home (Lowry's Dollarton cabin, destroyed by a fire). By the end of *La Mordida*, Wilderness has resolved to rebuild paradise in Dollarton, but in the same paragraph he is beginning to mourn Mexico all over again. How secure will his future be when the past remains perpetually unsettled?

We leave Wilderness in the Laredo hotel, but his loss will echo through Lowry's late writing. In "Through the Panama" it sounds shrill and bitter ("[an] excommunication," he calls his deportation, "[an infringement] of spiritual rights of man" [Lowry, "Panama" 69]). In "The Garden of Etla," Mexico is once again the "infernal paradise," a place of self-gnosis all the more mythic for his inability to return ("the person who falls in love with Mexico . . . is involved, in the deepest sense with a mystery . . . man himself is a mystery, and perhaps that is part of the point") (Lowry, "Garden" 45). Perhaps most succinct are a few lines he gave the Consul in a late draft of *Volcano* (Mordida, 351). They are not particularly memorable lines—an odd display of etymological gymnastics from a half-soused wit starting up his final binge. But reading them after Lowry's exile, their struggle to find commonality across languages, their struggle to translate, their failure to translate—more than anything they just seem sad: "Consider the word remorse. *Remors. Mordeo, mordere. La Mordida!*" (Lowry, *Volcano* 262) If only he could have paid the damned debt.

NOTES

1.   The actual pull quote reads, "Prosperity, Inflation, *and Tourists* are Changing Beautiful Mexico into Ugly Mexico" (emphasis added). See Rendon, 27.
2.   While Wilderness was working in Mexico, gathering material for *The Valley*, in the 1930s, the American government, at all levels, was passing laws and fomenting hysteria to force Mexicans and Mexican-Americans out of the country in order to secure jobs for "Americans." The repatriation ultimately undermines the ideality of American citizenship that Wilderness celebrates at the novel's end. See Balderrama and Rodríguez, 1–5.
3.   Lowry had envisioned that the novel would conclude his cycle *The Voyage That Never Ends* in a triumphant manner. See Bowker, 490.

WORKS CITED

Agamben, Giorgio. *Homo Sacer: Sovereign Power and Bare Life.* Translated by Daniel Heller-Roazen, Stanford, CA: Stanford UP, 1998.

Balderrama, Francisco E., and Raymond Rodríguez. *Decade of Betrayal: Mexican Repatriation in the 1930s.* Albuquerque: U of New Mexico P, 2006.

Berger, Dina. *The Development of Mexico's Tourism Industry: Pyramids by Day, Martinis by Night.* New York: Palgrave, 2006.

Bowker, Gordon. *Pursued By Furies: A Life of Malcolm Lowry.* New York: St. Martin's P, 1993.

Brady, Mary Pat. *Extinct Lands, Temporal Geographies.* Durham, NC: Duke UP, 2002.

Clancy, Michael. *Exporting Paradise: Tourism and Development in Mexico.* Oxford, UK: Pergamon, 2001.

Coronado, Gabriela. "Discourses of Anti-corruption in Mexico. Culture of Corruption or Corruption of Culture?" *Journal of Multidisciplinary International Studies*, vol. 5, no. 1, 2008.

de Sousa Santos, Boaventura. "Beyond Abyssal Thinking." *Eurozine.* 29 June 2007.

Deleuze, Gilles. *The Logic of Sense.* Translated by Constantin V. Boundas, New York: Columbia UP, 1990.

Grace, Sherrill E. *Strange Comfort: Essays on the Work of Malcolm Lowry.* Vancouver: Talonbooks, 2009.

Krauze, Enrique. *Mexico: Biography of Power.* Translated by Hank Heifetz, New York: Harper-Collins, 1997.

Lowry, Malcolm. *Dark as the Grave Wherein My Friend is Laid.* Edited by Douglas Day and Margerie Bonner Lowry, Toronto: General Publishing, 1968.

——. "Garden of Etla." *United Nations World*, IV (June 1950), pp. 45–47.

——. *Malcolm Lowry's La Mordida: A Scholarly Edition.* Edited by Patrick McCarthy. Athens: U of Georgia P, 1996.

——. "Through the Panama." *The Voyage That Never Ends*, edited by Michael Hofmann, New York: New York Review of Books, 2007.

——. *Under the Volcano.* 1947. New York: Penguin, 1985.

McCarthy, Patrick. *Forests of Symbols.* Athens: U of Georgia P, 1994.

Meyer, Lorenzo. "The Expropriation and Great Britain." *The Mexican Petroleum Industry in the Twentieth Century*, edited by Jonathan C. Brown and Alan Knight, Austin: U of Texas P, 1992.

Miller, Andrew John. "Under the Nation-State: Modernist Deterritorialization in Malcolm Lowry's *Under the Volcano.*" *Twentieth-Century Literature*, vol. 50, no. 1, 2004, pp. 1–17.

Ramirez, Luz Elena. *British Representations of Latin America.* Gainesville: UP of Florida, 2007.

Rendon, Eduardo Bolio. "Vanishing Enchantment?" *Modern Mexico*, vol. 18, no. 9, 1946, pp. 14–28.

Saragoza, Alex. "The Selling of Mexico: Tourism and the State, 1929–1952." *Fragments of a Golden Age: The Politics of Culture in Mexico Since 1940*, edited by Gilbert Joseph et al., Durham: Duke UP, 2001.

15

The Poetics of Exposed, Irreparable Space in Lunar Caustic; or, Reading Lowry Through Agamben

RICHARD J. LANE

ABANDONED AND EXPOSED

In *Homo Sacer: Sovereign Power and Bare Life*, Giorgio Agamben discusses the abandoned subject as not being "set outside the law" but being "abandoned by it ... exposed and threatened on the threshold in which life and law, outside and inside, become indistinguishable" (28). Subjectivity, within modernity, is fragile and, in many respects, *irreparable*, whereby, as Agamben argues, "Irreparable means ... [being] consigned without remedy to ... being-thus ... irreparable also means that ... there is literally no shelter possible, that in ... being-thus they [modern subjects] are absolutely exposed, absolutely abandoned" (Agamben, *Coming* 39). The modern subject is also subject to biopolitical analysis, seen when the protagonist of Malcolm Lowry's *Lunar Caustic*, a character named Plantagenet, on his own volition, walks in to the psychiatric ward of a New York hospital. His mobility (or, his existential choice expressed through his freedom of movement within an otherwise oppressive institution that normally constrains one's mobility in a closely defined space) is paradoxical, since it signifies that the sovereign biopolitical power of the state is both strangely affirmed (its governance of a defined space) yet also suspended (its control appears limited and even non-existent). Plantagenet appears relatively at home in the building, yet also spends much of his time gazing out at the surrounding urban, port environment. Is his gaze, therefore, imprisoned or free, or, as Christiane Barucoa puts it, "Du regard emprisonné / Entre ses quatre murs de pierre" ("Of a gaze imprisoned / Between its four stone walls," qtd. in Bachelard 34)? In entering this space, is Plantagenet subjecting himself further to a more closely defined biopolitics? Is he eventually abandoned, in the sense of being banished from the ward (banished as a free agent, yet paradoxically exiled into his freedom), or is he "exposed and threatened" because of his threshold or liminal status? How do readers understand the space of the building Plantagenet is briefly, and paradoxically, "at home" in (a home, that is of course both *heimlich* and *unheimlich*)? The intensification of suffering among the abandoned subjects of *Lunar Caustic* leads to their abjection, the creaturely aesthetic of which is articulated by Lowry in a metaphysical, theological language, while he simultaneously appears to deconstruct the transcendent and the sacred. The text is "surnaturel" presenting, as with Jean Cocteau's *Opium*, "a theory of art related to the invasion of the self by dreams, portents, and the unknown" (McAlice 6). Daydreams of the sort that occur in *Lunar Caustic*, while dystopian, belong to "topoanalysis," to use Bachelard's term, not psychoanalysis; in other words, Plantagenet's introjection and projection of subjectivity via architecture and the urban/port environment is one that maps the subject in, and via, spatiality.

Filipczak argues that "Bellevue reflects and exposes mechanisms of oppression and violence that operate in the reality outside" (395), a reality where any notion of salvation "is revealed as absurd" (396). Exposure is, in this reading, the opposite of "Origen's vision of *apokatastasis*, i.e., total renewal, [where] everything is included in the plan of salvation" (397). What has been uncovered or exposed here? Precisely the "torment," "torture," and "source" of accused being, which is also its "limit" (all of these being Agamben's terms from *The Coming Community*). The accused are also the irreparable, those subjects "consigned without remedy to their being-thus" (39), a being-thus which, subject to the "originary fracture" of the philosophical question of essence/existence, reveals a subject that paradoxically appears open to all, or free, while also as such condemned to being at the mercy of judgment, decision, opinion, and trial. As *Lunar Caustic* makes clear, modern existence is not a question of some future *renovatio* but rather the lack of shelter leading to absolute exposure and abandonment. Under certain conditions—that is, recognition of the exposure of freedom— the person flees from, recovers, or shelters from this exposure. Throughout *The Arcades Project*, for example, Walter Benjamin calls this fleeing a form of forgetting and sleeping, whereas in *Being and Time* Heidegger calls it "tranquillized self-assurance" (233). Fully recognizing Agamben's notion of exposure is, thus, anxiety inducing. As Heidegger argues: "Anxiety brings [the human being] . . . face to face with its *Being-free for*" (232), which is an uncanny moment (233); in other words, it is the recognition that exposure is "not-being-at-home" (*das Nicht-zuhause-sein*).

The space of exposure in *Lunar Caustic* is analogous to that of Agamben's paradoxically described "coming community," where "*Quodlibet ens* is not 'being, it does not matter which,' but rather, 'being such that it always matters'" (*Coming* 1). In this space, subjectivity is akin to Nigel Dennis's portrayal of humanity "not-being-at-home" in *A House in Order*, that is, situated within a transparent skin (the glass house or greenhouse) that does not so much shelter as expose the human occupant. Dennis's protagonist actually desires the security of a proper enclosure or prison, such as the concentration camp that he can see from his greenhouse, expressed in the following exchange, during which the camp guards reveal embarrassment because they initially failed to notice him.

> Q: This is a very tedious charade. With every lie you add to it you step closer to the hole in the ground you are going to. . . . Do you ask us to believe that you sat all day on that greenhouse chair and were not observed?
> A: What else can I ask, when it's true? I hoped and prayed to be observed . . .
> Q: *Why?*
> A: Why, because I hoped to go to prison.
> (Dennis 19)

Hope in the prison camp, defined as a release from exposure, is indicative of the discomfort Dennis's protagonist endures while being permanently on display (ironically, he later learns that the prisoners, in observing him, have been interpreting signs of his cowardice and despair as actions of defiance to the authorities). In *Lunar Caustic*, hope is expressed on a pilgrimage, not to a church, which is regarded by the protagonist as merely being a temporary waystation, a cool place to drink alcohol in a heatwave, but to a hospital: "all day he has hovered round it; now it looms up closer than ever. This is his objective" (Lowry 11). Inside the church Plantagenet had observed depictions on the walls of "the stages of the cross" (11), preparing the reader for a potential teleological journey inside the hospital; Plantagenet is a superior theologian, however, since he eventually reveals that the "stages" of suffering lead not to some simplistic notion of an ultimate cure, but instead to the revelation that he is to remain in the moment of suffering once he has been expelled from the hospital. These stages, then, are the "Augenblick Kreuzwig" or the notion that Franz Rosenzweig makes clear in *The Star of Redemption*, that "every station" is potentially a moment of universal suffering, that is, "the way of the cross" (see my discussion in Lane, "Sacred Space" 370). Plantagenet's suffering includes not just the lidless eye or the lacerated mind, but also the consequences of having a panoptical gaze. Critics have compared Plantagenet's entry into the hospital with a descent into hell (i.e., following the Dante allusions throughout the text), but spatially this entry is more a raising up, an elevation, and a revealing. As noted, the building's skin becomes transparent, partly because of its glass windows, but partly as a *surnatural* phenomenon:

Plantagenet suddenly caught sight, through the bars, of four operations being performed simultaneously in the wing opposite in high sunlit rooms of glass, so that it seemed as though the front of that part of the hospital had suddenly become *open*, revealing, as in the cabin plans of the 'Cunard' or in charts of the human anatomy itself, the activities behind the wraith of iron or brick or shin: and it was strange to watch these white-masked figures working behind the glass that now glittered like a mirage. At the same time the whole scene that lay before them suddenly, like the looming swift white hand of a traffic policeman, reeled towards him; he felt he had only to stretch out his fingers to touch the doctor working on the right side of the table sewing up the incision, or the nurse plastering and binding the patient or placing the blanket over the body; and it seemed to him that all these dressings and redressings in these hours of north light were at the same time being placed, torn away and replaced, on a laceration of his own mind. (Lowry 25–26)

The transparent skin reveals a palimpsest composed of four main structures: the hospital, a ship, the human body, and the mind. Logically, these structures all occupy a different space, but Plantagenet's vision (or nightmare) brings them together in a complex gestalt, one which fundamentally involves witnessing. The voyeuristic aspect of this witnessing creates a physical intimacy: Plantagenet feels that he can literally touch these overlayered scenes. Yet he is also *touched by* the scenes, transferring himself into them, becoming the patient whose lacerated mind is being painfully re-lacerated by a constant ripping off and reapplication of a bandage. The exposed structures are, in effect, wounds, and Plantagenet undergoes transference in his vulnerable witnessing and taking on such wounds. Plantagenet is not a scapegoat figure, and as a witness he clearly cannot save or redeem the other, but the witness can go in the other's stead; in other words, his existential *Jemeinigkeit* (or "in each case mine-ness") can be for others. The gestalt creates a complex image, one which has a heightened graphicness, or *Anschaulichkeit* ("heightened graphicness). The transparent skin exposes what usually remains hidden, or at the least private; exposure here involves light and time, perhaps being analogous to the amount of light and the length of time that a film negative is exposed to. Too much light and the negative is bleached out; too much time, and movement is blurred; yet it is increased exposure that allows the witness to capture and illuminate that which would otherwise not be seen or photographed.

SINDON—OR, THE COVERING

The witness does not remain silent in *Lunar Caustic*; in fact, the opposite occurs in the fourth chapter, in a discussion in the office of the hospital psychiatrist, Doctor Claggart. The discussion is primarily Claggart's opportunity to expel or banish Plantagenet from the hospital, because he is "a foreigner" (46), as well as being a liar (47), a troublemaker or non-conformist (50), a "conceited Englishman" (50), a "back-alley drunk" (50), and a time-waster or tourist (perhaps with the implication that Plantagenet is slumming it, gaining material for his writing) (62). On one level, the discussion appears quite reasonable, an encounter between analyst and analysand, with the latter claiming artistic and creative insight into institutional life, and the former claiming that Plantagenet's own blind spots lead to his misrecognizing and misunderstanding his compatriots. At another level, however, the chapter develops some of the Christian imagery of the novella as a whole, in particular that of baptism and the *sindon*, the "cloth" or sheet with which Plantagenet dries himself. In fact, the chapter opens with an allusion to *sindon*: "The doctor, in a white robe, seemed to people the room with phantoms" (46). This robe is multiplied and confused with the white curtains that "blow in" from the open windows: "He couldn't find the doctor among the phantoms, for the curtains, blowing in at that moment, made one whiteness with his robe" (46). The priestly robe further foreshadows Plantagenet's use of Christian terms of reference for washing after the sports game that was played in bare feet; the other players conform to the order not to wash, not daring "to take a shower before supper at all, or even, like the disciples, to wash their feet" (48). Plantagenet, however, does wash, throwing water on his face, then drying himself on a bed sheet, for which he is told he is "*going to suffer*" (50). The baptismal rebirthing imagery is made clear with the italics in Plantagenet's monologue: "many who are supposed to be mad here . . . are simply people who perhaps once saw, however confusedly, the necessity for change in themselves, for *rebirth*, that's the word" (52). Rather bluntly and obviously, the chapter is also punctuated with the invocations "My God" and "good Christ," or variations thereof. The chapter would therefore appear to oppose the priestly representative of the Sanhedrin—or at the least a Pharisee—with that of a disciple, a follower or representative of Christ, and an Everyman figure, the abjected banished human soul exposed and subjected to oppressive law. I suggest that Lowry is playing a much deeper game than this, and that such a binary opposition, while almost crudely foregrounded, muddies the potentially baptismal waters.

Plantagenet, drying his post-baptismal self with a sheet, is closer to the mysterious young man of the Gospel of Mark: "Now a certain young man followed

Him, having a linen cloth thrown around his naked body. And the young men laid hold of him, and he left the linen cloth and fled from them naked" (Mark 14:51–52, NKJV). The *sindon* is here both clothing and remainder, as it is all that is left behind when the young man flees Christ's arrest. Clement of Alexandria refers to, and indeed quotes, a Gnostic version of Mark in which the young man is to receive initiation through baptism; as Frank Kermode explains, "the young man in Mark's account of the arrest is on his way to be baptized; that is why he is naked under his *sindon*, a garment appropriate to symbolic as well as to real burial, and appropriate also to symbolic resurrection, both to be enacted in the ceremony" (Kermode 58). Turning to Farrer, Kermode finds the themes of betrayal and escape: "the young man is related to . . . two Old Testament types, one in Amos (2:16)—'on that day the bravest of warriors shall be stripped of his arms and run away'—and the other in Genesis (39:12), where Joseph escapes from the seduction attempt of Potiphar's wife by running away and leaving his cloak in her hands" (61). Plantagenet's ban from the hospital is also his abandonment of his compatriots; his initiation into the fellowship of suffering is, however, a potential seduction into their world. At an even deeper level, however, Lowry has overlayered this episode that occurs in Mark, both authorized and Gnostic, with more subtle Christ imagery, since it is Christ who leaves or abandons the disciples, his *sindon* or shroud being left behind in the otherwise empty tomb. Filipczak argues that the Christ imagery is present by allusion to the Gospel of John, with the episode of Christ washing each of the disciple's feet, which "can be regarded as the structural equivalent of the Last Supper" (Filipczak 402). As Filipczak suggests, "In the novella the towel is compared to a winding sheet, which evokes associations with death and burial. The towel or sheet used by Jesus also anticipates winding sheets and therefore his death" (402). Unfortunately, while this argument is strong and is undoubtedly correct in terms of the tracing of the allusion, in the novella Plantagenet is the only one who washes/is baptized, and the only one who uses the sheet: on himself, not the others/the disciples. What, then, is the purpose of this overlayering of the young man's *sindon* imagery with a Christ who abandons humanity through his death and disappearance from the tomb? In other words, why has Lowry chosen the Christ of the Gospel of Mark, with its infamous original sudden and shocking ending: "So they went out quickly and fled from the tomb, for they trembled and were amazed. And they said nothing to anyone, for they were afraid" (Mark 16:8, NKJV)? These questions may of course be answered through an understanding of what *does not* get written about in Mark prior to the addition of a textual supplement (Mark 16:9–20, NKJV) used to create the previously absent ending: a resurrected Christ. Furthermore, following Filipczak's reading, the Christ (or "pseudo-Christ") of *Lunar Caustic* is a failure: "the theological elements of *Lunar Caustic* are diffuse traces of a religious system that is no longer available to or salvific for the characters" (Filipczak 94); "The very attempt at salvation is revealed as absurd" (396); "The pseudo-Christ of the novella is too weak to lead anybody out of bondage. His yearning to free everybody is revealed as merely a parody of redemption" (397); and "The world that emerges from Plantagenet's vision of reality is cut off from grace or the possibility of renewal. It is 'condemned'" (399). I suggest that even the name of Christ being spoken in this text is a scandal, or a *skandalon*, a stumbling block, within a profane world.

Lowry, in my reading, appears to offer two pictures of Christ: the Gnostic and the powerless; the first holds secret knowledge, and the second denies the efficacy of knowledge. The allusion to the Gnostic Mark suggests that there is a secret power available to the redeemer or his disciple, once he has gone through initiation. Plantagenet clearly rejects the knowledge set and application of modern-day western medicine, but he opposes it partly with his recognition of suffering, and partly with an aesthetic vision: "If you'd read them, the first thing you'd notice would be the curious symbolism and if you had ever read any French poetry—or any poetry at all for that matter—you would see some similarity in the process of selectivity to, say, that of Rimbaud, taking an obvious example ... Forests, soleils, rivers, savanes" (Lowry 57). Plantagenet is suggesting that it is through the profane illumination of modernist aesthetics that the abandoned subjects of the hospital are to be understood, and yet his subsequent illuminating examples—that Garry's lack of education has meant that he cannot read—are "the Pentateuch, the Revelation of St John and the Song of Songs" (58). The implication is, of course, that it is only through interpreting these texts as modernist symbolist dreamscapes that they will make any sense. Yet such modernist gnosis is rejected (as is all gnosis) by the suffering Christ (Plantagenet's other option or experience), the Christ of power through weakness and the fellowship of suffering. Plantagenet identifies with both Christs, although the profane illumination of gnosis is ultimately emptied out by the banishment back into the world of suffering, that is to say, the community "inside" the hospital, which is even more extensively present in the outside city spaces.

THE SPACE OF THE CREATURELY

Plantagenet's reference to the Cunard cabin plans, as quoted above, provides another clue to the spatial and intertextual dynamics of *Lunar Caustic*; the reference is less about luxury-cruise-liner accommodation and more to do with the "ship of fools" who willingly place themselves in constricted spaces at sea. As

Robert Burton says in *The Anatomy of Melancholy*, "What is a ship but a prison?,," while Samuel Johnson famously asserted that "A man in jail has more room, better food, and commonly better company." Critics have long pointed out the analogous ship or "freighter" in *Lunar Caustic*: a pseudo ark with its cargo of animals "bound for a zoo" (69; the other closely related intertextual network in the novella functions through reference to Melville's *Moby Dick*). The word "bound" here is intriguing, meaning both "constriction" and "destination," both being, in this example, "inhumane." In other words, whether it is being bound at sea in a storm, or trapped in small cages in a zoo, it is the essentially "inhumane" treatment of the animals that is disturbing, foregrounding the paradox in the word "inhumane"; that conditions not fit for humans are also considered not fit for animals. Indeed, in the novella the animals cry in a way that "was perhaps more human than the one now heard" (69) in the hospital. This chiasmus can be read as straightforward ethical commentary (conditions in the hospital are terribly inhumane) or as a moment whereby the proximity of the animal/human—their similarity and differences—reveals *the space of the creaturely*. As Eric Santner argues, "human beings are not just creatures among other creatures but are in some sense *more creaturely* than other creatures by virtue of an excess that is produced in the space of the political" (26). In *Lunar Caustic*, it is not the case that conditions in the hospital are somehow more troubling than those aboard the freighter: it is that the humans themselves are more creaturely than the animals.

> Noting the derivation of the word "creature" from the future-active participle of the Latin *creare*, [Julia] Lupton writes that the "*creatura* is a thing always in the process of undergoing creation; the creature is actively passive or, better, *passionate*, perpetually becoming created, subject to transformations at the behest of the arbitrary commands of an Other." "Creature" is not so much the name of a determinate state of being as the signifier of an ongoing *exposure*, of being caught up in the process of *becoming creature* through the dictates of divine alterity. This dimension of radical subjection—of created thing to creator—has induced, in the history of the concept, a series of further articulations, ultimately becoming generalized to signify "anyone or anything that is produced or controlled by an agent, author, master, or tyrant." (Santner 28)

If *Lunar Caustic*, then, is a textual space in which Plantagenet's state-of-exception reveals the biopolitical "radical subjection" of the creaturely, then the question needs to be asked "why make this text so deeply Christological?" Ironically, the very signs of messianic failure listed above are only such from a Davidic kings or

Old Testament perspective (see Horbury), not from a Pauline or New Testament perspective of the counterintuitive "power through weakness." The one who dares to "go forward" in the novella is "the carpenter" (Lowry 69), while Plantagenet desires the freedom for human beings "to suffer like animals" (69). Santner notes that humans may enter the zone of the creaturely, but *that does not make them animal*; rather, the shared suffering leads in human beings to "biopolitical animation" (Santner 39), of the sort that Plantagenet expresses at the close of the novella, moving back into the world yet not entirely leaving behind the fellowship of the hospital patients. Plantagenet may leave the hospital in despair, but as Kierkegaard says, this despair—or sickness—is what ultimately *distinguishes* the animated subject from the animal (Kierkegaard 15). In other words, the creaturely condition that Plantagenet exhibits is composed of recognition (sharing the deep anxiety and fear expressed by the animals on board the ship) and difference (precisely the self-reflexive stepping away and observing of the condition of being-animal or being-subjected, which is constitutive of difference).

It is not so much that Plantagenet's recognition that the spatial biopolitical dynamics of the hospital are to be found outside the hospital that torments Plantagenet, rather, it is that he "failed" to be a Davidic messiah king that is consuming him after the event; again, as Kierkegaard says, it is not the "failure" over which the subject despairs, rather, it is not losing the old subject—or remaining the same subject—that creates the despair; in this case, if Plantagenet did not become a Davidic messiah king then he is still the same creaturely, abjected, and weak person, precisely that which torments him. This person is of course typological, the clue being found in the notion that "the despair has inflamed something that cannot burn or be burned up in the self" (Kierkegaard 19). Plantagenet, then, leaves the hospital in despair, plunging back into the profane world without abandoning his typological self, or, "eternity's claim upon him" (Kierkegaard 21). Plantagenet, in other words, exists "meta-ethically" to use Rosenzweig's term. The "metaethical" suggests that the subject is always exposed in its receptivity, in its waiting or receptiveness to the Other (be that Other read via secular or sacred ethics). The metaethical stance implies that this receptivity is constitutive, and that such receptivity is both a weakness and a strength (it is the "passive" creaturely and the more active *animation*). As noted above, Plantagenet's modernist mode of perception—his profane *illumination*—creates an aesthetics of heightened graphicness (*Anschaulichkeit*), which is also the dialectical image of the metaethical state: the "graphic" situation, say, of the hospital and its patients/inmates, and the intense psychological/aesthetic imagery of lacerated being, or, the perspective of the *Lebenschauung* or life-view, where "we view the human as it in fact is, always individual" (Samuelson 11). In the

Lebenschauung, the human "receives from another its obligations" and "can only be understood from a perspective beyond itself" (12).

The space of the creaturely in Lunar Caustic, then, appears always to be inter-penetrated with that which it is not, or should not be. For example, the closed cell is "opened" in multiple ways: through its skinless state or transparency; through the fact that the cell is part of a larger structure that is literally and metaphysi-cally on a journey (the opposite of the static cell, dungeon, or cave); and through its openness (i.e., Plantagenet can simply leave it). Typologically, the space of the creaturely is that which is sacred and profane, awaiting the event (of release, redemption, a "cure," etc.) and having witnessed or experienced the event. The interpenetration of inside and outside throughout the novella thus gives it a certain porosity, almost as if it were a poetical Arcades Project, with labyrinthine glass passages heading off in myriad directions. Even though the novella func-tions normally in its linear, progressive narrative movement, this interpenetrated creaturely space is also non-linear and three-dimensional; it is perhaps closer to B. S. Johnson's Albert Angelo (1964), simply for the latter's hole cut through several pages, allowing a glimpse further on or into the unfolding narrative, and conceivably, Lowry has also created the conceptual grounds for a more radi-cal textuality, such as that to be found in Johnson's The Unfortunates (1969): an unbound collection of chapters stored in a box, that can be shuffled by the reader in any order. These references are not as far-fetched as they might sound, since Lowry later sliced through his own copy of Ultramarine, literally cutting words out of the text with a sharp knife, and to complete the analogy, this annotated or cut text is now housed in its own specially constructed box (see Lane, "Cutting"). Lunar Caustic, to stick with the novella in question, did not need cutting because it is already so cutting, being lacerated and exposed in its torture that is also its limit, to cite Agamben: "To exist means to take on qualities, to submit to the torment of being such (inqualieren). Hence quality, the being-such of each thing, is its torture and its source—its limit. How you are—your face—is your torture and your source. And each being is and must be its mode of being, its manner of rising forth: being such as it is" (Coming 98).

PLANTAGENET THE (PAULINE) MILITANT

Critical readings of Lunar Caustic, whatever their methodology, tend to be struck by the sudden ending, whereby Plantagenet goes back into the world. Biographically, this allows for the connection of the text, or its sublation (in the Hegelian sense), with the texts that follow that "re-entry" by Lowry. In other words, the Christological, as a merely interpretive and aesthetic "problem," is cathartically worked through in *Lunar Caustic* and dialectically resolved (cancelled out and incorporated) in(to) *Under The Volcano*. Richard Cross, for example, argues that "the novella was never itself a masterpiece-in-embryo but that, like *Ultramarine*, its importance lies in its having prepared the artist to write *Under the Volcano*" (25). Plunging "back" into the world is, however, not quite so straightforward as it might seem, since by this point in the novella different spatial zones or domains have been thoroughly interpenetrated or made transparent; that is to say (or question), what does it mean to move to the "outside" when inside and outside are now thoroughly permeable and interpenetrated by one another? Plantagenet appears in the "outside" to be just as skeptical and interrogative as he was on the "inside," these terms in scare quotes needing, of course, to be placed under Derridean erasure. Further, in *Lunar Caustic* Doctor Claggart critiques Plantagenet's notion of the other patients to the extent that where Plantagenet sees suffering inside the ward, Claggart sees shelter, treatment, and an environment that is better than the home one that the patients come from. The spaces of shelter or suffering are, throughout the novella, represented as an outcome of economics, such as in Plantagenet and Claggart's constant references to lack of time or resources to truly focus on each individual subject in the city's care. In other words, even though the hospital is a public institution, it is still a marketplace, and as such it homogenizes its inhabitants and their "territory" so that they may "be exposed in the same way as others to the uniform prerogatives of the market" (Badiou 11). Plantagenet's crime has been to attempt to deterritorialize this market, whereby each subject is considered once more as a person (although, ironically, Doctor Claggart argues that, inadvertently, all Plantagenet does is imagine or fantasize each subject's personhood). Plantagenet is truly a foreigner in the sense of contaminating capitalist space, and yet he returns to the "outside" (under erasure) and becomes, in effect, a customer or consumer. Doctor Claggart, from the position of a state functionary, has resisted Plantagenet's biopolitical militancy, whereby Plantagenet wishes to reinstate the "universal singularity" (11) of personhood. Plantagenet, then, can only gain traction from his exilic existence as a mode of subtraction, whereby what he perceives, from the perspective of the creaturely as the truth (and from the perspective of the truth-event), "is subtracted from the organization of subsets prescribed by that state. The subjectivity corresponding to this subtraction constitutes a necessary *distance* from the State and from what corresponds to the State in people's consciousness: the apparatus of opinion" (15). Plantagenet's post-exilic existence, rather than being some kind of failure, is instead what Badiou calls *a fidelity to the event*, or "the 'process' of continuing with a situation *from the point of view of the event that has come to supplement it*" (Gibson 147; italics in the original). As Andrew Gibson explains, "For Badiou, the event is what comes to *supplement* being, the multiplicity of a given situation, in that it both pertains to that situation and yet it is also outside and detached from the latter's rules" (147). Plantagenet's "event" could perhaps be described, using Girard's term, as being that of "mimetic desire," with the concomitant recognition that the scapegoating process has always already happened (it is what, according to Girard, stops society collapsing into an abyss of uncontrollable violence). Fidelity to the event, for Plantagenet, is fidelity to exposed subjectivity; thus the closing reversal of the novella's opening narrative sequence is also its retraversing (tavern to church; church to tavern) and its re-territorialization. The sacramental imagery is not contaminated as such by the alcoholic drink in the church because Plantagenet is merely subtracting from the state's positioning or demarcating of the sacred and the profane. From the creaturely, at the close of the novella, Plantagenet moves in to the realm of *kratos*; his violent smashing of the bottle against "an obscene sketch of a girl chalked on" to a washroom wall (Lowry 75) could be called *krateros*, "a term that admirably displays the conjunction of good and bad violence within the sacred" (Girard 264). Such violence is thus militant, that exemplary position for Badiou which is found, paradoxically, in the Apostle Paul: "For me, Paul is a poet-thinker of the event, as well a one who practices and states the invariant traits of what can be called the militant figure. He brings forth the entirely human connection, whose destiny fascinates me, between the general idea of a rupture, an overturning, and that of a thought-practice that is this rupture's subjective materiality" (Badiou 2). The militant is "heterogeneous to the law" (57), just as Plantagenet is heterogeneous to the demarcated space of therapeutic biopower. Finally, then, it is crucial to recognize that *Lunar Caustic*'s evental modernist space—Schoenberg's twelve-tone system is given by Badiou as an example of an event (Gibson 147)—is deeply ethical: "Ethics arrives as a supplement to the subject, making the subject more and other than he or she has thitherto been; or rather, better still, it even 'induces' a subject" (148). *Lunar Caustic* stands alone as a modernist ethical text, needing no dialectical sublation or Davidic messianism to repair what remains vulnerable: the human subject.

WORKS CITED

Agamben, Giorgio. *Homo Sacer: Sovereign Power and Bare Life.* Translated by Daniel Heller-Roazen, Stanford, CA: Stanford UP, 1998.

——. *The Coming Community.* Translated by Michael Hardt, London & Minneapolis: U of Minnesota P, 2007.

Bachelard, Gaston. *The Poetics of Space.* Translated by Maria Jolas, Boston: Beacon, 1969.

Badiou, Alain. *Saint Paul: The Foundation of Universalism.* Translated by Ray Brassier, Stanford, California: Stanford UP, 2003.

Benjamin, Walter. *The Arcades Project.* Translated by Howard Eiland and Kevin McLaughlin, Cambridge, MA, and London, UK: The Belknap P of Harvard UP, 1999.

Cross, Richard K. *Malcolm Lowry: A Preface to His Fiction.* Chicago & London: The U of Chicago P, 1980.

Dennis, Nigel. *A House in Order.* Middlesex, UK: Penguin, 1969.

Filipczak, Dorota. "Theology in Asylum: The Failure of Salvific Story in Malcolm Lowry's *Lunar Caustic.*" *Literature and Theology*, vol. 8, no. 4, 1994, pp. 394–404.

Gibson, Andrew. *Postmodernity, Ethics and the Novel: From Leavis to Levinas.* London and New York: Routledge, 1999.

Girard, René. *Violence and the Sacred.* Translated by Patrick Gregory, Baltimore: Johns Hopkins UP, 1979.

Heidegger, Martin. *Being and Time.* Translated by John Macquarrie and Edward Robinson, Oxford, UK: Blackwell, 1990.

Horbury, William. *Jewish Messianism and the Cult of Christ.* London: SCM, 1998.

Johnson, B.S. *Albert Angelo.* London: Constable, 1964.

——. *The Unfortunates.* London: Panther, 1969.

Kermode, Frank. *The Genesis of Secrecy: On the Interpretation of Narrative.* Cambridge, MA: Harvard UP, 1996.

Kierkegaard, Søren, *The Sickness Unto Death.* Translated by Howard V. Hong and Edna H. Hong, Princeton, NJ: Princeton UP, 1983.

Lane, Richard J. "Cutting *Ultramarine*: Some Thoughts on the Annotated Edition at UBC Special Collections," *The Malcolm Lowry Review*, vol. 47–48, Fall 2000/ Spring 2001, pp. 128–139.

——. "Sacred Space and the Fellowship of Suffering in the Postmodern Sublime," *Through A Glass Darkly: Suffering, the Sacred, and the Sublime in Literature and Theory*, edited by Holly Faith Nelson, Lynn R. Szabo, and Jens Zimmerman, Waterloo, ON: Wilfrid Laurier UP, 2010, pp. 363–375.

Lowry, Malcom. *Lunar Caustic.* London: Jonathan Cape, 1977. Originally published in *The Paris Review*, no. 29, 1963.

McAlice, Edward. "A Cocteau Allusion in Lowry's *Lunar Caustic.*" *Notes on Contemporary Literature*, vol. 25, no. 3, 1995, pp. 6–7.

Rosenzweig, Franz. *The Star of Redemption.* Translated by William W. Hallo, London and Notre Dame: U of Notre Dame P, 1985.

Samuelson, Norbert M. *A User's Guide to Franz Rosenzweig's Star of Redemption.* Richmond, Surrey: Curzon, 1999.

Santner, Eric L. *On Creaturely Life: Rilke, Benjamin, Sebald.* Chicago and London: U of Chicago P, 2006.

Coda

After Lowry: A Film Essay

MIGUEL MOTA

The accompanying film essay, *After Lowry*,[1] attempts to complicate, in productive ways, the experience (ideally conceived as unmediated) of the Malcolm Lowry Walk, a landscape currently occupying a curious space between the natural and the cultivated, the private and the public. The Malcolm Lowry Walk, located in Cates Park in the village of Dollarton in the district of North Vancouver, British Columbia, commemorates the author of the great twentieth-century novel *Under the Volcano*, who with his wife, Margerie Bonner Lowry, lived there from 1940 to 1954 in a squatter's shack on the beach. It was here that Lowry finished *Under the Volcano*, and here too that he would compose his long story set in Dollarton itself, "The Forest Path to the Spring," a sometimes ecstatic, sometimes contemplative meditation on the human relationship with nature and with history. The longer Lowry lived in Dollarton, the more complex his fictional ruminations on the landscape became. A great deal of his work is dedicated to rethinking his personal and literary challenges against the backdrop of Burrard Inlet and the larger sweep of coastal history, and the potential redemption it embodied for him. This space became for Lowry, to use the words of English historian Simon Schama, "a text on which [he wrote his] recurring obsessions" (Schama 12). The sense of, and belief in, Dollarton as a place to begin anew in an unspoiled world returns repeatedly in Lowry's writing, and "The Forest Path to the Spring," a story he worked on until late in his life, has frequently been read as a kind of psalm to the simple, solitary, and hopeful existence that could be led in a squatters's shack by the sea.

This particular landscape became for Lowry a natural emblem of his desire for a simpler, nobler, less complicated life and world. It was here that Lowry was finally able to finish his great work and here that he most successfully (even if only temporarily) found respite from a deeply troubled, because deeply felt, life. It is hardly surprising, then, that Lowry's years on the beach at Dollarton have repeatedly been seen as a paradise, however temporary it may have turned out to be. And so it is to this space, this "paradise," that many readers of Lowry's life and work have continuously returned, as pilgrims to a kind of literary shrine, a place of proximity and connectedness to the writer himself. In the late 1980s, the district of North Vancouver even reclaimed Lowry as one of its own after having hounded him off its beaches decades earlier with numerous eviction notices. A commemorative plaque was erected in 1987 in honour of the years he spent living and working in Dollarton. A path through the forest was christened the Malcolm Lowry Walk, and roughly halfway along it a set of steps was built leading down to a wood platform on the beach to mark the site of the Lowrys' shack.[2]

Yet this landscape, a kind of sacred place to many, is also of course a fictional space, the product of both Lowry's and his readers' desires. *After Lowry* calls attention to the mediation involved in any attempt to recreate the Lowrys' experience in Dollarton. The film juxtaposes the "natural" sounds and images of the park with a number of self-consciously artificial interjections into that "natural" space, including additional sound recordings of that very same space, various iconic images associated with the Lowrys' days there, and textual material produced by both Lowry and his readers/critics, in an attempt to offer a critique of the park's utopian function (a function that fulfills a desire for proximity and connectedness) in the context of Lowry's life and work. *After Lowry* explores the extent to which this "natural" space is repeatedly and inevitably turned into an aesthetic object, whether mediated sonically through the aural landscape, textually through Lowry's narratives, or culturally through the gaze of the literary tourist. In the end, the film essay considers the extent to which the "natural" space of the Malcolm Lowry Walk functions not as an unmediated connection to some imagined origin and "authentic" author, but rather as a historical and geographical document, a living, changing text, itself always subject to media manipulation and cultural desire.[3]

NOTES

1. The film is available on the Modernist Commons website at http://modernistcommons. ca/islandora/object/emic%3A74f79dfc-a933-434b-b535-04f825920ea8/sources

2. The exact location of the original shack has been a matter of some conjecture and controversy, and it is perhaps both ironic and fitting that the gaze of the literary tourist searching for the "authentic" paradisical home of Malcolm Lowry should be directed at the precise spot where he may have never lived.

3. For their help in funding the production of this film, I would like to thank the Hampton Research Fund at the University of British Columbia.

WORKS CITED

Lowry, Malcolm. "The Forest Path to the Spring." *Hear Us O Lord from Heaven Thy Dwelling Place*. Vancouver, Toronto: Douglas & McIntyre, 1961.

———. *Under the Volcano*. 1947. Harmondsworth, UK: Penguin, 1961.

Schama, Simon. *Landscape and Memory*. Toronto: Random House, 1995.

Contributors

Ailsa Cox is professor of short fiction at Edge Hill University in the UK. Her books include *Alice Munro* (Northcote House, 2004) and *Writing Short Stories* (Routledge, 2005); she is also the editor of the journal *Short Fiction in Theory & Practice* (Intellect Press). Her story "No Se Puede Vivir Sin Amar" appears in *Malcolm Lowry: From the Mersey to the World* (Liverpool University Press, 2009). Other short stories are collected in *The Real Louise* (Headland Press, 2009).

Catherine Delesalle is an assistant professor at Université Jean Moulin Lyon 3, where she teaches modern English literature and translation. In addition to writing her PhD dissertation on the concept of exile in Lowry's fiction, she has published numerous articles on Lowry, Joseph Conrad, and other modern and contemporary writers. She has recently published *La Divine Comédie ivre: répétition, ressassement et reprise dans l'œuvre en prose de Malcolm Lowry* (Michel Houdiard, 2010).

Annick Drösdal-Levillain teaches English at the University of Strasbourg. Since writing her PhD dissertation on Malcolm Lowry and Joseph Conrad, she has focused her research on the "Lowryan echo-system," the links between the artist's life and work, tracking down the Lacanian symptom and metaphors embedded in the body of the text, exploring landscapes and soulscapes. Her research is presently heading north, toward Norwegian writers and artists and their interaction with Lowry and Conrad.

Mathieu Duplay is professor of American literature at Université Paris Diderot (Paris 7). His research focuses on the relationship between literature and philosophy, with a particular emphasis on the question of voice and its linguistic, aesthetic, ethical, and political implications. He is the author of numerous articles on Malcolm Lowry, as well as the critical monograph *William Gaddis, Carpenter's Gothic: le scandale de l'écriture* (Éditions Ellipses, 2001). His latest research focuses on the operas of contemporary American composer John Adams.

Mark Goodall is lecturer in media communications at the Bradford Media School, University of Bradford. He is the author of *Sweet and Savage: the World through the Shockumentary Film Lens* (Headpress, 2006) and the editor of *Crash Cinema: Representation in Film* (Cambridge Scholars, 2007). He has written numerous articles on cult film, art, and music. He currently edits *The Firminist*, a periodical about Malcolm Lowry. His next book from Headpress is *The Gathering of the Tribe: Music and Heavy Conscious Creation*.

W. M. Hagen teaches courses in modern literature, film, and Western civilization at Oklahoma Baptist University in Shawnee, Oklahoma. His article on Margerie Bonner Lowry's proposed screenplay is the second such feasibility study of a Lowry film project, following his previous exploration of Malcolm Lowry's screenplay of *Tender is the Night* for *The Malcolm Lowry Review*. Other film articles include critiques of *Apocalypse Now*, *Under the Volcano*, *Diva*, *Shadowlands*, and silent, Oklahoma-based Westerns.

Charles Hoge teaches English literature, composition, and children's literature classes at the Metropolitan State University of Denver. His research attempts to engage folkloric traditions as a heuristic approach through which to encounter literature, and in doing so explore the productivity of the intertwining relationship that emerges between the two. He has published articles on the extinction of the dodo and the monstrous footprint its eulogists left on the landscape of the Enlightenment; the obscure but influential shadows cast by medieval folklore upon the development of the twentieth-century iterations of the zombie and the vampire; and the potential for re-reading fan fiction through the filters of ludology. His PhD dissertation (University of Denver, 2015) works with the tenuous persistence of folklore in Victorian culture in regard to death rituals and the unstable human corpse.

Richard J. Lane teaches English at Vancouver Island University, where he is the Principal Investigator of the Canada Foundation for Innovation MeTA Digital Humanities Lab, and the director of the Literary Theory Research Group and the Seminar for Advanced Studies in the Humanities. He has published articles on Lowry's *Last Notebook* and *Ultramarine*, as well as numerous essays on Canadian, British, and post-colonial literature. He has also published a number of critical books, including *Beckett and Philosophy* (ed., Palgrave, 2002), *Reading Walter Benjamin* (Manchester University Press, 2005), *Image Technologies in Canadian Literature* (ed., Lang, 2009), and *The Routledge Concise History of Canadian Literature* (Routledge, 2011).

Miguel Mota, associate professor in the Department of English at the University of British Columbia, has published numerous articles on modern and contemporary writers and filmmakers, including William Carlos Williams, John King, Jeanette Winterson, Derek Jarman, and Mike Leigh. His publications on Lowry include numerous articles as well as *The Cinema of Malcolm Lowry* (with Paul Tiessen, UBC Press, 1990). He has most recently, with four other Lowry scholars, published critical editions of three Lowry novels (*Swinging the Maelstrom, In Ballast to the White Sea*, and *The 1940 Under the Volcano*) with the University of Ottawa Press.

Josiane Paccaud-Huguet is professor of modern English literature and literary theory at Université Lumière Lyon 2, where she is also dean of the Faculty of Languages. She has published extensively on modernist authors (Conrad, Joyce, Woolf, Mansfield, Lawrence, Lowry) both in France and abroad. Her latest publications include *Joseph Conrad: l'écrivain et l'étrangeté de la langue* (éditions Minard, 2006) and "Psychoanalysis after Freud," in *Literary Theory and Criticism, An Oxford Guide* (ed. Patricia Waugh, Oxford University Press, 2006). She is currently working on a translation of Virginia Woolf's *Between the Acts* for Bibliothèque de la Pléiade and is finishing a book on the modernist "moment of vision."

Laurence Piercy has recently embarked on a PhD in English literature at the University of Sheffield. He is currently working on a comparative study of European exile literature, psychoanalysis, and the philosophy of free will.

Ryan Rashotte is the author of *Narco Cinema: Sex, Drugs, and Banda Music in Mexico's B-Filmography*. He has a Ph.D. in English from the University of Guelph.

Pierre Schaeffer teaches English in the Faculty of Law at the University of Strasbourg. He is the author of numerous articles on Lowry, Virginia Woolf, and Jack Hodgins. His current research interests include work on Joyce Carol Oates' *The Falls* as well as on the enigmatic aspect of the literary voice in contemporary British and North American fiction.

Paul Tiessen is professor emeritus of English and film studies at Wilfrid Laurier University. His volumes on Malcolm Lowry include *A Darkness That Murmured: Essays on Malcolm Lowry and the Twentieth Century* (2000), with F. Asals; *Joyce/Lowry: Critical Perspectives* (1997), with P. McCarthy; *The Cinema of Malcolm Lowry: A Scholarly Edition of Lowry's 'Tender Is the Night'* (1990), with M. Mota; and *The Letters of Malcolm Lowry and Gerald Noxon, 1940–1952* (1988). From 1984 to 2002 he edited the *Malcolm Lowry Review*. He is a collaborator on a fully annotated 1936–1944 Lowry trilogy, published by the University of Ottawa Press: *Swinging the Maelstrom* (2013), *In Ballast to the White Sea* (2014), and *The 1940 Under the Volcano* (2015).

Pascale Tollance is professor of English at Université Lumière Lyon 2. She has written extensively on Malcolm Lowry, as well as on British contemporary authors such as Graham Swift, Julian Barnes, Kazuo Ishiguro, Angela Carter, A. S. Byatt, Jeanette Winterson, and Rachel Seiffert. She is the author of a book on Graham Swift (*Graham Swift. La Scène de la voix*, Presses Universitaires du Septentrion, 2011) which focuses on the staging of voice in Swift's fiction. She is on the editorial board of *L'Atelier*, and has co-edited volume 5.1 (*Survivance*) and 6.2. (*La Transmission*). Her interests include post-colonial literatures; and she has worked recently on the fiction of Janet Frame, J. M. Coetzee, and Alice Munro.

Christine Vandamme is a lecturer at Grenoble Alpes University, where she teaches British literature in the premodernist and modernist periods as well as post-colonial literature. Her field of specialty is that of space and literature from pre-modernism to modernism and also, more recently, post-colonial literature, especially Australian literature. She has published extensively on Joseph Conrad, Malcolm Lowry, and Patrick White, the three authors she studied in her PhD dissertation on space and hermeneutics in those three authors' works. She is the author of *Lord Jim* (Bréal, 2004) and co-editor of *Science and Empire in the Nineteenth Century: A Journey of Imperial Conquest and Scientific Progress* (Cambridge Scholars, 2010). Regarding the work of Lowry, her interest in the ethical and political aspects of space representation and narrative space have led her to explore the highly deconstructive power of a prose which, far from celebrating nihilistic volcanic explosion, ceaselessly breaks new ground for alternative formations to be born.

CANADIAN LITERATURE COLLECTION /
COLLECTION DE LITTÉRATURE CANADIENNE

Series Editor: Dean Irvine

The Canadian Literature Collection / Collection de la littérature canadienne (CLC) is a series of nineteenth- to mid-twentieth-century literary texts produced in critical editions. All texts selected for the series were either out of print or previously unpublished. Each text appears in a print edition with a basic apparatus (critical introduction, explanatory notes, textual notes, and a statement of editorial principles) together with an expanded web-based apparatus (which may include alternate versions, expanded textual notes, previous editions, correspondence, photographs, source materials, and other related texts by the author).

The Literary Studies sub-series of the CLC features monographs and edited collections that complement the historical focus of these critical editions.

Previous titles in this collection

Emily Ballantyne, Marta Dvořák and Dean Irvine (editors), *Translocated Modernisms: Paris and Other Lost Generations*, 2016

Lee Skallerup Bessette, *A Journey in Translation*, 2016

Laurie Kruk, *Double-Voicing the Canadian Short Story*, 2016

Bart Vautour and Emily Robins Sharpe (editors), *Meet Me on the Barricades* by Charles Yale Harrison, 2016

Kailin Wright (editor), *The God of Gods: A Canadian Play* by Carroll Aikins, 2016

Miguel Mota and Paul Tiessen (editors), Chris Ackerley and David Large (annotations), *The 1940 Under the Volcano* by Malcolm Lowry, 2015

Robert D. Denham (author), *Northrop Frye and Others: Twelve Writers Who Helped Shape His Thinking*, 2015

Emily Robins Sharpe (editor), *Hugh Garner's Best Stories*, 2015

Bart Vautour (editor), *This Time a Better Earth* by Ted Allan, 2015

For a complete list of our titles in this collection, see: https://press.uottawa.ca/series/french-and-canadian-studies/canadian-literature-collection.html